CONSCIOUSNESS

D0162017

Consciousness is arguably the most important interdisciplinary area in contemporary philosophy of mind, with an explosion of research over the past thirty years from philosophers, psychologists, and scientists. It is also perhaps the most puzzling aspect of the world despite the fact that it is familiar to each of us. Consciousness also seems resistant to any straightforward physical explanation.

This book introduces readers to the contemporary problem of consciousness, providing a clear introduction to the overall landscape and a fair-minded critical survey of various theories of consciousness. Beginning with essential historical background to the problem of consciousness, Rocco Gennaro explores the following key topics and debates:

- the metaphysical problem of consciousness, including varieties of dualism and materialism;
- consciousness and neuroscience, particularly the question of whether consciousness can be reduced to brain activity or attentional mechanisms;
- representational and cognitive theories of consciousness;
- consciousness and psychopathology;
- animals, machines, and consciousness.

Extensive use is made of interesting phenomena throughout the book, ranging from blindsight, synesthesia, and change blindness to phantom limb syndrome, split-brain cases, and dissociative identity disorder (DID).

The inclusion of chapter summaries, annotated further reading, and a glossary make this book essential reading for anyone seeking a clear and informative overview of the problem of consciousness, not only in philosophy but also related fields such as psychology and cognitive science.

Rocco J. Gennaro is Professor of Philosophy at the University of Southern Indiana, USA. His most recent books are The Consciousness Paradox: Consciousness, Concepts, and Higher-Order Thoughts (2012) and Disturbed Consciousness: New Essays on Psychopathologies and Theories of Consciousness (2015).

NEW PROBLEMS OF PHILOSOPHY

Series Editor: José Luis Bermúdez

'Routledge's *New Problems of Philosophy* series has a most impressive line-up of topical volumes aimed at upper-level undergraduate and graduate students in philosophy and at others with interests in cutting edge philosophical work. The authors are influential figures in their respective fields and notably adept at synthesizing and explaining intricate topics fairly and comprehensively.'
— *John Heil, Monash University, Australia, and Washington University, St Louis, USA*

'This is an outstanding collection of volumes. The topics are well chosen and the authors are outstanding. They will be fine texts in a wide range of courses.'
— *Stephen Stich, Rutgers University, USA*

The *New Problems of Philosophy* series provides accessible and engaging surveys of the most important problems in contemporary philosophy. Each book examines a topic or theme that has either emerged on the philosophical landscape in recent years, or a longstanding problem refreshed in light of recent work in philosophy and related disciplines. Clearly explaining the nature of the problem at hand and assessing attempts to answer it, books in the series are excellent starting-points for undergraduate and graduate students wishing to study a single topic in depth. They will also be essential reading for professional philosophers. Additional features include chapter summaries, further reading and a glossary of technical terms.

Also available:

The Metaphysics of Identity
André Gallois

Images
John V. Kulvicki

Disjunctivism
Matthew Soteriou

Attention
Wayne Wu

Cognitive Phenomenology
Elijah Chudnoff

Consequentialism
Julia Driver

Egalitarianism
Iwao Hirose

Semantic Externalism
Jesper Kallestrup

For further titles in the series, see www.routledge.com/New-Problems-of-Philosophy/book-series/NPOP

CONSCIOUSNESS

Rocco J. Gennaro

Routledge
Taylor & Francis Group

LONDON AND NEW YORK

First published 2017
by Routledge
2 Park Square, Milton Park, Abingdon, Oxon OX14 4RN

and by Routledge
711 Third Avenue, New York, NY 10017

Routledge is an imprint of the Taylor & Francis Group, an informa business

British Library Cataloguing in Publication Data
A catalogue record for this book is available from the British Library

Names: Gennaro, Rocco J., author.
Title: Consciousness / by Rocco J. Gennaro.
Description: 1 [edition]. | New York : Routledge, 2016. | Series: New problems of
    philosophy | Includes bibliographical references and index.
Identifiers: LCCN 2016015201| ISBN 9781138827707 (hardback : alk. paper) |
    ISBN 9781138827714 (pbk. : alk. paper) | ISBN 9781315521534 (e-book)
Subjects: LCSH: Consciousness.
Classification: LCC B808.9 .G458 2016 | DDC 128/.2—dc23
LC record available at https://lccn.loc.gov/2016015201

ISBN: 978-1-138-82770-7 (hbk)
ISBN: 978-1-138-82771-4 (pbk)
ISBN: 978-1-315-52153-4 (ebk)

Typeset in Joanna
by Swales & Willis Ltd, Exeter, Devon, UK

CONTENTS

ACKNOWLEDGEMENTS

I would like to thank Tony Bruce and Adam Johnson at Routledge for their support and diligent work throughout this project. Their timely feedback and continued encouragement have been invaluable during my work on this book. In addition, I thank three anonymous referees for numerous helpful suggestions on a previous draft of this manuscript and I would also like to thank four anonymous reviewers of my initial proposal. I thank the University of Southern Indiana for a sabbatical leave during Fall 2015 during which I completed a draft of this manuscript. I also thank The MIT Press for permission to use occasional paragraphs or short sub-sections, still usually somewhat modified, from *The Consciousness Paradox* (2012) and *Disturbed Consciousness* (2015), especially in Chapters 3 and 4. Substantial direct quotations from those books are noted as such in the text. Finally, I dedicate this book to my family who allowed me the space and time to work mostly at home during my sabbatical leave – Deidra, Olivia, and Joey.

INTRODUCTION: THE PROBLEM OF CONSCIOUSNESS

General introduction and book outline

Consciousness is arguably the most important area within contemporary philosophy of mind with an explosion of research over the past thirty years from philosophers, psychologists, and scientists. It is also perhaps the most puzzling aspect of the world despite the fact that it is so very familiar to each of us. Although some features of mental states can perhaps be explained without reference to consciousness, it is consciousness that seems most resistant to a straightforward explanation. Can conscious experience be explained in terms of brain activity? Is the conscious mind physical or non-physical in some way? This book introduces readers to the contemporary problem of consciousness, providing both a clear explanation of the overall landscape and a critical survey of various theories of consciousness. It also explains how consciousness impacts a number of importantly related issues in the philosophy of mind, such as the traditional mind–body problem, the nature of psychopathology, and animal consciousness. The emphasis whenever possible will be on fairly recent empirical and interdisciplinary work. Although there is much of contemporary interest on consciousness in

Eastern thought, especially Indian philosophy (Siderits et al. 2011; Coseru 2012), I will mostly restrict my discussion to Western philosophy.

This book is primarily for upper-level undergraduates who have completed a first or second course in core philosophy subjects, but it can also be used in a graduate seminar on consciousness as a complement to an anthology of readings. It is also a good starting point for professionals in other academic areas since the existing literature can often make it difficult to navigate through the main positions and philosophical debates.

The remainder of this section presents an overall picture of the book. In the next section, I introduce the reader to some key terminology such as the numerous and often confusing senses of the term "conscious." In the final section, I briefly outline some of the background history on the topic, especially some major figures in the history of Western philosophy (such as Descartes, Locke, Leibniz, and Kant).

Chapter 1 ("The metaphysics of consciousness") introduces the reader to the major metaphysical positions on the problem of consciousness. There are two broad traditional and competing views concerning the nature of the mind and conscious mental states: dualism and materialism. This chapter summarizes some of the main reasons given for accepting and rejecting both materialism and dualism. It includes a discussion of several different flavors of materialism and dualism, including identity theory, eliminative materialism, functionalism, substance dualism, property dualism, and epiphenomenalism. While there are many versions of each, dualism generally holds that the conscious mind or a conscious mental state is non-physical in some sense. On the other hand, materialists believe that the mind is the brain, or, as identity theorists would put it, that conscious mental activity is identical with neural activity. Some form of materialism is probably more widely held today than in centuries past. Part of the reason has to do with the explosion in scientific knowledge about the workings of the brain and its intimate connection with consciousness, including the clear connection between brain damage and various states of consciousness. Stimulation to very specific areas of the brain results in very specific conscious experiences. Nonetheless, major problems remain such as the so-called "hard problem of consciousness" (Chalmers 1995) which basically refers to the difficulty of explaining just how physical processes in the brain give rise to subjective conscious experiences. Materialist responses to these objections are explained.

There is also discussion of various other metaphysical views such as idealism, panpsychism, and emergentism. Several other related philosophical problems will also be addressed in this context, such as the possibility of immortality and the nature of free will. The nature of out-of-body and near-death experiences (OBEs and NDEs) is briefly discussed as well.

Chapter 2 ("Consciousness, neuroscience, and attention") outlines and explains the growing importance of neuroscience in consciousness studies. Neural and materialist theories of consciousness are critically discussed, including Francis Crick and Christof Koch's neurobiological temporal synchrony theory, David Edelman and Gulio Tononi's dynamic core hypothesis, Victor Lamme's recurrent processing theory, and Jesse Prinz's attended intermediate-level representation theory. The ongoing search for the "neural correlates of consciousness" (NCCs) is also explained.

Some important and fascinating phenomena are described in this chapter, such as inattentional and change blindness, which raise the interesting question of the relationship between attention and consciousness. The so-called "binding problem" is also introduced with some discussion of the "unity" of consciousness. It is also important to be clear about what is meant by the "unity of consciousness"; explaining how the brain achieves such unity has become a central topic in the study of consciousness. There are many different senses of "unity," but perhaps most common is the notion that, from the first-person point of view, we experience the world in an integrated way and as a single phenomenal field of experience. However, when one looks at how the brain processes information, one only sees discrete regions of the cortex processing separate aspects of perceptual objects. Even different aspects of the same object, such as its color and shape, are processed in different parts of the brain. The problem of exactly how the brain integrates the information processed by different regions of the brain is known as the binding problem. Chapter 2 ends with sections on a few alternative theories of consciousness, including integrated information theory (IIT), the enactive or sensorimotor theory, and quantum theories of consciousness.

The focus of Chapter 3 ("Representational and cognitive theories of consciousness") is on so-called "representational theories of consciousness" which attempt to reduce consciousness to "mental representations" of some kind. Mental states are intentional; that is, they are directed at (or "about") objects or properties. Examples include Michael Tye's (2000) first-order representationalism (FOR) which aims to explain conscious experience primarily in terms of world-directed (or "first-order") intentional states, and higher-order representationalism (HOR) which holds that what makes a mental state M conscious is that it is the object of some kind of higher-order state directed at M (Rosenthal 2005; Gennaro 2012). In addition, the somewhat related "self-representational" approach to consciousness is critically discussed (Kriegel 2009). One key guiding question that should be answered by any theory of consciousness is: What makes a mental state a *conscious* mental state? Common objections and replies to the above are explained and assessed. Finally, the cognitive theories of Daniel Dennett (multiple drafts theory) and Bernard Baars (global workspace theory) are also critically addressed in Chapter 3. Dennett is most concerned that materialists avoid falling prey to what he calls the "myth of the Cartesian theater," the notion that there is some privileged place in the brain where everything comes together to produce conscious experience. For Baars, the basic idea is that we should think of the cognitive system as built on a "blackboard architecture" which is a kind of global workspace. According to his global workspace theory (GWT), unconscious processes and mental states compete for the spotlight of attention, from which information is "broadcast globally" throughout the system. Consciousness consists in such global broadcasting.

Chapter 4 ("Consciousness and psychopathology") outlines the growing and cutting-edge interdisciplinary field of consciousness and psychopathology, including so-called "philosophical psychopathology" and "philosophy of psychiatry." Various cognitive deficits and abnormal phenomena are explained with the focus on how they negatively impact consciousness, such as phantom limb pain, amnesia, split-brain cases, somatoparaphrenia, schizophrenia, visual agnosia, and dissociative identity disorder (DID). One source of interest in these areas comes from the provocative and accessible writings of several neurologists, most notably Oliver Sacks, Todd Feinberg, and V. S. Ramachandran.

Philosophers have of course long been intrigued by disorders of the mind and consciousness. Part of the interest stems from the idea that if we can understand how consciousness goes wrong in some cases, then that leaves important clues about how to theorize about the normal functioning mind. Going back at least as far as John Locke (1689/1975), there has been discussion about the philosophical implications of multiple personality disorder (MPD) which is now called "dissociative identity disorder" (DID). Questions abound: could there be two centers of consciousness in one body? What makes a person the same person over time? These questions are closely linked to the traditional philosophical problem of personal identity. Much the same can be said for memory disorders, such as various forms of amnesia. Does consciousness require some kind of autobiographical memory or psychological continuity? On a related front, there is significant interest in experimental results from patients who have undergone a commissurotomy, which is performed to relieve symptoms of severe epilepsy when all else fails. During this procedure, the nerve fibers connecting the two brain hemispheres (the "corpus callosum") are cut, resulting in so-called "split-brain" patients. The remainder of Chapter 4 is devoted to the "philosophy of psychiatry" which includes such topics as the nature of mental illness, our notions of free will and moral responsibility, and the disorders of schizophrenia and psychopathy. What exactly is a mental illness? Can psychopaths really be morally responsible for their actions? If not, how should they be punished? Does moral responsibility require consciousness?

Chapter 5 ("Animal and machine consciousness") assesses the extent to which animals are conscious and whether or not machines could be conscious. This importantly extends the overall problem of consciousness beyond human consciousness to two major areas in contemporary research. Regarding animals, perhaps most important is what criteria should be used when inferring that an animal is conscious. In addition, I highlight some important recent experimental results in cognitive ethology, such as in determining whether animals have so-called "mindreading" ability; that is, the ability to think about others' mental states. It is clear that we have come a long way from the Cartesian view that animals are mere automata and do not even have conscious experience. In addition to the significant behavioral similarities between humans and many animals, much more is known today about other physiological similarities, such as our brain and DNA structures.

The possibility of machine (or robot) consciousness has intrigued philosophers and non-philosophers alike for decades, including in numerous science fiction books and movies. Could a machine really think or be conscious? Could a robot really subjectively experience the smelling of a rose or the feeling of pain? One important early launching point was a well-known paper by the mathematician Alan Turing (1950) who proposed what is known as the "Turing test" for machine intelligence and thought (and perhaps consciousness as well). The basic idea is that if a machine could fool an interrogator (who cannot see the machine) into thinking that it is human, then we should say it thinks or, at the very least, has intelligence. However, even if a machine or robot could pass the Turing test, many remain very skeptical as to whether this demonstrates genuine thinking, let alone consciousness. Another much-discussed argument is John Searle's (1980) famous Chinese room argument which has spawned an enormous amount of literature since its original publication. Searle is concerned to reject what he calls "strong AI" which is the view that a suitably programmed computer literally has a mind; that is, it really understands language and has other mental capacities similar to humans. The similarities and differences between human brains and computer programs (and robots) are also assessed and the nature of "connectionist" networks is described. What is the best way to create an artificial intelligence? Significant ethical questions also arise: If we eventually can create conscious robots, then shouldn't we treat them as morally significant?

Finally, in a concluding chapter, I draw together the main topics that have been discussed and offer further assessment of some of them. I summarize some of the outstanding issues and present some likely future directions in the field.

Key terminology

It is well understood that the concept of consciousness is notoriously ambiguous. It is important to make several distinctions and to define key terms. The noun "consciousness," especially in some abstract sense, is not used very often in the contemporary literature, though it originally derives from the Latin *con* (with) and *scire* (to know). One can have knowledge of the external world or one's own mental states through consciousness. The primary contemporary interest lies more in the use of the expressions "x is conscious" or "x is conscious of y." Under the former category, perhaps most important is the distinction between state and creature consciousness (Rosenthal 1993). We sometimes speak of an individual mental state, such as a desire or perception, as being conscious. On the other hand, we also often talk about organisms or creatures as conscious, such as when we say that "human beings are conscious" or "dogs are conscious." Creature consciousness is simply meant to refer to the fact that an organism is awake, as opposed to sleeping or in a coma. However, some kind of state consciousness is normally implied by creature consciousness; that is, if a creature is conscious, then it must have conscious mental states. On the other hand, perhaps there can be state consciousness without creature consciousness, such as in the case of vivid dreams. Due to the lack of a direct object in "x is conscious," this is usually referred to as intransitive consciousness, in contrast to transitive consciousness, where the phrase "x is conscious of y" is used (Rosenthal 1993). We might say that a person is conscious or aware of a dog in front of her. Most contemporary theories of consciousness are aimed at explaining state consciousness; that is, what makes a mental state conscious.

It might seem that the term "conscious" is synonymous with, say, "awareness" or "experience" or "attention." However, it is crucial to recognize that this is not generally accepted today. For example, one might hold that there are unconscious experiences depending on how the term "experience" is defined (Carruthers 2000), though this is perhaps somewhat atypical. More common is the belief that we can be aware of external objects in some unconscious sense, such as during instances of subliminal perception. The expression "conscious awareness" does not seem to be redundant. Finally, it is not clear that consciousness ought to be restricted to attention. It seems plausible to suppose, for example, that one is conscious of objects to some extent in one's peripheral visual field even though one is attending to a more narrow (or focal) set of objects within that visual field. Needless to say, contemporary philosophers and psychologists are nearly unanimous in allowing for unconscious mental states or representations, though they differ as to whether this applies to all kinds of mental states including, say, pains and emotions.

Perhaps the most commonly used notion of "conscious" is captured by Thomas Nagel's famous "what it is like" sense (Nagel 1974). When I am in a conscious mental state, there is "something it is like" for me to be in that state from the subjective or first-person point of view. When I smell a flower or have a conscious visual perception, there is something it "seems" or "feels like" from my perspective. An organism such as a bat is conscious if it is able to experience the world through its echolocation senses. There is also something it is like to be a conscious creature whereas there is nothing it is like to be a table or tree. This is primarily the sense of "conscious state" that I use throughout the book. "What it's like" basically means "how a conscious state is for the subject." When it comes to capturing the main phenomenon to be explained, it seems to me that we most often have Nagel's "something it is like" sense in mind.

There are still, though, a cluster of expressions and technical terms associated with Nagel's sense, and some authors simply stipulate the way that they use them. For example, philosophers often refer to conscious states as *phenomenal* or *qualitative* states. More technically, philosophers frequently describe such states as having qualitative properties called "qualia" (singular, quale). Chalmers explains that a "mental state is conscious if there is something it is like to be in that mental state. . . . We can say that a mental state is conscious if it has a qualitative feel. . . . These qualitative feels are also known as phenomenal qualities, or qualia for short" (1996, 4). There is significant disagreement over the nature, and even the existence, of qualia, but they are often understood as the felt properties or qualities of conscious states (Wright 2008; Kind 2008). Others might, more neutrally, say that qualia are qualitative features present in experience. What it feels like, experientially, to see a red rose is different from what it feels like to see a yellow rose. Likewise for hearing a musical note played by a piano and hearing the same musical note played by a tuba. The qualia of these experiences are what give each of them its characteristic "feel" and also what distinguish them from one another. In any case, qualia are most often treated as properties of some mental states, though some use the term "qualia" in the more external sense of "the qualities of what is represented." I will use it in the former sense.

One also finds closely allied expressions like "phenomenal character" and "subjective character" in the literature. Tye (2015), for example, tells us that the "phenomenal character of an experience is what it is like subjectively to undergo the experience." More explicitly, Uriah Kriegel (2009) is at great pains to distinguish what he calls "qualitative character" from "subjective character" under the larger umbrella of "phenomenal character" because they play such a central role in his theory of consciousness. He explains that "a phenomenally conscious state's qualitative character is what makes it the phenomenally conscious state it is, while its subjective character is what makes it a phenomenally conscious state at all" (Kriegel 2009, 1). In his view, then, the phenomenally conscious experience of the blue sky should be divided into two components: (1) its qualitative character, which is the "bluish" component of the experience (or the *what* of the experience), and

(2) its subjective character, which is what he calls the "for-me" component (or what determines that it is conscious).

Ned Block (1995) makes a well-known distinction between phenomenal consciousness (or "phenomenality") and access consciousness. Phenomenal consciousness is very much in line with Nagel's notion described earlier. However, Block defines the quite different notion of access consciousness in terms of a mental state's relationship with other mental states; for example, a mental state's "availability for use in reasoning and rationality guiding speech and action" (Block 1995, 227). This view would, for example, count a visual perception as (access) conscious not because it has the "what it's likeness" of phenomenal states but because it carries visual information that is generally available for use by the organism, regardless of whether it has any qualitative properties. Access consciousness is therefore a functional notion concerned with what such states do. Although something like this idea is certainly important in cognitive science and philosophy of mind generally, not everyone agrees that access consciousness deserves to be called "consciousness" in any important sense. Block himself argues that neither sense of consciousness implies the other, while others urge that a more intimate connection holds between the two.

Finally, it is helpful to distinguish between consciousness and *self-consciousness*, which plausibly involves some kind of awareness or consciousness of one's own mental states (instead of something out in the world). Self-consciousness arguably comes in degrees of sophistication ranging from minimal bodily self-awareness to the ability to reason and reflect on one's own mental states, such as one's beliefs and desires. The term "introspection" is often used for this latter, more reflective, notion. Some important historical figures have even held that consciousness entails some form of self-consciousness (Kant 1781/1965; Sartre 1956), a view shared by some contemporary philosophers (Gennaro 1996; Kriegel 2004).

My overall sense, however, is that some authors only add to the terminological confusion by introducing new (or not so new) distinctions into the literature instead of clarifying existing meanings of "consciousness" or simply adopting a prior definition over others. Has, for example, Block's distinction between access and phenomenal consciousness really clarified the matter? It is important to resist the urge to introduce our own special terminology, though we are all perhaps guilty to some extent. I make a plea for more uniform usage whenever possible. Unless I specifically indicate otherwise, I will use the terms "phenomenal," "qualitative," and "experience" as conscious in Nagel's sense, but I will allow for unconscious awareness and unconscious representations directed at the outer world or one's own mental states. So, for me, there are no unconscious experiences or unconscious qualitative states (or unconscious qualia). There is little reason to have an unconscious counterpart for each of the terms above. I will also avoid using as much of the foregoing technical jargon as possible throughout this book without sacrificing rigor or accuracy.

A brief sketch of some history

Interest in the nature of conscious experience has of course been around for as long as there have been reflective humans. It would be impossible to survey the entire history here and this book series is designed to emphasize recent work (and "new problems"), but a few highlights are in order. In the history of Western philosophy, important writings on human nature and the soul and mind go back to ancient philosophers, such as Plato who famously held that our non-physical minds pre-date our bodies and continue to exist after bodily death. More sophisticated work on the nature of consciousness and perception can be found in the work of Plato's most famous student, Aristotle, who describes the mind (nous, often also translated as "intellect" or "reason") as the part of the soul by which it knows and understands (Caston 2002), and then throughout the later Medieval period, such as in the work of Thomas Aquinas and others.

It is, however, with the writings of seventeenth-century philosopher René Descartes (1641/1993) and his successors in the early modern period of philosophy that consciousness and the relationship between the mind and body took center stage. As we shall see in Chapter 1, Descartes argued that the mind is a non-physical substance distinct from the body. He also did not believe in the existence of unconscious mental states, a view certainly not widely held today. Descartes defined "thinking" very broadly to include virtually every kind of mental state and urged that consciousness is essential to thought. Our mental states are, according to Descartes, infallibly transparent to introspection. John Locke (1689/1975) held a somewhat similar position regarding the connection between mental states and consciousness, but was far less committal on the exact metaphysical nature of the mind. Locke's definition of "person" explicitly mentions consciousness:

[A person] is a thinking intelligent Being, that has reason and reflection, and can consider it self as it self, the same thinking thing in different times and places; which it does only by that consciousness, which is inseparable from thinking, and as it seems to me essential to it: It being impossible for any one to perceive, without perceiving, that he does perceive.

(1689/1975, II.27.9)

Perhaps the most important philosopher of the early modern period explicitly to endorse the existence of unconscious mental states was Gottfried Leibniz (1686/1991, 1720/1925). Although Leibniz also believed in the immaterial nature of mental substances (which he called "monads"), he recognized the existence of what he called *petit perceptions*, which are basically unconscious perceptions. In this sense, Leibniz was particularly ahead of his time. Leibniz also importantly distinguished between perception and "apperception," which is roughly the difference between outer-directed consciousness and self-consciousness (see Gennaro 1999).

The most detailed theory of mind in the early modern period was developed by Immanuel Kant. His main work *Critique of Pure Reason* (1781/1965) is as dense as it is important and cannot easily be summarized. Although he owes a great debt to his immediate predecessors, Kant is arguably the most important Western philosopher since Plato and Aristotle and remains highly relevant today. Kant basically thought that an adequate account of phenomenal consciousness involved far more than any of his predecessors had considered. There are important innate mental structures which are "presupposed" in conscious experience. Kant presented an elaborate theory as to what those structures are, which, in turn, had other important implications. Kant, like Leibniz, saw the need to postulate the existence of unconscious mental states and underlying "mechanisms" or "faculties" to provide an adequate theory of mind. For example, he distinguished between the faculties of *sensibility* and *understanding* which must work together to make experience possible. He emphasized the passive nature of the sensibility (through which outer objects are given to us) as opposed to the active and more cognitive nature of the understanding, which thinks about and applies concepts to that which enters via sensibility. Kant uses the term *Begriff* for "concept." *Begriff*, unlike its English counterpart, is a more active term meaning "a grasping." The verb is *begreifen*, meaning "to grasp," thus emphasizing the active role played by the understanding.

So the idea is that we first passively receive information via our senses in what Kant (1781/1965) calls our "faculty of sensibility," which we might think of today as early perceptual processing. Some of this information will then rise to the level of unconscious mental states which can also cause our behavior in various ways. But these mental states do not become conscious until the faculty of understanding operates on them via the application of concepts. Kant explains that "Objects are *given* to us by means of sensibility. . . . They are *thought* through the understanding, and from the understanding arise concepts" (A19/B33); there must be significant unconscious (synthesizing) activity implicit in each conscious state. He famously claimed that "thoughts without content are empty, intuitions [= sensory experiences] without concepts are blind" (Kant 1781/1965, A51/B75). The Kantian Categories applied to experience include such concepts as substance, cause, and number, and Kant called the two central notions of space and time the "two pure forms of intuition." Unified conscious experience must be the product of the (presupposed) synthesizing work of the mind, including the application of various concepts or "categories." Kant argued that it is difficult to make sense of having coherent conscious experience unless we presuppose that outer objects persist in time. If we did not make such a presupposition, then we would not be able to distinguish the fleeting subjective succession of our conscious experiences of objects from the enduring nature of the outer objects themselves. Kant famously called the activity of such synthesizing (or binding) the "transcendental unity of apperception." Although Kant had nothing to say about such mechanisms in neurophysiological terms, he still had much of value to say about them in cognitive terms.

Over the past one hundred years or so, however, research on consciousness has taken off in many important directions. In psychology, with the notable exception of the virtual banishment of consciousness by behaviorist psychologists (e.g. Skinner 1953), there were also those deeply interested in consciousness and introspective (or "first-person") methods of investigating the mind. The writings of Wilhelm Wundt (1897), William James (1890), and Alfred Titchener (1901) are good examples of this approach. Franz Brentano (1874/1973) also had a profound effect on some contemporary theories of consciousness, such as the self-representationalist approach to be discussed in Chapter 3. Similar introspectionist approaches were taken by those in the so-called "phenomenological" tradition in philosophy, such as Edmund Husserl (1913/1931) and Martin Heidegger (1927/1962). The work of Sigmund Freud was of course also very important, at minimum, in bringing about the near universal acceptance of the existence of unconscious mental states and processes.

It must, however, be kept in mind that none of the above had very much knowledge about the detailed workings of the brain (especially compared to today). The relatively recent development of neurophysiology is, in part, also responsible for the exciting interdisciplinary research interest in consciousness, particularly since the 1980s. There is no doubt that some form of materialism is much more widely held today than in centuries past. Part of the reason has to do with the explosion in scientific knowledge about the brain and its intimate connection with consciousness, as for example revealed in the association between brain damage and disorders of consciousness (such as in amnesia and Alzheimer's disease). Brain death is now the main criterion used to establish when someone has died. Stimulation of specific areas of the brain results in specific conscious experiences. We now have several ways to learn about how the brain works. For example, nuclear magnetic resonance imaging (MRI) measures the radio signals emitted by some atomic nuclei. The radiation emitted provides detailed information about the chemical nature of the nuclei. When used in neuroscience, MRI can give us information about the anatomy of the brain. Functional magnetic resonance imaging (fMRI) is a related method that measures changes in blood flow associated with neuronal activity within the brain while the subject is engaged in various cognitive or perceptual tasks.

In any case, Chapter 1 introduces the reader to the very substantial metaphysical issues surrounding the problem of consciousness.

Summary

This book mainly introduces readers to the contemporary problem of consciousness, providing both a clear explanation of the overall landscape and a critical survey of various theories of consciousness. It also explains how consciousness impacts a number of importantly related issues in the philosophy of mind, such as the traditional mind–body problem, the nature of psychopathology, and animal consciousness. Key terminology was introduced such as the numerous and often confusing senses of the term "conscious" and the more technical term "qualia." We also took a brief tour of the background history on consciousness via discussion of several major figures in the history of Western philosophy including Plato, Descartes, Locke, Leibniz, and Kant.

Further reading

Among the best anthologies on consciousness are Metzinger 1995, Block, Flanagan, and Güzeldere 1997, Metzinger 2000, Baars, Banks, and Newman 2003, Smith and Jokic 2003, Zelazo, Moscovitch, and Thompson 2007, Velmans and Schneider 2007, Bayne, Cleeremans, and Wilken 2009, Smithies and Stoljar 2012, and Alter and Howell 2012.

For a sample of other single-author introductions, see Revonsuo 2010, Blackmore 2012, P. M. Churchland 2013, Weisberg 2014, and Seager 2016.

See Brook 1994, 2005 and Kitcher 1990, 2010 for excellent books on Kant's theory of mind which also illustrate the importance of Kant's theory today. See Jorgensen 2010 for much more on seventeenth-century theories of consciousness.

For much more on the sometimes difficult definitional matters, see the 2009 special issue "Defining Consciousness" in the *Journal of Consciousness Studies* 16 (5), as well as DeQuincey (2006) and the peer commentary that follows.

There are also many useful articles with expansive references in the online *Stanford Encyclopedia of Philosophy* (http://plato.stanford.edu/) and the *Internet Encyclopedia of Philosophy* (http://www.iep.utm.edu/), but of course most of them tend to provide a much more cursory look at various sub-topics in the field. Moreover, annual conferences such as "The Science of Consciousness" and the "Association for the Scientific Study of Consciousness" as well as journals such as *Philosophical Psychology*, *Journal of Consciousness Studies*, and *Consciousness and Cognition* have offered quality places for disseminating work in the field. The same is true for the wonderful database and bibliography PhilPapers (http://philpapers.org/).

1

THE METAPHYSICS OF CONSCIOUSNESS

1.1 Dualism and materialism

Metaphysics is the branch of philosophy concerned with the ultimate nature of reality. As such, the issue of the nature of human beings arises and, in particular, how the human mind is related to the human body. Are we exclusively physical things with a physical mind (or brain)? Are our minds something over and above our physical bodies? Can our conscious minds continue to exist after bodily death? There are two broad traditional and competing metaphysical views concerning the nature of the mind and conscious mental states: dualism and materialism. While there are many versions of each, the former generally holds that the conscious mind, or a conscious mental state, is non-physical in some sense. On the other hand, materialists typically hold that the mind is the brain or that conscious mental activity is identical to neural activity. More generally, one can define materialism as the view that everything is material. One might instead opt for the somewhat weaker claim that mental activity *depends upon* brain activity without being identical or reducible to it.

It is important to recognize that by "non-physical," dualists do not merely mean "not visible to the naked eye." Many physical things fit this description, such as the atoms that make up the air in a typical room. For something to be non-physical, it must literally be outside the realm of physics; that is, not in space at all and undetectable in principle by the instruments of physics (though some dualists, such as Descartes in the seventeenth century, may have had "material" in mind when he used the term "physical"). It is equally important to understand that the category "physical" is broader than the category "material." Materialists are called such because there is the understandable tendency to view the brain, a material thing, as the most likely physical candidate to identify with the mind. However, something might be physical but not material such as an electromagnetic or energy field. One might therefore instead be a "physicalist" in some broader sense and still not a dualist. Some authors prefer to use the term "physicalist" anyway but it is still no easy task to interpret the basic thesis that "everything is physical" (Stoljar 2008). Still, to say that the mind is non-physical is to say something much stronger than that it is non-material. Dualists, then, tend to believe that conscious mental states are radically different from anything in the physical world at all.

1.2 Dualism

There are a number of reasons why some version of dualism has been held throughout the centuries. For one thing, especially from the introspective or first-person perspective, our conscious mental states just do not seem like physical things or processes. That is, when we reflect on our conscious perceptions, pains, and desires, they do not seem to be physical in any sense. It was especially difficult, say, at the time of Descartes, to conceive of how a chunk of matter of any complexity could be conscious, let alone perform mental activities such as reasoning. That is, at that time, it was hard to understand how mental activity in general, not just conscious activity, could be wholly material. Consciousness seems to be a unique aspect of the world not to be understood in any physical way. Although materialists will urge that this completely ignores the more scientific third-person perspective on the nature of consciousness and mind, this idea continues to have force for many today. Indeed, as we shall see, it is arguably the crucial underlying intuition behind historically significant "conceivability arguments" against materialism and for dualism. Such arguments typically reason from the premise that one can conceive of one's conscious states existing without one's body or, conversely, that one can conceive of one's own physical duplicate without consciousness at all. The metaphysical conclusion ultimately drawn is that consciousness cannot be identical to anything physical, partly because there is no essential conceptual connection between the mental and the physical. Arguments such as these go back to Descartes and continue to be used today in various ways (Kripke 1972; Chalmers 1996), but it is highly controversial as to whether they succeed in showing that materialism is false. As we shall see later in this chapter, materialists have replied to such arguments and the relevant literature has grown dramatically in recent years.

Historically there has been a link between dualism and a belief in immortality, and hence a more theistic perspective than one tends to find among materialists. Indeed, belief in dualism is sometimes even explicitly theologically motivated. If the conscious mind is not physical, it seems more plausible to believe in the possibility of life after bodily death. On the other hand, if conscious mental activity is *identical to*, or even merely *depends on*, brain activity, then it would seem that when all brain activity ceases, so do all conscious experiences and thus no immortality. After all, what do many people believe continues after bodily death? Presumably, one's own conscious thoughts, memories, experiences, beliefs, and so on. Nonetheless, we should try to evaluate the dualism–materialist debate on its own merits to the extent possible.

One might of course wonder, "even if the mind is physical, what about the soul?" Maybe it's the soul, not the mind, which is non-physical as one might have learned in many religious traditions. While it is true that the term 'soul' (or 'spirit') is often used instead of 'mind' in such religious contexts, it is unclear just how the soul is supposed to differ from the mind. The terms are often even used interchangeably in many historical texts and by most philosophers because it is unclear what else the soul could be other than "the mental substance." It is difficult to describe the soul in any way that doesn't make it sound like what we mean by "the mind." Again, that is what many believe goes on after bodily death, namely conscious mental activity. The term 'soul' carries a more theological connotation, but it doesn't follow that the words 'soul' and 'mind' *refer* to entirely different things. Further, relying purely on religion to answer a scientific question has been disastrous in many past cases, such as the age of the Earth, that diseases were punishments from God, and that schizophrenia involved demon possession. Time after time, there has been long-standing resistance to scientific progress based on religious belief, with little to justify it especially when one looks back in retrospect.

1.2.1 Near-death and out-of-body experiences

Somewhat related to the issue of immortality, the existence of near-death experiences (NDEs) is also used as some evidence for dualism and immortality. Some patients, often in cardiac arrest at a hospital, experience a peaceful moving through a tunnel-like structure to a light and are often able to see doctors working on their bodies while hovering over them in an emergency room (sometimes akin to what is called an "out-of-body experience" or an OBE). These are often very moving emotional experiences which have a profound effect on those who experience them. In some cases, the patient sees other deceased relatives and exhibits little or no electroencephalograph (EEG) activity. In response, materialists will point out that such experiences can be artificially induced in various experimental situations, and that starving the brain of oxygen is known to cause hallucinations. This "dying brain hypothesis" is also bolstered by the notion that the release of endorphins during times of stress and fear can explain the feelings of peacefulness and pleasure. Interestingly, air force pilots can have at least somewhat similar experiences and often pass out when testing their ability to handle centrifugal force while training in a centrifuge which whips pilots around in a circle at high speeds. We must remember that NDEs are supposed to be "near death" not "after death," and thus some brain activity is presumably still present during the time of the NDE (even if not always detected by the EEG which measures only very surface brain activity). Of course, if it could ever be shown that one is having a conscious experience *at the time* there is *no* brain activity, then this would indeed be strong evidence for dualism. I am not aware of this scenario actually occurring. Part of the problem of course is the methodological difficulty of performing controlled and repeatable experiments. Some mystical and religious experiences can often share some of the features of NDEs but some also result from temporal lobe epilepsy.[1]

An OBE occurs when one seems to perceive the world (and often one's own body) from above or outside one's body. You feel like you have left your body and are "floating" above it. This seems to indicate a separate "mind" or "soul" separating out from the body. However, materialists explain how very similar experiences can be easily induced by stimulating neurons in the temporoparietal junction in the right side of the temporal lobe (Blanke et al. 2004; Blanke and Arzy 2005). In the late 1960s and 1970s, five-digit numbers were placed on a shelf above an emergency room bed with very poor results as patients having OBEs were unable to "see" the numbers. As odd as it sounds, it seems that the normal correlation between body image and visual input can become dissociated, which is sometimes also seen in patients with seizures. This would seem to take much of the force out of the OBE-related arguments in favor of dualism. Also, how exactly is dualism supposed to help to explain these phenomena? What is the "phantom body" made out of? How can it interact with the physical body? If it is really non-physical, then how can it have a physical location over one's body?

Various paranormal and psychic phenomena, such as clairvoyance, faith healing, and mindreading, are sometimes also cited as evidence for dualism. However, materialists (and even many dualists) will first likely wish to be skeptical of the alleged phenomena themselves for numerous reasons. There are many modern-day charlatans who should make us seriously question whether there really are such phenomena or mental abilities in the first place. They unethically take advantage of the gullible and vulnerable, often with methods used by magicians. One might think that such astounding abilities could be captured on video and really lead to some incredible repeatable results and accurate predictions. Second, it is again not quite clear just how dualism follows from such phenomena, even if they are genuine. A materialist, or physicalist at least, might insist that though such phenomena, if genuine, are puzzling and perhaps currently difficult to explain in physical terms, they are nonetheless ultimately physical in nature; for example, having to do with very unusual transfers of energy in the physical world. The dualist advantage is perhaps not as obvious as one might think, and we need not jump to supernatural conclusions so quickly.

1.3 Substance dualism and objections

1.3.1 Interactionism

Interactionist dualism, or interactionism, is the most common form of "substance dualism." Its name derives from the widely accepted fact that mental states and bodily states causally interact with each other. For example, my desire to drink something cold causes my body to move to the refrigerator and get something to drink and, conversely, kicking me in the shin will cause me to feel pain and get angry. Due to Descartes' influence, it is also sometimes referred to as "Cartesian dualism." Knowing nothing about just where such causal interaction could take place, Descartes speculated that it was through the pineal gland, a now almost humorous conjecture. The pineal gland is a small gland in the vertebrate brain located between the two hemispheres. But a modern-day interactionist would certainly wish to treat various areas of the brain as the location of such interactions.

Three serious objections are worth mentioning here: (1) One is simply the issue of just how do or could such radically different substances causally interact. How does anything non-physical causally interact with something physical, such as the brain? No such explanation is forthcoming or even seems in principle possible since one side of the causal relation is, by definition, non-physical. Gilbert Ryle (1949) mockingly calls the Cartesian view about the nature of mind a belief in the "ghost in the machine." Moreover, if causation involves a transfer of *energy* from cause to effect, then how is that possible if the mind is really non-physical? Energy is still a physical constant embedded in every system of physics.

(2) Assuming that some such energy transfer makes any sense at all, it is also then often alleged that interactionism is inconsistent with the well-established scientific Conservation of Energy principle, which says that the total amount of energy in the universe, or any controlled part of it, remains constant. So any loss of energy in the cause must be passed along as a corresponding gain of energy in the effect, as in standard billiard ball examples. But if interactionism is true, then when mental events cause physical events, such as when my desire to drink something cold causes my body to move to the refrigerator, energy would literally come into the physical world. On the other hand, when bodily events cause mental events, energy would literally go out of the physical world. At the least, there is a very peculiar and unique notion of energy involved, unless one wished even more radically to deny the conservation principle itself.

(3) Perhaps most importantly, a materialist might use the well-known fact that brain damage (even to very specific areas of the brain) causes mental defects as a serious objection to interactionism (and thus indirectly as support for materialism). Surely the most straightforward explanation for this fact is that the brain area in question is identical to the normal

mental activity in question. It has long been known that brain damage has negative effects on one's mental state and alters (or even eliminates) one's ability to have certain conscious experiences. Even centuries ago, a person would much prefer to suffer trauma to one's leg, for example, than to one's head. The implications of this have not been completely lost on most philosophers. For example, it thus stands to reason that when all of one's brain activity ceases upon death, consciousness is no longer possible and so neither is an afterlife. It seems clear from all the empirical evidence that human consciousness is at least *dependent upon* the functioning of individual brains. Having a functioning brain is, at minimum, *necessary* for having conscious experience, and thus conscious experience must end when the brain ceases to function.

The level of detailed knowledge about the mental function of brain areas has of course increased dramatically in recent years. Very specific mental changes occur when, and only when, very specific brain damage occurs. It is true that such a "correlation" is not the same as an identity or cause, but the simplest explanation for the neuropsychological evidence is clearly that conscious mental activity is, or at least depends upon, the relevant brain activity. For example, in humans, damage to particular brain regions, such as due to disease, trauma, or stroke, is associated with specific impairments of perception, memory, cognition, emotion, and decision-making. Drugs that alter brain activity produce corresponding changes in perception, memory, cognition, emotion, or personality, depending upon the neurotransmitter systems involved and particular brain regions affected. Loss of vision results from damage to areas of the visual cortex (in the back of the brain). Loss of hearing or the ability to recognize sounds, including speech, results from damage to regions of auditory cortex within the temporal lobes. Prosopagnosia, the inability to recognize familiar faces, is typically caused by damage to the occipito-temporal cortex (the fusiform gyrus). Damage to brain regions involved in emotional regulation, which include the limbic system, particularly the amygdala, commonly results in impaired processing of emotional stimuli. Furthermore, numerous neurological disorders and diseases, such as Alzheimer's, bipolar disorder, amnesia, depression, schizophrenia, epilepsy, and mental retardation, which are all characterized by profound changes in cognitive function and awareness, are all associated with specific biochemical, neurophysiological, or neuroanatomical changes in the brain (see Chapter 4 as well).

While some of the specifics are still not fully understood, what is no longer in dispute is that these mental disorders and diseases are direct consequences of aberrant, and often very specific, brain function (Gennaro and Fishman 2015; Piccinini and Bahar 2015).

A dualist might reply that such phenomena do not absolutely refute her metaphysical position since it could be replied that damage to the brain simply *causes* corresponding damage to the (non-physical) mind. However, this raises a host of other related questions: Why not opt for the simpler explanation that brain damage causes mental damage because mental processes simply *are* brain processes? Substance dualism posits the existence of an additional substance associated with each human body, namely a non-physical mind. Further, if the non-physical mind is damaged when brain damage occurs, how would that leave one's mind according to the dualist's conception of an afterlife? Will the severe amnesic at the end of life on Earth retain such a deficit in the afterlife? If proper mental functioning still *depends* on proper brain functioning, then is dualism really in no better position to offer hope for immortality? Wishful thinking or a purely theological rationale for belief in brainless minds cannot outweigh the scientific evidence against the prospect of personal survival after bodily death; that is, against the idea that oneself as a *person* with one's memories, desires, beliefs, and so on continues to exist after brain activity ceases. The dominant Western conception of immortality involves the view that not only some "mind" or "soul" continues into the afterlife, but that it is my consciousness, my memories, and so on which continue. Moreover, what kind of horrible afterlife would it be if all mental damage, such as from a stroke, were to be carried over to the afterlife? This would certainly not be what believers have in mind, especially if one hopes for an eternally blissful or heavenly existence. I do not mean to suggest that the only or main reason to embrace all forms of dualism is based on religion or a desire for immortality. As we shall see later in this chapter, some versions of dualism (such as contemporary property dualism) are motivated mainly by arguments against materialism and dissatisfaction with its ability to explain consciousness.

1.3.2 Parallelism

It is worth pointing out here that there is, historically at least, another less popular form of substance dualism called *parallelism* which denies the causal interaction between the non-physical mental and physical bodily realms (often attributed to Leibniz). The idea is our minds and our bodies run along parallel tracks, so to speak, with each unfolding according to its own laws. Leibniz used the analogy of two watches which are perfectly synchronized so that mental states and bodily states are timed perfectly. So, for example, when you kick me in the shin, I feel pain at about that same time, but the kick didn't cause the pain. Or I decide to get up and get a drink from the refrigerator and then my body moves accordingly, but there's really no cause and effect between my decision and my bodily movement. It *appears* that the mental and physical causally interact but it is not really the case.

The good news is that parallelism avoids the standard objections to interactionism raised above. However, it seems fair to say that it encounters even more serious objections than interactionism. (1) Most obviously, there is the problematic denial of any causal interaction between the mental and physical. Perhaps this won't bother a parallelist but most do not wish to stray that far from common sense such that so many of our ordinary statements come out as false. (2) What keeps our mental and physical "clocks" from getting out of synch? What keeps them running so perfectly together in each of our lives? The parallelist would say that the answer is God who has the knowledge (with foreknowledge) and power to engineer things so perfectly in a "pre-established harmony." Otherwise, for example, I might have strange auditory perceptions of being at a concert while my body is in class or feel the pain prior to your kick to my shin. This is surely difficult to swallow – it would be better if the parallelist did not have to rely on a yet further controversial metaphysical belief to explain the mind–body relation. To be fair to Leibniz, he of course believed that he had already proven that God exists. (3) But suppose, just hypothetically, that God decided to destroy all minds. What would happen according to parallelism? Oddly, absolutely nothing would change with respect to our bodily movements. All human physical behavior, including going to work, having conversations, and so on, would continue on in the same way despite the lack of any mentality behind it or caused by it. This seems like a very bizarre consequence of parallelism. For these reasons, few have turned to parallelism as a defensible form of substance dualism.

In any case, substance dualism has generally fallen out of favor in at least most philosophical circles, though there are exceptions (Swinburne 1986;

Foster 1996). Nonetheless, it often continues to be held, or even presup-posed, in various theological traditions and a belief in immortality.

1.4 Epiphenomenalism and property dualism

Epiphenomenalism has also been attractive to some through the years. It holds that mental events are caused by, but not reducible to, brain events such that those mental events are mere "epiphenomena" which do not, in turn, cause anything physical, despite appearances to the contrary (Robinson 2004). Mental states or events are caused by physical states or events in the brain but do not themselves cause anything. Our conscious lives are, we might say, just "along for the ride." It seems as if our mental life affects our body and the physical world surrounding us: it seems that fear makes our heart beat faster. In reality, however, the causal sequence of events leading to the increased heart beat is not fear, but the state of our nervous system which causes the fear. In this sense, we can at least be assured that all physical events are caused by other physical events, perhaps a desirable view in itself. According to a famous analogy of Thomas Huxley (1874), the relationship between mind and brain is like the relationship between the steam-whistle which accompanies the work of a locomotive engine and the engine itself. Just as the steam-whistle is caused by the engine's operations but has no causal influence upon it, so too the mental is caused by neural mechanisms but in turn has no causal influence on anything physical.

But problems for epiphenomenalism abound. First, it is incredibly coun-terintuitive, for whatever that is worth. But what could be more obvious than my pain makes me cry or that the visual experience of the charging lion makes me run away? At the very least, the epiphenomenalist, like the parallelist, also owes us an explanation of the *appearance* of interaction. Why does it appear as though my pain causes me to cry? Second, if conscious mental states really cause nothing, then there is no reason why they should have evolved. If conscious states clearly modify our behavior in certain ways, then they should be very useful from an evolutionary perspective. Moreover, like the parallelist, the epiphenomenalist also seems committed to the view that ceasing to have any conscious mental states will not affect our bodily behavior at all.

While a detailed survey of all varieties of dualism would take us far afield, it is important to point out that the most popular form of dualism today is called *property dualism*. Property dualism holds that there are mental *properties* (i.e. characteristics or aspects of things), as opposed to substances, that are neither identical nor reducible to physical properties. A property is a way that something is. Redness is a property of roses and pains feel a certain way (e.g. sharp) but the brain has neurophysiological properties. There are different versions of property dualism but what they have in common is the idea that conscious properties, such as the color qualia involved in a conscious visual perception, cannot be explained in purely physical terms and, thus, are not themselves to be identified with any brain state or process. The sharpness of pain, for example, is surely not a property of a brain state. Similarly, if I am hallucinating a yellow rat, the property of being yellow is not a property of a brain state and not a property of anything existing at the time of my experience. Neither the yellowness nor the sharpness can be observed as a brain property from the outside. As we shall see later in this chapter, some have used various anti-materialist arguments as an indirect argument for property dualism.

But one might also wonder what it even means to say that a "property" is mental (and "non-physical" in some sense) without inhering in at least some kind of substance. Does it even make sense to say that some instances of non-physical properties occur in one's physical body? A property dualist does hold that some physical objects or events have both some physical and some non-physical properties. As long as the properties themselves are not reducible, there will be something that exists but cannot be fully accounted for solely by physical objects, events, and properties. In contrast, when we give an explanation of a physical property (such as liquidity), we say that it has been "reduced to" or "constructed from" other physical properties of its parts (such as the atoms or molecules that compose the liquid). The main claim of property dualism is, then, that there are some properties that are *not* reducible to physical properties.

1.5 Idealism, panpsychism, and emergentism

Although not a form of dualism, *idealism* holds that there are only immaterial mental substances, a view more commonly held in the Eastern tradition. The most prominent Western proponent of idealism was eighteenth-century empiricist George Berkeley. So the idealist agrees with the substance dualist that minds are non-physical but denies the existence of mind-independent

physical substances altogether. Idealists, however, agree with the materialist that there is only one kind of thing, a view called "monism," but differ
with respect to what that type of thing is. Yet another version of monism is
called "neutral monism" according to which fundamental entities are neither mental nor physical (Russell 1927; Alter and Nagasawa 2012).

Part of Berkeley's rationale for idealism was that we are really only directly
aware of our conscious or "sensory" states and that Locke's "indirect realist"
inference to mind-independent objects is unwarranted. He also challenged
Locke's distinction between entirely mind-independent primary qualities of
objects, such as size and shape, and secondary qualities of objects, such as
color and sounds, where only the latter are mind-dependent to some extent.
For example, according to Berkeley, the size and shapes of things can vary
from perceiver to perceiver in the same way as colors and sounds. So physical objects are thus really collections of sensory ideas.

But idealism faces a number of serious objections and it often seems to
require a belief in the existence of God. For example, one central question
is: What, outside of us, causes these sensory states? After all, even Berkeley
conceded that something (or someone) else must cause our conscious states;
we certainly don't seem to be constantly causing such states in ourselves;
that is, conjuring up in imagination, say, our visual perceptions as we walk
down the street. Thus, his answer was that God is constantly causing sensory
ideas in each of us. Some in the Eastern tradition might call "God" something more like "pure consciousness" instead. So Berkeley had to invoke a
very busy "hands-on" God to answer such a question about what causes our
sensory perceptions. Well, according to Bishop Berkeley, God is omnipotent and omniscient and so is obviously up to the task! But we should note
that Berkeley is making no less of an inference than the indirect realist who
instead infers that mind-independent physical objects likely cause our sensory
states. There are also other significant standard problems for any idealist view:

First, when ten of us see a table that we are all sitting around, is there
one table or ten? If ten, then how can any science be done at all and why do
our experiences cohere so well? If just one, then isn't it mind-independent
in some sense? Second, when a completely new astronomical observation
or discovery is made, such as the discovery of a very distant galaxy, didn't
the galaxy have to exist first and mind-independently? If so, how can that
be if idealism is true? Wasn't there a time lag from when the light left the
galaxy and our visual conscious perception of the galaxy? How could that
be if there is only consciousness and sensory ideas?

Third, if we do not allow for any inferences from each of our own minds to other things, then it also seems that we shouldn't infer or claim to know that there are other minds either. This seems to lead to an untenable solipsist view such that each person can only know, or even reasonably believe, that he or she exists. Fourth, if idealism is true, how does mind or consciousness "create" the appearance of matter? This is notoriously difficult to answer. Attempts to address this sort of problem by the likes of Berkeley, Leibniz, and some Indian scholars are fraught with difficulties.[2]

Emergentism is the view that consciousness is an emergent property of physical systems. A property P is emergent if P is a novel property of a system or entity that arises when that system or entity has reached a certain level of complexity. P is distinct from and not reducible to the properties of the parts of the system from which it emerges. Although there are several notions of emergence, we might say more generally that the emergent "whole" is greater than the sum of the "parts." The claim here is that consciousness is an emergent property of the brain.

One problem with at least some robust notion of emergence is raised by Kim (1999); namely, that emergent properties would seem to be epiphenomenal. He partly relies on arguments he had previously used to challenge the coherence of what is sometimes called "nonreductive physicalism" (Kim 1989). For example, Kim's "causal exclusion argument" points out that events don't normally have two separate full causes of a physical event (sometimes called "overdetermination"). The previous physical cause would be enough; there would be nothing physical for an emergent property P to cause over and above its "lower-level" parts (or "base"). Thus, P is superfluous or causally impotent at best since the "emergent base" is causally sufficient to produce any subsequent physical changes.

Panpsychism is the somewhat eccentric, but recently resurgent, view that all things in physical reality have some mental properties, even down to micro-particles (Skrbina 2005, 2014; Strawson 2006). All things have some degree of mentality or consciousness. Panpsychism derives from the two Greek words *pan* (all) and *psyche* (soul or mind). Such a view can be attractive to those who reject any kind of reductive materialism. If consciousness didn't arise or emerge at some point from "dead matter" or during the evolution of life, then perhaps it always existed in some form. This basic idea is sometimes called the argument from continuity. If one becomes convinced that consciousness cannot be explained by or reduced to the workings of the brain, one might opt for the view that some form of consciousness or mentality must have been present in all matter from the very start. Panpsychists must of course be careful not to commit the fallacy of division which basically says that if something is true of the whole, it must be true of the parts. This inference is clearly not automatically warranted, for example, water (= H_2O) extinguishes fire but oxygen (O) does not! What is true of an entire house is not automatically true of each part of the house, and so on. So the panpsychist must give us good reason to think that human consciousness cannot be reduced to "something else" before urging us to entertain the possibility that it exists in all matter, albeit in a more primitive form.

One major objection to panpsychism is the so-called "combination problem": If mind or consciousness is supposed to exist in quarks, atoms, photons, or cells, then human minds must be some kind of combination or sum of these lesser minds. But how do the experiences of fundamental entities combine to produce the familiar human conscious experience that we have? It is even very difficult to see how this question could be answered (Goff 2006, 2009; Chalmers 2016). Further, if a panpsychist is motivated to reject materialism due to its inability to explain the connection between the brain and consciousness, doesn't a similar problem simply reappear at the micro-level?

Another obvious problem with panpsychism is simply the lack of evidence that such fundamental entities possess minds, let alone some level of consciousness. Atoms and photons, not to mention tables, rocks, and planets, lack characteristic evidence of consciousness, such as complex behavior, an ability to learn, requisite brain activity, and so on. We may disagree about consciousness in, say, fish, insects, or even some plants, but what *positive* reason is there for attributing consciousness to a table or a quark? Further, what ethical implications are there for panpsychism? Does cutting down a tree literally cause suffering or pain? What about mowing your lawn or tearing down a building to put up a new house?

1.6 Materialism: some general support

As we saw earlier in this chapter, some form of materialism is probably much more widely held today than in centuries past due to the explosion in scientific knowledge about the workings of the brain and its intimate connection with consciousness. Stimulation of specific areas of the brain results in modality-specific conscious experiences. Indeed, materialism often seems to be a working assumption in neurophysiology. The idea is that science is showing us that conscious mental states, such as visual perceptions, are really just identical to a certain neurochemical brain process, much like the science of chemistry taught us that water just *is* H_2O.

There are also other theoretical factors on the side of materialism, such as adherence to the so-called "principle of simplicity" or "Occam's razor," which says that if two theories can equally explain a given phenomenon, then we should accept the one that posits fewer objects or forces. In this case, even if dualism could equally explain consciousness (which would of course be disputed by materialists), materialism is clearly the simpler theory in so far as it does not posit any objects or processes over and above physical ones. Materialists will wonder *why* there is a *need* to believe in the existence of such mysterious non-physical entities. Moreover, in the aftermath of the Darwinian revolution, it would seem that materialism is on even stronger ground provided that one accepts basic evolutionary theory and the notion that most animals are conscious. Given the similarities between the more primitive parts of the human brain and the brains of other animals, it seems most natural to conclude that, through evolution, increasing layers of brain areas correspond to increased mental abilities. For example, having a well-developed prefrontal cortex allows humans to reason and plan in ways not available to dogs and cats. At the same time, it seems reasonable to attribute fear and pain to most animals who share those corresponding brain areas with humans (and behave in similar ways to us). Much the same goes for visual and olfactory states. It seems much less controversial to hold that we should be materialists about the minds of animals. If so, then it would be odd indeed to hold that non-physical conscious states suddenly appear on the scene with humans.

There are still, however, a number of much-discussed and important objections to materialism, most of which question the notion that materialism can adequately *explain* conscious experience.

1.7 Materialism: problems and replies

1.7.1 The explanatory gap and the hard problem

Joseph Levine (1983) coined the expression "the explanatory gap" to express a difficulty for any materialistic attempt to explain consciousness. Although not really concerned to reject the metaphysics of materialism,

Levine gives eloquent expression to the idea that there is a key gap in our ability to explain the connection between phenomenal properties and brain properties (see also Levine 2001). The basic problem is that it is, at least at present, very difficult for us to understand the relationship between brain properties and phenomenal properties in any explanatory satisfying way, especially given the fact that it seems possible for one to be present without the other. There is an odd kind of arbitrariness involved: Why or how does some particular brain process produce that particular taste or visual sensation? It is difficult to see any real explanatory connection between specific conscious states and brain states in a way that explains just how or why the former are identical to the latter. There is therefore an explanatory gap between the physical and mental. Levine argues that this difficulty in explaining consciousness is unique; that is, we do not have similar worries about other scientific identities, such as that "water is H_2O" or that "heat is mean molecular kinetic energy."

David Chalmers (1995) has articulated a similar worry by using the catchy phrase "the hard problem of consciousness," which basically refers to the difficulty of explaining just how physical processes in the brain give rise to subjective conscious experiences.

> [The] really hard problem is the problem of *experience*. . . . How can we explain why there is something it is like to entertain a mental image, or to experience an emotion? It is widely agreed that experience arises from a physical basis, but we have no good explanation of why and how it so arises.
>
> (1995, 201)

Others have made similar points, as Chalmers acknowledges, but reference to the phrase "the hard problem" has now become commonplace in the literature. Unlike Levine, however, Chalmers is much more inclined to draw anti-materialist metaphysical conclusions from these and other considerations. Chalmers distinguishes the hard problem of consciousness from what he calls the (relatively) "easy problems" of consciousness, such as the ability to discriminate and categorize stimuli, the ability of a cognitive system to access its own internal states, and the difference between wakefulness and sleep. The easy problems generally have more to do with the functions of consciousness, but Chalmers urges that solving them does not touch the hard problem of phenomenal consciousness (see also Shear 1997).

There are many responses by materialists to the above charges, but it is worth emphasizing that Levine does not reject the metaphysics of materialism. Instead, he sees the "explanatory gap [as] primarily an epistemological problem" (Levine 2001, 10). That is, it is primarily a problem having to do with knowledge or understanding.

Perhaps most important for the materialist, however, is recognition of the fact that different concepts can pick out the same property or object in the world (Loar 1997). Out in the world there is only the one "stuff," which we can conceptualize either as water or as H_2O. The traditional distinction, made most notably by Gottlob Frege in the late nineteenth century, between "meaning" (or "sense") and "reference" is also relevant here. Two or more concepts, which can have different meanings, can refer to the same property or object, much like 'Venus' and 'The Morning Star.' One strategy, then, is for materialists to explain that it is essential to distinguish between mental properties and our concepts of those properties. There are so-called "phenomenal concepts" which use a phenomenal or "first-person" property to refer to a conscious mental state, such as a sensation of red (Alter and Walter 2007; Carruthers and Veillet 2007). In contrast, we can also use various concepts couched in physical or neurophysiological terms to refer to that same mental state from the third-person point of view. There is thus one conscious mental state which can be conceptualized in two different ways: either by employing first-person experiential phenomenal concepts or by employing third-person neurophysiological concepts. It may then just be a "brute fact" about the world that there are such identities and the appearance of arbitrariness between brain properties and mental properties is just that – an *apparent* problem leading many to wonder about the alleged explanatory gap. Qualia would then still be identical to physical properties. Moreover, this response provides a diagnosis for why there even *seems* to be such a gap, namely that we use very different concepts to pick out the same property. The explanatory gap at best reflects our current conceptual or imaginative capacities and not any real division between objective metaphysical substances in the world.

Further, materialists urge that science will be able, in principle, to close the gap and solve the hard problem of consciousness in an analogous way that we now have a very good understanding for why "water is H_2O" or "heat is mean molecular kinetic energy" that was lacking centuries ago. Maybe the hard problem isn't so hard after all – it will just take some more time. After all, the science of chemistry didn't develop overnight and we are relatively early in the history of neurophysiology and our understanding of phenomenal consciousness. Perhaps the hard problem is more like the old "vitalism" problem of how "life" emerges from "matter" (Dennett 1991; Churchland 1996). How can success for a reductionistic strategy be ruled out so soon? Given the relative infancy of neurophysiology, it seems premature to declare that any kind of successful physicalist reduction is hopeless. This problem starts to sound like the claim that since we cannot now understand the brain-consciousness link, we'll never be able to understand it (which applies more to "mysterianism" discussed below in section 1.7.5). This is partly why Daniel Dennett said that "accepting dualism is giving up" (Dennett 1991, 37). Patricia Churchland (1996) also argues that our inability to imagine or not to imagine a mechanism for consciousness is more of an uninteresting psychological fact about us, not an interesting metaphysical fact about the world or the true nature of consciousness.

Further, it seems reasonable at some point to turn the tables on the dualist: How exactly does simply claiming that conscious mental states occur non-physically *explain* anything? How can one explain the intricate workings of the human mind in terms of a non-physical substance? How or why does a non-physical mind "give rise" to consciousness?

1.7.2 *The knowledge argument*

There is a pair of very widely discussed and related objections to materialism which come from the seminal writings of Thomas Nagel (1974) and Frank Jackson (1982). These arguments, especially Jackson's, have come to be known as examples of the "knowledge argument" against materialism, due to their clear emphases on the epistemological (that is, knowledge-related) limitations of materialism. Like Levine, Nagel does not reject the metaphysics of materialism. Jackson had originally intended for his argument to yield a dualistic conclusion (epiphenomenalism), but he no longer holds that view (Jackson 1998, 2004). The general pattern of each argument is to assume that all the physical facts are known about some conscious mind or conscious experience. Yet, the argument goes, not all is known about the mind or experience. It is then inferred that the missing knowledge is non-physical in some sense which is surely an anti-materialist conclusion in some sense (Alter 2005).

Nagel imagines a future where we know everything physical there is to know about some other conscious creature's mind, such as a bat. However, it seems clear that we would still not know something crucial, namely "what it is like to be a bat." It will not do to imagine what it is like for us to be a bat. We would still not know what it is like to be a bat from the bat's subjective or first-person point of view. The idea, then, is that if we accept the hypothesis that we know all of the (objective) physical facts about bat minds, and yet some (subjective) knowledge about bat minds is left out, then materialism is inherently flawed when it comes to explaining consciousness. Even in an ideal future in which everything physical is known by us, something would still be left out. Jackson's somewhat similar, but no less influential, argument begins by asking us to imagine a future where a person, Mary, is kept in a black and white room from birth, during which time she becomes a brilliant neuroscientist and an expert on color perception. Mary never sees red, for example, but she learns all of the physical facts and everything neurophysiologically about human color vision. Eventually she is released from the room and sees red for the first time. Jackson argues that it is clear that Mary comes to learn something new, namely what it is like to experience red. This is a new piece of knowledge and hence she must have come to know some non-physical fact (since, by hypothesis, she already knew all of the physical facts). Thus, not all knowledge about the conscious mind is physical knowledge.

More formally, we might put Jackson's (1982) argument as follows:

(1) Mary (before her release from the black and white room) knows *everything physical* there is to know about seeing red, but
(2) Mary (before her release) does *not* know everything there is to know *about seeing red* because she clearly learns something new about it upon her release.
(3) *Therefore,* There are some truths or facts about seeing red that escape a physicalist (and thus materialist) explanation.
(4) *Therefore,* Physicalism (and thus materialism) is false and phenomenal properties or qualities (i.e. "qualia") cannot be explained as (or identified with) physical properties.

The influence and quantity of work that these ideas have generated cannot be exaggerated. Numerous materialist responses to Nagel's argument have been presented (such as Van Gulick 1985) and there is an entire anthology devoted to Jackson's knowledge argument (Ludlow et al. 2004). Some materialists have even wondered if we should concede up front that Mary wouldn't be able to imagine the color red even before leaving the room, so that maybe she wouldn't be surprised upon seeing red for the first time. Various suspicions about the effectiveness of such thought experiments also usually accompany this response. That is, perhaps premise 1 should not even be conceded in the sense that we can't judge right now if such a futuristic omniscient neuropsychologist could know everything physical but still not be able to form an image of redness.

Another well-known reply is the "ability hypothesis" put forth by David Lewis (1983, 1988) and Lawrence Nemirow (1990). Mary does not acquire any new factual or propositional knowledge after release, but only a set of abilities such as the ability to imagine, remember, and recognize colors or color experiences. Lewis and Nemirow argue that Mary's epistemic progress after release consists in the acquisition of knowing what it is like (e.g. to experience a certain color) but they both think that knowing what it is like just is to have certain practical abilities. According to Nemirow, "knowing what an experience is like is the same as knowing how to imagine having the experience" (Nemirow 1990, 495). Lewis explains that "knowing what it is like is the possession of abilities: abilities to recognize, abilities to imagine, abilities to predict one's behavior by imaginative experiments" (Lewis 1983, 131).

More commonly, however, materialists reply to premise 2 by arguing that Mary does not learn a *new fact* when seeing red for the first time, but rather learns the same fact in a *different way*. Recalling the distinction between concepts and objects or properties, the materialist will urge that there is only the one physical fact about color vision, but there are two ways to come to know it: either by employing neurophysiological concepts or by actually undergoing the relevant experience and so by employing phenomenal concepts. We might say that Mary, upon leaving the black and white room, becomes acquainted with the same neural property as before, but only now from the first-person point of view. The property itself isn't new, only the perspective (or "mode of presentation") is different. In short, coming to learn or know something new does not always entail learning some new fact about the world. Analogies are given in other less controversial areas; for example, one can come to know about some historical fact or event by reading a (reliable) third-person historical account or by having observed that event oneself. But there is still only the one objective fact under two different descriptions.

Finally, it is crucial to remember that, according to most, the metaphysics of materialism remains unaffected. Drawing a metaphysical conclusion from such purely epistemological premises is always a questionable practice. For example, Nagel's argument doesn't show, and doesn't even intend to show, that bat mental states are not identical to bat brain states. Indeed, a materialist might even expect the conclusion that Nagel reaches. After all, given that our brains are so different from bat brains, it almost seems natural for there to be certain aspects of bat experience that we could never fully comprehend. Only the bat actually *undergoes* the relevant brain processes. Similarly, Jackson's argument doesn't show that Mary's color experience is distinct from her brain processes.

Despite the plethora of materialist responses, vigorous debate continues since many still think that something profound must always be missing from any materialist attempt to explain consciousness. Part of the underlying intuition is that understanding subjective phenomenal consciousness is an inherently first-person activity which cannot be captured by any objective third-person scientific means, no matter how much scientific knowledge is accumulated. Some knowledge about consciousness is essentially limited to first-person knowledge.

1.7.3 Zombies

Unlike many of the above objections to materialism, the appeal to the possibility of zombies is often taken as both a problem for materialism and a more positive argument for some form of dualism, such as property dualism. The philosophical notion of a "zombie" basically refers to conceivable creatures which are physically and behaviorally indistinguishable from us but lack consciousness entirely (Chalmers 1996). It certainly seems logically *possible* for there to be such creatures: "the conceivability of zombies seems . . . obvious to me. . . . While this possibility is probably empirically impossible, it certainly seems that a coherent situation is described; I can discern no contradiction in the description" (Chalmers 1996, 96). Philosophers often contrast what is logically possible (in the sense of "that which is not self-contradictory") from what is empirically possible given the actual laws of nature. Thus, it is logically possible for me to jump fifty feet in the air, but not empirically possible. Philosophers often use the notion of "possible worlds" – that is, different ways that the world might have been – in describing such non-actual situations or possibilities. The objection, then, typically proceeds from such a possibility to the conclusion that materialism is false because materialism would seem to rule out that possibility. Part of the reason is because it has been fairly widely accepted (since Kripke 1972) that all identity statements are necessarily true (that is, "true in all possible worlds") and the same should therefore go for mind–brain identity claims. Since the possibility of zombies shows that it doesn't go for mind–brain identity claims, we should conclude that materialism is false. The metaphysical conclusion ultimately drawn is that consciousness cannot be identical to anything physical, partly because there is no essential conceptual connection between the mental and the physical. More formally:

(1)   We can conceive of zombies, which are creatures just like us but lacking consciousness.
(2)   If we can conceive of zombies, then they are possible.
(3)   If zombies are possible, then materialism is false.
Therefore, (4) materialism is false.

It is impossible to do justice to all of the subtleties and replies here. The literature in response to zombie and related "conceivability" arguments is enormous.[3] A few lines of reply are as follows: First, perhaps some things or scenarios just *seem* conceivable but really aren't; that is, premise 1 might be false. Perhaps we can also conceive of water not being H_2O, since there seems to be no logical contradiction in doing so, but, according to received wisdom from Kripke, that is not really possible. And there may be a very good reason why such zombie scenarios *seem* possible, namely that we do not (or at least not yet) see what the necessary connection is between neural events and conscious mental events. On the one side, we are dealing with scientific third-person concepts and, on the other, we are employing phenomenal concepts. We are, perhaps, simply currently not in a position to understand completely such a necessary connection.

Second, it is sometimes objected that the conceivability of something does not really entail its possibility (so premise 2 is false). Much of the debate centers on various alleged similarities or dissimilarities between the mind–brain and water–H$_2$O cases (or other such scientific identities). Indeed, the issue of the exact relationship between conceivability and possibility is the subject of an entire anthology on the topic (Gendler and Hawthorne 2002).

Third, even if zombies are conceivable in the sense of "logically possible" or "not self-contradictory," how can any substantial metaphysical conclusion be drawn about the actual world? Premise 3 incorrectly assumes again that one can infer from an epistemic claim to a metaphysical conclusion. There is often suspicion about what philosophers' "thought experiments" can teach us about the nature of our minds. It seems that one could take virtually any philosophical or scientific identity claim, conceive that it is possibly false, and then conclude that it is actually false. The same would then have to go for Chalmers' own "naturalistic dualism" which conjectures that consciousness is tied to "fundamental information." But surely it is not *self-contradictory* to suppose that consciousness is not a fundamental ontological feature of the world. Surely it is at least *conceivable* that consciousness is not tied to "information" in the way that Chalmers has argued (Chalmers 1996, 2007). Much the same is true for any theory of consciousness which identifies it with virtually anything physical or in nature. And if Chalmers accepts this possibility, he presumably would not take it as proving that his ontological view about the actual world is false. This also calls into question the central notion that identity statements must be necessarily true; that is, true in all possible worlds. Perhaps there is a difference between "logical" and "metaphysical" necessity such that the latter is somewhat weaker than the former.

Depending on how one is inclined to respond to the above antimaterialist arguments, one can be classified as either a "type-A" or "type-B" materialist (Chalmers 2010a). According to type-A materialists such as Dennett (1991) and Dretske (1995), "there is no epistemic gap between physical and phenomenal truths, or at least any apparent epistemic gap is easily closed" (Chalmers 2010a, 111). Type-A materialists, for example, argue that it is not even conceivable that there are zombies (and so reject premise 1). They deny that there is even an *epistemic* gap between the physical and phenomenal consciousness. They also deny that truths about consciousness cannot be *deduced from* the complete physical truth, as is claimed in the knowledge argument.

So type-A materialists think that Mary could deduce what red looks like from her knowledge of all of the physical facts. For this reason, type-A materialism has also come to be known as "*a priori* physicalism." For type-A materialists, then, there really isn't a special hard problem of consciousness over and above the so-called "easy" problems.

Type-B materialism is the more commonly held position. It concedes that there is an epistemic gap between the physical and phenomenal consciousness but argues that there is no metaphysical gap. So, for the reasons discussed above, zombies are conceivable but not really metaphysically possible. Premise 2 is false according to type-B materialists. Mary is indeed ignorant of something prior to leaving the room but it's not a new fact (rather, an old fact learned in a new way). Block and Stalnaker (1999), Perry (2001), and Papineau (2002), for example, favor this line of argument. By way of contrast, it has therefore come to be known as "*a posteriori* physicalism" which basically says that all truths about consciousness follow by *metaphysical necessity* from the complete physical truth, even though the complete physical truth does *not logically entail* all truths about consciousness. The type-B materialist will concede that there is a hard problem of consciousness but urge that it doesn't pose any special problems for the metaphysics of materialism.

1.7.4 Leibniz's Law and intensional contexts

Let us return more generally to the notion of conceivability and its use in arguments for dualism. There is a different kind of systematic worry about any argument of this kind (see Churchland 2013, chapter two).

Consider the following sentences:

(1)   There is *water* in the pool.
(2)   There is H_2O in the pool.

If (1) is true, then so is (2). If (1) is false, then so is (2). We would, of course, normally expect this when one *co-referring* term or expression is replaced by another. No problem so far. But now consider the following and let's assume that Karen is a four-year-old who knows nothing about chemistry:

(3)   Karen knows that her pool is filled with *water*.
(4)   Karen knows that her pool is filled with H_2O.

(3) is true while (4) is false. Additional examples like (3) and (4) can be constructed very easily, whenever someone is ignorant of even a well-established identity.

Now consider for example the following "argument from introspection" for mind–body dualism or against materialism as discussed by Churchland (2013, 49–56):

(1) Mental states are knowable through introspection.
(2) Brain states are *not* knowable through introspection.
Therefore, (3) Mental states are *not* brain states.

The premises seem clearly true. I can learn about my mental states via introspection but I cannot know about my brain purely through introspection. The conclusion is supposed to follow from what has been called "Leibniz's Law"; that is, if x and y have any different properties, then x cannot be identical to y. Alternatively: If x has all the same properties as y, then x = y. The problem is that Leibniz's Law fails in *intensional contexts;* that is, cases where replacing one co-referring term with another can change a statement's truth-value, such as in the Karen-water sentences (3) and (4) above. Terms like "know," "believe," and "conceive" are indications of such contexts.

So it *seems* that mental states have a property that brain states lack – that is, the property "knowable through introspection" – and thus they must be distinct. But this argument fails because it is mistakenly using Leibniz's Law in an intensional context. If we were allowed to use this law in such contexts, then we could prove the non-identity of anything, even water and H_2O, Venus and the Morning Star, Muhammad Ali and Cassius Clay, and so on. For example, water has a property that H_2O lacks ("known by Karen to be in her pool"), so they are distinct. Something has clearly gone wrong. The dualist cannot prove the non-identity of brain states and mental states by using Leibniz's Law in this way.

Similar problems confront Descartes' well-known divisibility argument for substance dualism where he also relies on Leibniz's Law. This time the property in question is divisibility. For example, in the sixth Meditation, Descartes argues as follows:

(1) My body, which includes my brain, is divisible (i.e. has parts).
(2) I cannot conceive of my mind as divisible.
Therefore, (3) My mind is distinct from any part of my body.

First, Descartes rightly recognizes that "conceiving" is broader than "imagining." The former just means "understand" whereas the latter involves "forming an image of." So although I cannot imagine or picture a 1,000-sided figure, I can still understand the idea and it's possible that there is one (or could be one). On the other hand, a "round square" would even be inconceivable which we would normally take as indicating impossibility. Descartes has in mind "inconceivable" in his own meditations about the divisibility of minds. This is one reason he believed that nothing could be both physical and mental.

One might agree with Descartes that when we introspect our mind, we cannot understand it as divisible or as having parts, but why suppose that we can learn all of the truth about, or the essential nature of, our conscious minds solely through introspection? Can't we also learn about our minds via a third-person scientific point of view? If not, then what are neurophysiologists and psychiatrists doing? Even if I cannot understand my mind as divisible when I introspect, surely you can understand my mind as divisible. This also explains Descartes' rejection of unconscious mental states; after all, I can't introspect my unconscious states by definition. It also explains the failure of the argument from introspection since all it can really prove is that we could not learn of any potential mental state–brain state identity through introspection alone.

Another way to frame the problem is via the age-old distinction between appearance and reality. A materialist thinks that even though we do not *appear* to be introspecting our brain states, we *really* are. Our minds do not appear to have parts when we introspect, but in fact our minds really do have parts, namely the parts of our brain. An analogy to outer perception might help here. The water in the pool doesn't *appear* to be made up of hydrogen and oxygen but it *really* is. Scientific research, chemistry in this case, shows us that outer objects are not really the way they appear to us. It seems at least reasonable to believe that inner perception works in the same way. Actually, it would be very confusing and distracting if we were directly aware of our brain activity when we introspect.

One might modify Descartes' argument to avoid the above objection as follows:

(1)   My body is divisible (i.e. has parts).
(2)   My mind is not divisible (i.e. does not have parts).
Therefore, (3) My mind is distinct from any part of my body.

However, materialists will obviously respond that premise 2 simply begs the question against materialism. That is, it assumes that the mind is not physical (and this not any part of my body). Indeed, the main issue is whether the mind is really divisible.

So the above arguments do not really show the non-identity of mental states and brain states.

1.7.5 Mysterianism

Finally, Colin McGinn goes so far as to argue that we are simply not capable of solving the problem of consciousness (McGinn 1989, 1991). In short, "mysterians" believe that the hard problem can *never* be solved because of human cognitive limitations. The explanatory gap can never be filled. The hard problem becomes the "impossible problem." Once again, however, McGinn does not reject the metaphysics of materialism, but rather argues that we are epistemically "cognitively closed" with respect to this problem, much like a mouse or cat is cognitively incapable of solving, or even understanding, calculus problems. More specifically, McGinn claims that we are cognitively closed as to *how* the brain produces conscious awareness. McGinn concedes that some brain property produces conscious experience, but we cannot understand how this is so or even know what that brain property is. Our concept-forming mechanisms simply will not allow us to grasp the physical and causal basis of consciousness. As we have seen, even materialists tend to agree that there are radically different concepts involved.

McGinn does not entirely rest his argument on past failed attempts at explaining consciousness in materialist terms; instead, he presents another argument for his admittedly pessimistic conclusion. McGinn observes that we do not have a mental faculty that can access both consciousness and the brain. We access consciousness through introspection or the first-person perspective, but our access to the brain is through the use of outer spatial senses (e.g. vision) or a more third-person perspective. Thus we have no way to access both the brain and consciousness *together*, and therefore any explanatory link between them is forever beyond our reach.

Materialist responses are numerous: First, one might wonder why we can't combine the two perspectives within certain experimental contexts. Both first-person and third-person scientific data about the brain and consciousness can be acquired and used to solve the hard problem. Even if a single person cannot grasp consciousness from both perspectives *at the same time*, why can't a plausible physicalistic theory emerge from such a combined approach? Presumably, McGinn would say that we are not capable of putting such a theory together in any appropriate way. Second, despite McGinn's protests to the contrary, many view the problem of explaining consciousness as a merely temporary limit of our theorizing, and not something which is unsolvable in principle (Dennett 1991), such as we saw in response to the hard problem. Third, it may be that McGinn expects too much, namely grasping some causal link between the brain and consciousness. After all, if conscious mental states are simply identical to brain states, then there may simply be a "brute fact" that really does not need any further explaining. Indeed, this is sometimes also said in response to the explanatory gap and the hard problem, as we saw earlier. It may even be that some form of dualism is presupposed in McGinn's argument to the extent that brain states are said to "cause" or "give rise to" consciousness, instead of using the language of identity. Fourth, McGinn's analogy to lower animals and mathematics is not quite accurate. Rats, for example, have no concept of calculus at all. It is not as if they can grasp it to some extent but just haven't figured out the answer to some particular problem within mathematics. Rats are just completely oblivious to calculus problems. On the other hand, we humans obviously do have some grasp on consciousness and on the workings of the brain. It is not clear, then, why we should accept the extremely pessimistic and universally negative conclusion that we can *never* discover the answer to the problem of consciousness, or, more specifically, why we could never understand the link between consciousness and the brain.

1.8 Varieties of materialism

Despite the apparent simplicity of materialism – say, in terms of the identity between mental states and neural states – the fact is that there are many different forms of materialism. Behaviorism (Watson 1913; Skinner 1953) roughly held that mental states are nothing more than behavioral dispositional states (though there are in fact many different kinds of behaviorist views). For example, the mental state "desiring water to drink" is identical to the disposition to drink water in certain circumstances. But positing such a close connection between mental states and behavior has been fatal to behaviorism – there are few, if any, behaviorists today. It seems clear that one can have various mental states even in the total absence of a disposition to behave, such as in a paralyzed person. Conversely, a great actor might behave in ways that indicate suffering and pain (including verbal reports) while the actor is really in no such state. The main problem is that we tend to think that mental states *cause* behavior and so any identification seems too strong.

While a detailed survey of all varieties of materialism is beyond the scope of this section, it is at least important to acknowledge the commonly drawn distinction between two kinds of "identity theory": token-token and type-type materialism. Type-type identity theory is the stronger thesis and says that mental *properties*, such as "having a desire to drink some water" or "being in pain," are literally identical to a brain property of some kind. Again, such identities were originally meant to be understood as on a par with, for example, the scientific identity between "being water" and "being composed of H_2O" (Place 1956; Smart 1959). However, this view historically came under serious attack because it seems to rule out the so-called "multiple realizability" of conscious mental states. The idea is simply that it seems perfectly possible for there to be other conscious beings (aliens, radically different animals) who can have those same mental states but who are also radically different from us physiologically (Fodor 1974). It seems that commitment to type-type identity theory led to the undesirable result that only organisms with brains like ours can have conscious states. Somewhat more technically, most materialists wish to leave room for the possibility that mental properties can be "instantiated" or "realized" in different kinds of organisms. This point actually can even apply *within* a species. In our brain, for example, the areas responsible for a specific cognitive function can be different from person to person, especially in cases where brains are damaged early in life. This so-called "neuroplasticity" involves the brain "rewiring" to perform the same cognitive task in a different area.

As a consequence, a more modest "token-token" identity theory has become preferable to many materialists. This view simply holds that each particular conscious mental *event* in some organism is identical to some particular brain process or event in that organism. This seems to preserve much of what the materialist wants, yet allows for the multiple realizability of conscious states, because both the human and the alien can still have a conscious desire for something to drink while each mental event is identical to a (different) physical state in each organism. This could even be a problem across humans, not to mention across various animals on Earth. But token-identity has long been criticized for not being metaphysically robust enough since it doesn't identify a physical counterpart to mental-state types. Token-token identities do not seem general enough to do science. One appeal of type-identity theory is that it gives us generalizations like the ones we find in chemistry. Water is *always* H_2O. So we can actually do science with this knowledge and arrive at general laws of nature. We wouldn't be in as good a position if we only knew that this or that particular instance of water is H_2O.

Taking the notion of multiple realizability seriously has also led many to embrace *functionalism*, which is the view that conscious mental states should really only be identified with the functional role they play within an organism rather than what physically makes them up (Putnam 1975). Mental states are analogous to the function of the heart pumping blood throughout the body. It doesn't matter what the heart is made out of; just what it does. For example, conscious pains are defined more in terms of input and output, such as caused by bodily damage and causing avoidance behavior, as well as in terms of their relationship to other mental states. This is normally viewed as a form of materialism since virtually all functionalists also believe, like the token-token theorist, that something physical ultimately realizes that functional state in the organism, though functionalism does not necessarily entail materialism.

Critics of functionalism, however, have argued that such purely functional accounts cannot adequately explain the essential "feel" of conscious states and that it seems possible to have two functionally equivalent creatures, one of whom lacking qualia entirely (Block 1980; Shoemaker 1981). This is the "absent qualia" objection. Having the right inputs and outputs isn't enough to have pains and taste sensations. One might again think of zombies here but even a sophisticated unconscious robot suffices to make the point. There could be creatures functionally equivalent to normal humans whose mental states have no qualitative character at all.

The "inverted spectrum" objection to functionalism maintains that there could be an individual who, for example, satisfies the functional definition of our experience of red, but is experiencing yellow and yet is behaviorally indistinguishable from someone with normal color vision (Shoemaker 1982;

Horgan 1984). We learn color terms when we are young mainly by ostention; that is, pointing to objects with those colors (e.g. "that's red" when pointing to a stop sign, a fire truck, a ripe tomato, and so on). But how do I know that you experience the same color sensation as I do when I perceive a ripe tomato? Maybe it looks more like a lemon color to you and vice versa. It may be that some such cases can be ruled out given the actual structure of our perceptual apparatus, but it seems possible that there could be two people with inverted spectra while at the same time using the terms "red" and "yellow" in the same way. So their conscious experience would be different but the function would be the same.

These objections are based on the possibility that a creature with the same functional organization of normal human beings might still not have any (or the right kind of) qualia. In response, some claim that these arguments provide counterexamples only to very simplistic functional theories. A more sophisticated functionalism could call into doubt the notion that functional duplicates with absent or inverted qualia are really possible (Dennett 1978; Levin 1985).

Some go so far as to embrace *eliminative materialism* and even deny the very existence of mental states altogether, at least in the sense that the very concept of consciousness is hopelessly muddled (Wilkes 1988) or that the mentalistic notions found in "folk psychology," such as desires and beliefs, will eventually be eliminated and replaced by physicalistic terms as neurophysiology matures into the future (P. M. Churchland 1981, 1985; P. S. Churchland 1986). Our ordinary or common-sense understanding of the mind is deeply wrong. This is seen as analogous to past similar eliminations based on deeper scientific understanding; for example, we no longer need to speak of "ether" or "phlogiston." Eliminative materialists argue that folk psychology radically misdescribes cognitive processes and so the mental states of folk psychology do not really pick out anything that is real. Like dualists, eliminative materialists insist that ordinary mental states cannot in any way be reduced to or identified with neurological events or processes. That is, there is little reason to think that there will be one-to-one inter-theoretical matches between a folk psychological term and a brain state. However, unlike dualists, eliminativists claim there is nothing more to the mind than what occurs in the brain. The reason mental states are irreducible is not because they are non-physical but because mental states do not really exist. While it is true that we sometimes revise a theory instead of eliminating a concept entirely, eliminativists believe that the latter is (or will be) warranted in the case of mental concepts.

Some have argued that eliminative materialism is in some sense self-refuting (Baker 1987). They insist that the eliminativist herself, for example, requires the existence of beliefs to assert that mental states don't exist. But if the eliminativist has any such belief, then there are beliefs, and eliminativism must be false. It is also hard to imagine a future where we will no longer use mental terms, at least in everyday conversation or, say, in raising our children. To the extent that eliminative materialism is a prediction about the future elimination of the use of mental terms, it is difficult to understand how this could become a reality (unlike the elimination of "ether" and other such past terms).

Perhaps more closely related to consciousness, some eliminativists argue that there is no such thing as qualia when they are defined in certain problematic ways. Dennett (1988) challenges the plausibility of the alleged features of qualia, such as their inherent subjectivity and their private infallible nature. In so doing, he suggests that our qualia concepts do not really correspond to the actual workings of our cognitive system. Still, Dennett's arguments, even if successful, might instead be thought of as showing that qualia do not have some of the properties that many attribute to them instead of showing that qualia don't exist at all. Similarly, Hardcastle (2000) argues that the neurological basis for pain sensations is so complex that no one thing could underlie our folk conception of pain, and thus that pain is a myth. However, her arguments might really be thought of as not showing that pain doesn't exist, but rather that it is more complicated than is normally suggested by our ordinary folk conception.

Finally, it should be noted that not all materialists believe that conscious mentality can be explained in terms of the physical, at least in the sense that the former can be "reduced" to the latter (depending on what one means by "reduce"). Materialism is true as an ontological or metaphysical doctrine, but facts about the mind cannot be deduced from facts about the physical world, much like facts about economics cannot be reduced to facts about physics (Boyd 1980; Van Gulick 1992). Economic theory cannot be derived from facts about physics. In some ways, this might be viewed as a relatively harmless variation on materialist themes, but others object to the materialist credentials of this "non-reductive materialism" and even its very coherence. For example, as we saw with respect to emergence,

Kim (1989, 1999) uses his "causal exclusion argument" against this view. If mental states are something over and above their underlying physical reality, then there would be nothing physical for them to cause over and above their "lower-level" physical reality. Thus, mental states would be superfluous or causally impotent once again on the fairly common-sense assumption called "causal closure"; namely, that every physical event has a full physical cause. Indeed, the line between non-reductive materialism and property dualism (and even emergence) is not always so easy to draw (though see Van Gulick 2001).

On a related front, some are content to invoke a somewhat weaker "supervenience" relation between mind and matter. Although "superveni-ence" is a highly technical notion with many variations, the basic idea is one of *dependence* (instead of identity); for example, that the mental depends on the physical such that any mental change must be accompanied by some physical change (Kim 1993). Mental properties depend on physical properties in the sense that there can be no mental differences without physical differences. Even Kim (1999) has acknowledged that supervenience is too weak of a relation to be called a version of physicalism since it is, for example, compatible with property dualism.

1.9 Free will

At this point it is worth addressing the importantly related problem of free will, which is of course a major metaphysical problem in its own right (Kane 2011). It is also a central question about the nature of human beings and our relationship to the physical world. Like the dualist–materialist debate, much of the free will–determinism dispute often centers on how much weight to put on introspective evidence as opposed to third-person scientific evidence. After all, we frequently make decisions after some period of *conscious* deliberation and thought. "I" am the one who makes a conscious decision and I tend to think that my conscious thought or intention is responsible for causing the action. So it is crucial to recognize these connections between free will, personal identity, or the "self," and consciousness. A determinist might concede that it "feels" or "seems" like we have free will from the conscious first-person point of view when we make choices and decisions. However, the scientific third-person evidence regarding the nature of cause and effect in our bodies (including our brains) outweighs the first-person evidence and shows us that free will is really an illusion. To put it another way: if we are entirely physical beings, then mustn't all of the brain activity and behavior in question be determined by physical causes and the laws of nature? Although materialism may not logically rule out free will, materialists will likely often reply that any traditional beliefs in free will simply ought to be rejected to the extent that they conflict with materialism and the best science. After all, if the weight of the evidence points toward materialism and away from dualism, then so much the worse for dualism. For our purposes here, it suffices to say that, on some definitions of what it is to act freely, it seems to be almost "supernatural" in the sense that one's conscious decisions can alter an otherwise deterministic sequence of events in nature (or our bodies). It might seem easier to believe in free will on the dualist view, but then of course we are still faced with the same Cartesian problem of how a non-physical mental state or property can cause any bodily movements.

Some will even go further with regard to free will, determinism, and moral responsibility. Many philosophers and scientists deny that *any of us* ever have free will, even aside from the presence of psychopathologies or mental illness. Perhaps all of our actions, even in everyday normal life, are really not free in at least some sense of the term. We need to recognize that our actions result from a wide range of causes, including our conscious mental states (e.g. beliefs, desires, preferences, fears, etc.) but also including any relevant *unconscious* motives and desires, biological and genetic factors, and past experiences. This would be true of all of our actions and decisions, even the most trivial. I decide to bring my umbrella to work *because* of my *belief* that it will rain and my *desire* to keep dry. My belief and desire, in this somewhat oversimplified example, *cause* and *explain* my action. How could I have those mental states and then *not* bring my umbrella? Further, if our actions at any given time are caused by brain activity and our mental states are really just brain states, then it is difficult to see where "free will" fits in the brain. It is normally assumed that causes are *sufficient* to produce their effects, so then how could we ever do otherwise than what causes our behavior at any given time?

It is crucial to point out that, in philosophical circles at least, the notion of free will has two very different definitions, one much stronger than the other. The stronger "libertarian" free will is perhaps what most people tend to have in mind and seems presupposed in most legal systems and world religions.[4] On this view:

Libertarian Free Will = A person P does act A freely when, and only when, P could have done some other action B at that same time *and* P had some control over doing A.

For many, the core ideas of "could have done otherwise" and "control" over actions are essential for free will and for holding someone morally responsible for an action. After all, if one really couldn't do otherwise, then how could we blame, punish, or otherwise hold that person morally responsible? For example, if someone were violently to assault another person and he was compelled to do so given his state of mind at that time, then he really *couldn't* have done otherwise and so how can we really hold him morally responsible for the action? He can still of course be *guilty* of the crime in the sense that he caused it and is thus legally responsible for it, but that is different than a more robust kind of moral responsibility. Further, we might also wonder what the point of *regretting* a past action is if one couldn't have done otherwise at that time.

Thus, determinism is often thought to be incompatible with both libertarian free will and attributions of moral responsibility. It is important to keep in mind, however, that the libertarian does not think that *all* of our actions are free; only some of them are. But the very same action cannot be both free and determined.

Determinism, in this context, might be defined as follows:

Psychological Determinism = Given the entire conscious and unconscious psychological make-up of a person P at a particular time (which results jointly from P's heredity *and* past experiences), P is compelled to do what P actually does *at that time*.

The example above of bringing an umbrella is an oversimplified but still instructive case. How could one have those very same beliefs and desires and yet still decide not to bring the umbrella? Of course, no one could be expected to *know* every possible cause of another's, or even one's own, action. But the plausibility of determinism gains support from the more *general* determinist view about cause and effect in nature such that given the state of the universe (or any causally closed part of it) at any given time and the laws of nature, the next state of the universe (or part of it) is uniquely fixed. That is, there is only one physically possible future. The common idea is that causes *necessitate* their effects – in the case of human actions, the causes once again include conscious mental states (beliefs, desires, preferences, fears, and so on) but also include any relevant unconscious motives and desires, biological factors, and past experiences. Determinists thus hold that all human actions are determined. In any case, if all of one's actions are determined, then one can never really do something other than what one actually does at any time and so we can't have libertarian free will.

One might suppose that bizarre random happenings at the quantum (or subatomic) level show that determinism is false (at least at that level) and thus might support the case for libertarianism. However, as has been frequently pointed out by many others, this does not really help the libertarian case for free will because if, say, one of my actions (such as doing A instead of B) results from a random (uncaused?) quantum event in my brain, then I would not really have any *control* over such randomness and genuine free will requires that I do have control.

Like the libertarian, many determinists (often called "hard" determinists) believe that free will and determinism are incompatible; that is, the very same action cannot be both free and determined. Thus, they are called "incompatibilists." This seems to follow from the above definitions. Either we can sometimes do other than we actually do or we never can do other than what we actually do. Furthermore, libertarian free will begins to sound very mysterious and even "supernatural" in the sense that humans are somehow supposed to have a special power to alter the physical world, including our bodies or brain activity. We somehow "stand above" nature in a way that would be hard to understand. Again, and to use another example, how could I have had *the very same* beliefs, desires, preferences, and so on as when I decided to have pizza for lunch, but then *at that same time* still have chosen to do something else (such as eat a cheeseburger instead)? If I choose to eat a cheeseburger the next day for lunch, mustn't there have been *something different* about my state of mind at that later time? The same would go for any illegal or unethical actions, such as a violent assault. Given the way the person was at the time, he couldn't have done otherwise and was compelled to behave that way at that time.

Does this mean that criminals – say, a serial murderer – shouldn't be punished? If determinism is true, then it may be that we should rethink the whole point of punishment. Instead of treating it as some kind of *retribution* based on libertarian free will, perhaps the focus should only be on *deterring* others (and criminals themselves) from committing future crimes. Most people in a society fear, and thus wish to avoid, incarceration and so will behave accordingly. If we can cause certain mental states in people, then the desired societal behavior will usually follow. Indeed, this is presumably what most parents presuppose when disciplining a child. But for those who do harm others, incarceration is at least one way to keep them away from the general population. The first priority still has to be public safety and so some hard determinists will treat the matter on the model of a quarantine (Pereboom 2014). Someone with a contagious disease, acquired through no fault of their own, should rightly be kept away from others simply because of the danger. The safety of others in society must similarly take precedence with respect to violent criminals. By analogy, we normally don't think that wild animals have libertarian free will but it doesn't follow that we should allow them to live among us to wreak havoc. Maybe serial killers and pedophiles really can't help what they do and really aren't morally responsible, but that doesn't mean we should invite them over for a family barbecue or let them all out of prison. Just keep them away from everyone else! Still, something obviously causes them to behave in such a way. We are often fascinated with learning what that might be (e.g. in serial killers), partly to prevent future criminal behavior.

It is also important to note that to say that someone is determined does not necessarily mean that he is "legally insane," which is a far narrower legal notion. In the United States at least, to be legally insane has more to do with "not understanding the difference between right and wrong" or "not understanding the consequences of one's actions" which is a very high hurdle for a defense to prove. Simply taking steps to avoid getting caught seems to indicate that a criminal recognizes the immorality, or at least illegality, of an action. The same currently goes for some relatively rare criminal cases involving genuine "mental illness" where a juror or judge might reasonably conclude that a mental illness is the main cause of an illegal act. For example, even though the vast majority of schizophrenics don't commit any crimes, some paranoid schizophrenics can tend to violent behavior. (I will return to the issue of psychopathology, consciousness, and moral responsibility in Chapter 4.)

Nonetheless, there is also a long tradition of "compatibilism," sometimes called "soft determinism." Compatibilists agree with determinists that that there is no such thing as libertarian free will but they argue that a very important notion of freedom (and moral responsibility) remains, which is indeed compatible with determinism. As odd as it might initially sound, the very same action can be both free and determined. Thus, for various reasons, they argue that "freedom" is really best understood as something more like "the absence of external constraint" or "acting in accordance with one's desires and beliefs." A criminal's actions are determined by *internal* causes but he is still not being coerced by someone else and he is acting in accordance with his (albeit twisted) desires and beliefs. He is, for example, doing what he wants to do at that time.

So, for a compatibilist, "a person P does action A freely" basically means that "P is not compelled to do A by external causes at the time of the action." Thus, a free act can be both free (in this sense) and determined because P would still be compelled to do A by *internal* psychological causes, as any determinist maintains. The matter is actually somewhat more complicated than this in the end. For example, someone who is addicted to drugs or is a kleptomaniac but really wants to stop might also not be acting freely, according to a compatibilist, because she has a second-order desire to get rid of her first-order desire to take drugs or steal (Frankfurt 1969, 1971).

Libertarians are not satisfied with compatibilist free will and view it as too weak. However, compatibilists will rightly point out just how important, as a very practical matter, their notion of free will has been to people throughout history. Being able to do what one wants and not to be controlled by an oppressive government, for example, has been the motivating force behind many revolutions and wars (including the American Revolution). Being free from another's control or domination is surely an important aspect of liberty, autonomy, and self-determination. What is so awful about being a prisoner, held hostage, or afraid of a violent stalker? Precisely that one cannot do what one wants to do under conditions where significant external constraints are present. Why have so many over the years risked their lives to make it to the United States from Cuba? Same answer. Throughout all of this, it seems almost silly to ask "yeah, but does the Cuban refugee or prisoner have *libertarian* free will?" or "Could they really do otherwise?" What we arguably really want is compatibilist free will.

Compatibilists about free will and determinism tend also to be compatibilists about free will and moral responsibility. Suppose a man attacks and robs a woman. Did he act according to his desires at the time? It would seem so. Did anyone else coerce him into committing the robbery? No. For the compatibilist, this is pretty much enough to conclude that he is morally responsible for the action, even if he couldn't have done otherwise at the time. Compatibilists point out that the only sense to be made of "could have done otherwise" is something more like "if a person had different mental states at that time, then he would have done otherwise."

1.9.1 Libet's experiments

In recent years, the idea that we even make free conscious decisions and the accompanying natural view that our conscious intentions *cause* our actions has also been challenged by some empirical work, especially based on seminal experiments run by Benjamin Libet (1985). These studies seem to show that our conscious intention to act (or "conscious will") comes about 350 milliseconds (just over one-third of a second) *after* our brains have already initiated the action (in the "readiness potential") in the secondary motor cortex. Put another way, our brains begin to cause bodily movements *prior to* our conscious decision to make those movements. The conscious decision comes too late to cause the bodily movement, though it does occur about 200 milliseconds before the bodily movement. One-third of a second might not seem like very long but it is in terms of brain activity. This seems to indicate that the conscious intention is merely along for the ride and doesn't really cause the bodily movement. Thus, some have even used this data as evidence for epiphenomenalism.

Consider some further details: A subject would be asked to note the position of a dot on a timer when she was first aware of an urge to act. By comparing this time to the subject's conscious decision to act (flex her wrist), researchers could calculate the total time from the subject's initial volition to the action. Approximately 200 milliseconds (one-fifth of a second) elapsed on average between the first appearance of conscious will to the action. Researchers also analyzed electroencephalogram (EEG) recordings for each trial with respect to the timing of the action. It was observed that brain activity involved in the initiation of the action occurred on average approximately 500 milliseconds before the pushing of the button. So mounting brain activity related to the eventual action was seen about 300 milliseconds before subjects reported the first awareness of conscious will to act. Conscious decisions to act were *preceded* by an unconscious buildup of electrical activity within the brain. For this reason and others, it has seemed to many that we are under the illusion that our conscious intentions cause our actions (Wegner 2002). That is, we mistakenly infer that our conscious intentions cause our actions because we are not consciously aware of the real causal path from the unconscious cause (in the motor cortex) to the action, whereas we are aware of the conscious intention even closer in time to the action. Much like the materialist says about dualism, the first-person appearance of conscious control does not match the underlying physical reality.

There is significant disagreement about some of Libet's methodology and on how to interpret some of his results, such as the difficulty of identifying a precise time of "conscious will" and the rather simplistic nature of the task. Interestingly, Libet himself didn't think that his experiments showed that there is no free will, though he did claim that it would be better to think of free will as a kind of "veto power" over what we are about to do. The idea is that we at least sometimes have the ability to stop ourselves from acting upon a given inclination even if "we" didn't consciously initiate it. Indeed, this may partly explain why some people can stop themselves from acting out violently or inappropriately while others cannot.

Chapter summary

Metaphysics is the branch of philosophy concerned with the ultimate nature of reality. In this chapter, we primarily examined the two broad traditional and competing metaphysical views concerning the nature of the mind and conscious mental states: dualism and materialism. While there are many versions of each, the former generally holds that the conscious mind, or a conscious mental state, is non-physical in some sense. On the other hand, materialists typically hold that the mind is the brain or that conscious mental activity is identical to neural activity. We not only saw that there are objections, often very serious objections, to each view but also that there are some other alternative views such as panpsychism and emergentism. Further, the perennial and related metaphysical problem of free will and determinism somewhat parallels the disagreement between dualists and materialists, depending upon how much emphasis one puts on the first-person introspective evidence as opposed to the more third-person scientific approach.

Further reading

For more recent defenses of type-type identity theory, see Hill and McLaughlin 1998, Papineau 1998, Bickle 2003, and Polger 2004. See Van

Gulick 2001 for a more detailed overview of reduction, emergence, and non-reductive materialism. For more on the free will–determinism debate, see Perebooom 2009, Watson 2007, and Pink 2004. For much more on the Libet experiments in relation to free will and moral responsibility, see "The Volitional Brian: Towards a Neuroscience of Free Will" 1999 6 (8–9), a special issue of the *Journal of Consciousness Studies*, Mele 2014, and Sinnott-Armstrong and Nadel 2011.

Notes

1 For those who think that NDEs show a glimpse of a real afterlife, see Moody 1975, Alexander 2012, and van Lommel 2010. For the opposing view, see Mitchell-Yellin and Fischer 2014, Augustine 2015, and also Blackmore 2011, chapter 24. See Martin and Augustine 2015 for numerous skeptical pieces on the phenomena discussed in this section.

2 An alternative "middle-ground" position is Kant's "transcendental idealism" which basically says that there are mind-independent objects or things but we cannot know what they are like "in themselves." So Kant rejected both Berkeley's idealism and Locke's indirect realism.

3 For more critiques on conceivability and related arguments, see for example Van Gulick 1993, Hill 1997, Hill and McLaughlin 1998, Papineau 1998, 2002, Balog 1999, Block and Stalnaker 1999, Loar 1999, Yablo 1999, Perry 2001, Botterell 2001, Kirk 2005, Stoljar 2006, Alter and Howell 2009, 2012, and Pereboom 2011. For more on the opposing view, see Chalmers and Jackson 2001 in response to which Block and Stalnaker 1999, and Gertler 2002, 2012.

4 The term "libertarianism" in this context has nothing to do with the more political connotation.

2

CONSCIOUSNESS, NEUROSCIENCE, AND ATTENTION

Over the past several decades there has been an explosion of interdisciplinary work in the science and philosophy of consciousness. Some of the credit must go to the groundbreaking 1986 book by Patricia Churchland titled *Neurophilosophy*. In this chapter, I discuss a number of theories of consciousness which explicitly reference neuroscience, such as Crick and Koch's neurobiological temporal synchrony theory, Edelman and Tononi's dynamic core hypothesis, Lamme's recurrent processing theory, and Prinz's attended intermediate-level representation theory. These theories aim to say more specifically what neural mechanisms are responsible for consciousness, rather than merely making the more generic "mental states are brain states" claim. The ongoing search for the so-called "neural correlates of consciousness" (NCCs) is also discussed.

Further, some important and fascinating phenomena are described, such as inattentional and change blindness, which raise the interesting question of the relationship between attention and consciousness. The so-called neural "binding problem" is also introduced with some discussion of the "unity of consciousness." Making sure that we are clear about what is meant by the unity of consciousness and explaining how the brain achieves such unity has become a central topic in the study of consciousness. This chapter will close with sections on a few alternative theories of consciousness, including information integration theory (IIT), quantum theories of consciousness, and the enactive or sensorimotor theory.

2.1 The brain

Although there has been some reference to the brain and neurophysiology in previous chapters, this is a good place to say more about the basics of brain science and various imaging techniques. Most readers will be familiar with the general structure of the brain and have some knowledge of neurophysiology. But for those not too familiar, some background is in order (see also Baars and Gage 2010).

The brain is divided into the left and right hemispheres, which are connected by an extensive band of nerve fibers collectively called the corpus callosum. The main brain structures of the neocortex include four lobes: the frontal lobe, the parietal lobe (top of the brain), the occipital lobe (in the back of the head), and temporal lobes (on the sides of the brain). The cerebral cortex involves several major structures, such as the hindbrain, which includes the cerebellum. The cerebellum controls balance and some motor coordination along with the pons. The midbrain includes the reticular formation and the superior and inferior colliculus. The forebrain encompasses the diencephalon (with the thalamus and hypothalamus), the telencephalon (the basal ganglia, which include the amygdala), and the limbic system (which includes the cingulate gyrus and the hippocampus). The neocortex with its four lobes is also part of the forebrain.

Functionally specific areas are well known to be essential for various mental abilities, such as the visual cortex, the auditory cortex, and various deeper structures such as the cingulate gyrus, the basal ganglia, the hippocampus, and the thalamus. The thalamus is a subcortical structure that sends and receives signals from the cortical areas, including the primary sensory areas responsible for vision, hearing, and feeling. This interconnected set of systems is sometimes called the thalamocortical system. The visual cortex, for example, is responsible for vision and is located in the occipital lobe. The classic area is labeled V1, but other areas include V2 through V5, though V5 is also sometimes labeled MT. V5/MT, for example, is well understood to be responsible for motion perception. Other major brain areas include the motor cortex and the somatosensory cortex.

There are approximately 100 billion nerve cells, or neurons, in an average adult human brain. Neurons come in a variety of shapes, but they all have treelike projections called dendrites that receive synaptic connections (a synapse is the small distance between neurons), in some cases up to 10,000 such connections with other neurons. Dendrites project from the single longer projection, called an axon. The branchlike patterns of dendrites vary widely from neuron to neuron. In addition, given the incredible number of connections between neurons, there are many more neural connections than the mere number of neurons. Neurons fire and communicate with one another via electrochemical activity. More specifically, neurons have a resting potential of -70mV, which is the normal voltage across the nerve cell membrane. If a neuron is excited by a neurotransmitter, a chemical released from a presynaptic neuron, then it causes a depolarization of the postsynaptic neuron. The depolarization causes brief changes in the neuron's permeability to potassium and sodium ions that, in turn, cause an electrical impulse (called an action potential) to occur at -50mV. The nerve cell fires at this point and not until this point. The firing of neurons is an all-or-nothing matter; that is, neurons do not fire to a lesser degree at, say, -60mV or to a greater degree at -40mV. The firing will then cause the release of neurotransmitters into the synapse of the postsynaptic cells, and then the cycle continues. Some synapses receive inhibitory signals that slow or stop activation of the postsynaptic neuron. Other synapses receive excitatory signals that increase the firing rate of the receiving neuron. All of this occurs over periods of tens to hundreds of milliseconds – a millisecond is one one-thousandth of a second.

As we shall see, it is important to note that there are numerous "feedback loops" in the brain, also referred to as recurrent processing or reentrant feedback. That is, many neurons not only connect and transmit from early processing areas to higher areas but also back from the higher areas to the early areas. A good example can be found in the thalamocortical system which is a dense network of reentrant connectivity between the thalamus and the cortex. Due to feedback loops, some are inclined to think that conscious mental states must be somewhat distributed in the brain. That is, the neural structures involved in having those conscious states occur over a fairly large area in the brain.

It is worth briefly noting some of the methods used to detect and measure brain activity in relation to various mental tasks. An electroencephalogram (EEG) measures changes in electrical potential by placing electrodes on the scalp. X-ray computed tomography (CT scan) results in computer-generated images of tissue density. Positron-emission tomography (PET) is a way to construct brain images from the distribution of radioactivity following administration of a radioactive substance. PET scans measure brain metabolism and blood flow directly by measuring the atoms that emit positrons that are incorporated into oxygen or glucose molecules. Nuclear magnetic resonance imaging (MRI) measures the radio signals emitted by some atomic nuclei. The radiation emitted provides detailed information about the chemical nature of the nuclei. Functional MRI (fMRI) is a newer and more advanced method that allows for such imaging while the subject is engaged in various tasks. The level of detail is also much greater than can be achieved by an MRI. Transcranial magnetic stimulation (TMS), while not really a brain imaging technique, involves holding a coil over the head which generates a pulsed magnetic field that stimulates (or interferes with) neurons in a focused area in the brain. This can be very helpful in determining what brain areas are at least necessary for having specific kinds of conscious states.

The task at hand is not of course merely a theoretical exercise. For individuals thought to be in a persistent vegetative state (PVS) or for patients under anesthesia, it is exceedingly important to be able to ascertain from a scientific, third-person point of view to what extent (if any) consciousness is correlated with specific brain activity (Alkire, Hudetz, and Tononi 2008; Mashour 2010). Errors in accurately determining when a patient is having conscious states, such as conscious pains, can have catastrophic results. Imagine suffering in excruciating pain while unable to move one's muscles to inform others. There is also "locked-in syndrome" which is a medical condition where brain damage has affected only motor functions and has left a patient immobile and unresponsive to stimuli while consciousness remains normal. Mashour and LaRock (2008) refer to this as the "inverse zombie problem"; that is, cases of internally experienced consciousness without any behavioral sign, as opposed to the philosopher's "zombie," who is hypothetically not conscious but behaves in a manner indistinguishable from a conscious human.

Ethical issues surrounding PVS are also significant (Levy and Savulescu 2009; Shea and Bayne 2010). Similar ethical questions arise at the other end of the spectrum of life; namely, regarding potential fetal pain during an abortion procedure, especially from, say, five months on (Brugger 2012). Determining whether there is consciousness in these cases may not be the sole consideration, but it certainly seems highly relevant to making ethical decisions.

2.2 The neural correlates of consciousness

The search for the "neural correlates of consciousness" (NCCs) has been a major preoccupation for philosophers and scientists alike for decades (Metzinger 2000). Narrowing down the precise brain property responsible for consciousness is a different and far more difficult enterprise compared with merely holding a generic belief in some form of materialism. One early candidate was offered by Francis Crick and Christof Koch (1990). The basic idea is that mental states become conscious when large numbers of neurons all fire in synchrony with one another (oscillations within the 35–75-hertz range, or 35–75 cycles per second). I will return to this view below. Currently, one method used to discover NCCs is simply to examine some aspect of neural functioning with sophisticated detecting equipment (such as MRIs and PET scans) and then correlate it with first-person reports of conscious experience. Another method is to study the difference in brain activity between those under anesthesia and those not under any such influence. A detailed survey would be impossible to give here (see Metzinger 2000 for a start), but a number of other candidates for the NCC have emerged over the past two decades, including reentrant cortical feedback loops in the neural circuitry throughout the brain (Edelman and Tononi 2000a, 2000b), N-methyl-D-aspartate (NMDA)mediated transient neural assemblies (Flohr 1995), and emotive somatosensory homeostatic processes in the frontal lobe (Damasio 1999). To elaborate briefly on Flohr's theory, the idea is that anesthetics destroy conscious mental activity because they interfere with the functioning of NMDA synapses between neurons, which are those that are dependent on NMDA receptors. Many others have also emphasized the importance of the role of neurochemistry in having various kinds of conscious states. Indeed, an entire anthology on the neurochemistry of consciousness has examined this often ignored area of research (Perry, Ashton, and Young 2002). Over fifty neurotransmitters have been discovered thus far, such as acetylcholine which seems to play a major role in the difference between sleep (and dreaming) and waking forms of consciousness. Dopamine seems to contribute importantly to attention and working memory. It is also widely acknowledged that some mental disorders, such as depression, dementia, and schizophrenia, result from abnormalities in the levels of neurotransmitters.

However, in any discussion of NCCs, we must recognize several basic points:

One issue is determining exactly how the NCC is related to consciousness. For example, although a case can be made that many NCCs are necessary for conscious mentality, it is unclear that they are sufficient. For one thing, many of the above candidates for NCCs seem to occur unconsciously as well. Second, there are obviously other necessary background conditions that need to obtain for a given NCC to suffice for consciousness. Even pinning down a narrow-enough necessary condition is not as easy as it might seem.

A related worry has to do with the very use of the term "correlate." As any philosopher, scientist, and even undergraduate student should know, saying that "x is correlated with y" is rather weak (though it can be an important first step), especially if one wishes to establish the stronger identity claim between consciousness and neural activity. Even if a solid reliable correlation can be established, we cannot automatically conclude that there is an identity relation. And many view the search for NCCs as somewhat neutral with respect to the metaphysics of mind. Perhaps x causes y or y causes x, and that's why we find the correlation. Most dualists could even accept such a view. Maybe there is some other neural process z that causes both x and y. So "correlation" is not even the same as "cause," let alone enough to establish identity. Finally, some NCCs are put forth as candidates not for all conscious states but only for certain specific kinds of consciousness such as visual awareness.

Chalmers (2000) presents several useful distinctions and offers a number of clear definitions (cf. Block 2007; Hohwy 2007). For one thing, we should distinguish between a mental state (or "vehicle") and its content (or what the state is about). Thus Chalmers arrives at the following definitions:

> A *content* NCC is a neural representational system N such that the content of N directly correlates with the content of consciousness.
>
> (Chalmers 2000, 20)

> A *state* N1 of system B is a neural correlate of phenomenal property P if N's being in N1 directly correlates with the subject having P.
>
> (Chalmers 2000, 22)

It is then important to recognize that any interesting NCC would at least need to isolate the minimal area in the brain responsible for a conscious state. Thus:

> An NCC is a minimal neural system N such that there is a mapping from states of N to states of consciousness, where a given state of N is sufficient, under conditions C, for the corresponding state of consciousness.
>
> (Chalmers 2000, 31)

Block (2007, 489) similarly explains that a "minimal neural basis is a necessary part of a neural sufficient condition for conscious experience," and Koch (2004, 16) tells us that the NCC is "the minimal set of neuronal events and mechanisms jointly sufficient for a specific conscious percept."

The main point is to find a neural correlation that is a reasonably narrow subset of the entire brain activity at a given time (Chalmers 2000; Block 2007). It would be much less informative, and perhaps even trivial, to learn that the entire brain is sufficient for having a conscious state. In a similar vein, one might distinguish between the core and total NCC. The core neural basis of a conscious state is the part of the total neural basis that distinguishes conscious states from states with other conscious contents. The total neural basis of a conscious state is itself sufficient for the occurrence of that conscious state (Block 2007, 482). We thus also need to distinguish the NCC from what might be called "enabling conditions," which refer to other aspects of a functioning body, such as proper blood flow and functioning lungs or heart. It is crucial to design experiments with controls such that the only difference between a pair of trials is the presence of consciousness. We can then use fMRI to ascertain any neural difference between such cases.

2.3 Neural theories of consciousness

Some theories of consciousness have therefore attempted very direct reductionist approaches; that is, to reduce consciousness to specific kinds of neural activity. These theories might thus be called "neural theories of consciousness" and are usually offered by scientists and psychologists, not philosophers.

2.3.1 *The temporal synchrony account*

As was noted briefly above, perhaps the best-known early attempt at a neural theory of consciousness is the "temporal synchrony" theory offered by Francis Crick and Christof Koch (1990), partly based on studies of the cat visual cortex (see also Crick 1994; Koch 2004). The basic idea is that mental states become conscious when large numbers of neurons fire in synchrony and all have oscillations within the 35–75-hertz range (that is, 35–75 cycles per second). When neural firings are in synch, we have conscious experience even if the neural populations are somewhat distributed across different brain regions. One might think of this as somewhat analogous to the blinking lights on a Christmas tree: groups of lights might blink at different rates or speeds but sometimes there will be a temporal synchrony among some of the lights' blinks. But Crick and Koch were almost immediately faced with the problem of whether temporal synchrony is sufficient for consciousness, merely necessary for it, or both (Crick and Koch 2003). Ultimately, Koch (2004) concedes that the data do not really support the conclusion that synchronization of neural assemblies constitutes a sufficient or even a necessary condition for the production of conscious awareness. It turns out that some 40-Hz oscillations can occur unconsciously and consciousness can arise in the absence of such oscillations. Still, as we shall see, the idea that some kind of distributed brain property is mainly responsible for consciousness has been highly influential in certain circles. It is also relevant to the binding problem, as we'll see below.

2.3.2 *The dynamic core hypothesis*

David Edelman and Giulio Tononi have argued that feedback loops (or "reentrant pathways" or "back projections") in the neural circuitry of the brain are essential for conscious awareness (Edelman and Tononi 2000a, 2000b). The basic idea relies on the fact, as Churchland puts it,

> that some neurons carry signals from more peripheral to more central regions, such as from V1 to V2, while others convey more highly processed signals in the reverse direction. . . . It is a general rule of cortical organization that forward-projecting neurons are matched by an equal or greater number of back-projecting neurons.
>
> (2002, 148–149)

There is mutual interaction between the relevant neuronal levels. Edelman and Tononi, for example, emphasize the global nature of conscious states, and it is reasonable to interpret this as the view that conscious states comprise both the higher- and lower-order areas of the brain. As they describe it, the "dynamic core" is generally "spatially distributed and thus cannot be localized to a single place in the brain" (Edelman and Tononi 2000a, 146). They mainly locate reentrant cortical feedback loops in the thalamocortical system which is a dense network of reentrant connectivity between the thalamus and the cortex. The dynamic core is thus a functional cluster of multiple neuronal groups in the thalamocortical system which interact with each other. Nonetheless, it has become clear that feedback loops are not sufficient for consciousness (though perhaps necessary). There are certain kinds of feedback loops which occur without corresponding consciousness. Still, the idea that consciousness involves important functional integration among parts of the brain has become an important idea in the search for NCCs (see also Llinas 2001).

2.3.3 Recurrent processing theory

Victor Lamme, focusing especially on vision, also thinks that the NCCs must be somewhat distributed in the brain (Lamme 2003; Lamme and Roelfsema 2000) given that there are numerous feedback loops in the brain. That is, numerous neurons are transmitting not only from early processing areas to higher areas but also back from the higher areas to the early areas. Indeed, the speed with which the "forward" and "backward" processing occurs can be measured. Based on various experimental results, such as visual search tasks, Lamme argues further that the so-called "feedforward sweep" is not sufficient for consciousness. The feedforward sweep is processed in about 30–100msec from the appearance of a stimulus. But it takes another 100–300msec for the backward sweep to occur, at which point conscious experience of the stimulus occurs.

For example, Lamme explains that "backward masking" renders a visual stimulus invisible by presenting a second stimulus shortly afterward (about 40msec later but perhaps even up to 110msec). Nonetheless the masked (invisible) stimulus still evokes significant feedforward activation in visual and even nonvisual areas. It seems that the feedback interaction from higher to lower visual areas is suppressed by backward masking, thereby disrupting reentrant processing (Fahrenfort, Scholte, and Lamme 2007; Kouider and Dehaene 2007). Much the same seems to hold for when TMS is applied to the same areas. Nonetheless, even in these cases, some (unconscious) visual information is acquired via the feedforward sweep, as is the case in subliminal perception.

If there is extensive damage to early visual areas (such as V1), then there will of course also be no conscious vision, but that is mainly because the process of conscious vision has been damaged at such an early stage. It is also important to carefully distinguish between consciousness and reportability since asking subjects to report on what they see can require additional brain areas which can confound these experimental results.

2.3.4 Somatic marker hypothesis

Antonio Damasio (1994, 1999) ties having conscious states closely to the related, though murky, notion of a "self" and stresses the central role of emotions. He argues for what he calls the "somatic marker hypothesis" which is a theory about how emotions and their NCCs are involved in decision-making. Emotions are necessary for reasoning and they play a key role in the construction of increasingly complex notions of a "self" as well as in "social cognition" in the sense that consciousness requires bringing together a "self" and "outer objects." When one has a conscious state, one *feels* oneself to be one among many selves or objects. In this way, Damasio perhaps anticipates "enactive or sensorimotor theory" with its emphasis on the body and interaction with the environment (see section 2.6.3 below).

Damasio explains how there are kinds of consciousness related to a corresponding notion of "self." The most basic representation of self is what he calls the "protoself" which is really an unconscious state shared by all life forms, even single-celled organisms. Its function is to detect and record internal physical changes of the organism such as in the hypothalamus, the brain stem, and the insular cortex (whose function is linked to emotion). There is the constant process of collecting neural patterns to map the current status of the body's responses to environmental changes. The protoself does not require language to function.

When the body is modified by these neural patterns, a second layer of self emerges which Damasio calls "core consciousness." When an organism becomes consciously aware of feelings associated with its internal bodily state, it can recognize that its thoughts are its own and can develop a momentary sense of self. A relationship is established between the organism and other objects it is observing, and the brain creates images to represent the organism's experience. Consciousness is the feeling of being aware of a feeling. Core consciousness is concerned only with the present moment. It does not require language or memory, nor can it reflect on past experiences or project itself into the future.

Damasio explains that "extended consciousness" can now emerge. This level could not exist without the previous two but importantly requires the use of autobiographical memory. Therefore, an injury to a person's memory center can cause damage to their extended consciousness, without hurting the other layers. The "autobiographical self" draws on memory of past experiences which involves use of higher thought. Working memory is necessary for an extensive display of items to be recalled and referenced.

2.3.5 Attended intermediate-level representation theory

Another neural-based, or "neuro-cognitive," account of conscious-ness from a philosopher is Jesse Prinz's attended intermediate-level representation (AIR) theory. According to Prinz's theory (2007, 2011, 2012), a conscious perception requires both a cognitive and a neural component. Prinz explicitly follows the earlier work of Ray Jackendoff (1987) to the extent that a conscious perception must represent basic "intermediate" features of external objects such as colors, shapes, tones, and feels. This is the "IR" aspect of AIR. To be conscious, however, the represented content must also be attended (the "A"). Attention, accord-ing to Prinz, is essentially reduced to availability to working memory, a low-capacity storage center which holds information briefly in a way that aids cognitive operations upon it.

To the extent that Prinz's view invokes the notion of a "representation," it has some affinity to the representational theories of consciousness to be discussed in the next chapter. However, Prinz proposes a very specific neural correlate for both the IR and A. He identifies the intermediate-level repre-sentations with gamma (40–80Hz) vector activity in the sensory cortex and the attentional component with synchronized oscillations that can incorpo-rate that gamma vector activity. In this way, his proposed NCCs are perhaps more in the spirit of the views mentioned in the previous subsections.

For our purposes here, it is especially worth emphasizing that Prinz holds that there is a very tight connection between consciousness and attention (2011, 2012). Indeed, according to Prinz, "when we attend, perceptual states become conscious, and when attention is unavailable, consciousness does not arise. Attention, in other words, is necessary and sufficient for consciousness" (2012, 89). Again, Prinz ties attention to working memory: "attention can be identified with the processes that allow information to be encoded in working memory" (2012, 93). Thus: "Consciousness arises when and only when intermediate-level representations undergo changes that allow them to become available to working memory" (2012, 97). So when intermediate-level representations are attended to, they become conscious.

Interestingly, Graziano (2013) holds a view which also explicitly mentions attention and resembles the interpersonal approach we saw above in Damasio's view. Graziano presents a "social theory of consciousness" but emphasizes the importance of attention: "consciousness is an attention schema. A schema is an informational model, constantly recomputed, that represents something worth tracking and predicting" (Graziano 2013, 69). He explains that "[conscious] awareness is a description of attention" and "attention [is] a data-handling method in the brain" (Graziano 2013, 23). He also stresses eight key similarities between attention and conscious awareness (Graziano 2013, 26–27), such as both involve an agent, both are selective, and both involve information processing. He points to key brain areas which are also responsible for "social thinking" or for thinking about other minds, namely the temporo-parietal junction (TPJ) and the superior temporal sulcus (STS).

Of course, some philosophers will raise the same philosophical doubts about all of the above materialist theories as were raised in the previous chapter (in section 1.7), such as how they could solve the hard problem or respond to conceivability arguments. For example, one might ask Lamme exactly why or how reentrant feedback from higher areas to the early areas in the thalamocortical system results in conscious experience or qualia. I am not aware of any of the above authors providing a unique or different response than those we discussed in the last chapter. Indeed, many non-philosophers often seem to ignore those kinds of objections. I suspect that there are any number of possible reasons for this: (a) they are simply unaware of the objections, (b) they are aware of the objections but don't have very much to add to the extant responses, (c) they don't particularly care about or even see the importance of the problem (choosing to focus on the "easy problems"), or (d) they might even concede that there is a significant explanatory gap and thus have sympathy for, say, emergentism or panpsychism. For his own part, Prinz holds that zombies aren't really conceivable; they just *seem* to be conceivable:

> The real problem with zombie arguments is that [zombies] are impossible. If materialism is true, consciousness is identical with a functional or physical process, and if that identity obtains, there cannot be duplicates of us without consciousness. Those who believe that zombies are possible are dualists.
>
> (Prinz 2012, 211)[1]

Given the emphasis above on the notion of attention, this is a good place to transition to a more detailed discussion of the relationship between attention and consciousness, which has again become a major topic in recent years.[2]

2.4 Attention and consciousness

Attention and consciousness have been closely linked on some views but perhaps the most common historical quote comes from William James, who famously said that "Everyone knows what attention is. It is the taking possession by the mind, in clear and vivid form, of one out of what seem several simultaneously possible objects or trains of thought. Focalization, concentration, of consciousness are of its essence" (James 1890, 402–403). Unfortunately, as we'll see, it may be more complicated than James thought. Some have focused on the inner neurophysiological mechanisms of attention such as in the influential "bottleneck view" of Donald Broadbent (1958). The idea is that attention acts as a kind of bottleneck in the brain's information-processing capacity. Attention is what selects or filters information to pass through limited-capacity bottlenecks. We obviously cannot pay attention to everything all the time.

For my purposes here, the most interesting issue is still the relationship between attention and consciousness. Is attention *necessary* for having a conscious experience? If the answer is yes, then the claim is that:

(**CRA**) Consciousness Requires (or implies) Attention.

But is attention *sufficient* for having a conscious experience? If the answer is yes, then the claim is that:

(**ARC**) Attention Requires (or implies) Consciousness.

It might seem that CRA is true. However, consciousness seems to be a broader category than attention due, for example, to the existence of peripheral (conscious) awareness. Conscious peripheral vision, for example, seems to be a case of consciousness without attention. I seem to have some degree of conscious peripheral vision even though I am now consciously attending to my computer screen. It is not as if everything else becomes "dark" or "black." Much the same seems true of auditory perception, such as focusing on a guitar solo in a song while peripherally conscious of the drums and bass. So it does not seem that attention is *always* necessary for consciousness. There seem to be many cases of conscious perception where we only have focal awareness of a small portion of our conscious visual field or a limited attentional focus in an auditory experience. In the visual case, this is supported by experiments showing that it is only the center of the retina that has a high density of cones with high acuity in contrast to the periphery (or parafovea) of the retina, which allows for much lower resolution. Yet one does not actually attend to one's peripheral visual field. CRA therefore seems much too strong.

Some might urge that inattentional blindness shows that CRA is true (Mack and Rock 1998; Simons and Chabris 1999). For example, even when one is paying close attention to something within one's focal conscious-ness, one may not even be conscious of other objects within that awareness. In a well-known video, a group of people are passing a basketball among themselves, and observers are asked to count the number of passes within the group. Many observers do not even notice that someone dressed in a gorilla suit walks right into the center of the scene, pounds his chest, and then walks away. This is a shocking result to many of those tested. But one problem here is simply that CRA is too strong since some subjects *do* become consciously aware of the gorilla. Further, even if someone doesn't *notice* or *remember* some *specific* object or feature in one's peripheral visual field, it doesn't automatically follow that it is not part of one's conscious visual experience in some more generic sense.

Similar cases can be found when a magician performs sleight of hand even within an extremely narrow focal area of one's visual field, such as when performing a card trick. And, perhaps most surprisingly, this is accomplished even when we know that the magician is trying to fool us! By means of subtle diversions of attention and other techniques, magicians are almost universally able to cause inattentional blindness in their audiences (Martinez-Conde and Macknik 2008).

Consider also Dennett's case of the Marilyn Monroe wallpaper, where you walk into a room with wallpaper containing hundreds of her portraits (Dennett 1991, 354–355). Your initial sense might convince you that you are seeing hundreds of identical Marilyns. But Dennett persuasively argues that the real detail is not in your head but in the world. We simply assume that all the pictures are of Marilyn Monroe; that is, our brains "fill in" the rest of the scene. We thus mistakenly assume that all of the Marilyns are consciously represented in our experience. This likely occurs often when we experience a number of similar-looking objects at the same time unless one object is so different as to "pop out" to one's conscious experience. But even though you obviously do not attend to or focus in on each and every portrait, it seems that there is still *some* form of conscious awareness of the peripheral visual field.

Change blindness, on the other hand, occurs when normal subjects fail to notice what would seem to be an obvious change in some object or scene (Simons 2000). Even in cases where one can compare pictures side by side, subjects often take an extremely long time to notice the change. This suggests that we really do not have a very detailed sense of everything in our visual field. Examples here might include a change in one of the items on a desk or a difference in the number of windows of a building. People often greatly overestimate their ability to detect such changes. Moreover, it is well known that there are many quick and jerky eye saccades (or movements) when a subject is looking at a scene or picture. Our eyes dart around in ways that subjects are unaware of and, in the case of change blindness, there is a clear searching of the pictures to find the difference in question. So it is doubtful that all or most of a visual scene is really simultaneously perceived, which is sometimes used as an argument against the idea that our conscious perception is "rich."

With regard to ARC, the problem is that there also seem to be cases of attention without conscious awareness, such as when a subject's attention is attracted by a stimulus without conscious awareness (Jiang et al. 2006). Subjects are, for example, presented with attention-grabbing stimuli (such as erotic photographs) to just one eye which are shown to be unconsciously processed. The more vivid stimulus presented to the other eye, however, draws conscious attention. So one might conclude that the erotic pictures capture the subject's attention even though the subject is not conscious of them. Thus, ARC is also too strong and attention does not always require consciousness.

Similar conclusions might be drawn from much-discussed blindsight cases, where partially cortically blind patients often successfully guess at some characteristics of a stimulus that is not consciously seen (Weiskrantz 1986). It would seem that the blindsighted subject has no conscious perception of an object X but is still attending to X in some sense, albeit prompted by a questioner. Kentridge (2011) argues, in contrast to Prinz, that consciousness is not necessary for attention in part because blindsight subjects show that attention to an object can occur without conscious experience of that object. The claim that attention is not sufficient for consciousness is also sometimes made by those who argue that two distinct brain processes are responsible for attention and consciousness (Koch and Tsuchiya 2007).

Despite the above alleged counterexamples, Prinz maintains that attention is indeed necessary and sufficient for consciousness; that is, both ARC and CRA are true. For example, Prinz and others might reply that some of the above lines of evidence (e.g. blindsight) do not enable us to distinguish between attention to a thing and attention merely directed to a part of *space*, and so do not really demonstrate the presence of attention to a thing without consciousness. Prinz also would not say that inattentional blindness is really entirely "inattentional." Much like the difference between focal and peripheral consciousness, he would similarly hold that some degree of attention is present throughout one's visual field, just some areas more than others.

One puzzling abnormal phenomenon related to attention and consciousness is worth mentioning here, namely neglect or hemispatial neglect. It is often the result of damage to the temporo-parietal junction (TPJ) and the superior temporal sulcus (STS). It is not a visual problem in the sense of cortical damage to the visual cortex (as in blindsight) but rather arguably an abnormality of attention such that patients ignore the left side of their visual field. For example, while drawing a clock, they try to jam all twelve numbers into the right side of the clock's face. Prinz would say that where there's no attention to part of one's visual field, there's no consciousness of that part of one's visual field. Neglect is arguably an attentional deficit which clearly results in a consciousness deficit.[3]

One might understandably wonder at times if part of the overall problem has more to do with the use of terminology or overlooked distinctions. For example, we should distinguish between (mental) state and creature consciousness, voluntary and involuntary behavior, and personal and subpersonal awareness. Although these last two distinctions are sometimes used by the above authors, we might more directly say, for example, that the blindsighter is generally creature conscious but not state conscious of the object in the blind field (that is, not having a conscious visual perception of the object). Also, if we wish to hold that something has captured a subject's attention without state consciousness (as in the erotic photographs mentioned earlier), then the notion of attention at work is clearly some sort of involuntary creature consciousness such as occurs with involuntary eye saccades. In this sense, it is possible for one on a sub-personal level to attend to things of which one is not state conscious. On the other hand, some authors argue that attention is best understood in terms of personal (or subject)-level voluntary initiated action or as a way to select a task for or to control action (Smithies 2011; Mole 2011; Jennings 2015). This line of reasoning can also be seen in the common metaphorical characterization of attention as a theatrical spotlight. The metaphor tends to suppose that attention has to do with personal-level agency such that we can put the spotlight on whatever we choose. The metaphor tends to suggest that attention works within a field of conscious items which are selected for attention. For example, Smithies (2011) argues that the role of attention is the active rational control by a subject, which is often referred to as a "top-down" approach, as opposed to the "bottom-up" involuntary grabbing of attention in other cases. In any case, I am not suggesting that most authors entirely ignore the distinctions above or that all of the disagreements come down to mere semantics. However, some authors seem to overlook these distinctions at times which might result in unnecessary disputes.

Finally, the notion of attention is also relevant to Block's much-discussed argument (2007) that phenomenal consciousness "overflows" access which stresses results from Sperling's (1960) well-known work on iconic memory. One way to construe the results is that the experiments show we are conscious of more than we attend to (so that CRA is false). The main experiment begins by showing subjects an array of letters in the center of one's visual field for 50msec, such as an array composed of three rows of four letters each. A visual image of the stimulus was found to persist for

150msec after removing the stimulus. Subjects were then asked to report what they saw under two different conditions. In condition one, subjects were asked to identify as many letters as possible. In condition two, subjects were asked to identify letters in a single row, albeit after the offset of the stimulus. Sperling found that in condition one, subjects could identify only about one-third of the twelve letters, but in condition two they could still typically report correctly on at least three out of four letters. Some conclude from this that one's sensory memory (which fades quickly) still preserves information about the letter shapes in all rows although subjects cannot report on all the information. In condition one, however, it may be that the act of reporting just takes too long and the sensory memories have faded. In condition two, the sensory memory is still available enough to be able to report on most or all letters in a single row. It is worth noting that some experimental results seem to cast doubt on Block's interpretation of the Sperling results. De Gardelle, Sackur, and Kouider (2009) found that participants persisted in the belief that only letters were present when pseudo-letters were also included in the array. This belief persisted even when participants were made aware that they might be misled. An unwarranted overconfidence persists on the part of participants, also challenging the view that there is very rich conscious phenomenology in the brief visual presentation. There have been many other attempts to resist Block's conclusion which I won't delve into here. It is, for example, also not clear that subjects are conscious of all the letters in the initial array.[4]

2.5 The binding problem and the unity of consciousness

Given its prominence as an ongoing puzzle in neuroscience, it is worth briefly discussing the binding problem here. The "problem of integrating the information processed by different regions of the brain is known as the binding problem" (Cleeremans 2003, 1). The binding problem is also inextricably linked to the problem of explaining the unity of consciousness. Conscious experience seems to be unified in various ways. As we have seen, this central aspect of consciousness played an important role for Kant who argued that unified conscious experience must be the product of the (presupposed) synthesizing work of the mind. What exactly is meant by the "unity of consciousness" and explaining how the brain achieves such unity has become a major topic in the study of consciousness. There are many different senses of "unity" (see Tye 2003; Bayne and Chalmers 2003), but perhaps most common is the notion that, from the first-person point of view, we experience the world in an integrated way and as a single phenomenal field of experience. However, when one looks at how the brain processes information, one only sees discrete regions of the cortex processing separate aspects of perceptual objects. Even different aspects of the same object, such as the color, shape, and motion of a blue ball, are processed in different parts of the brain. Given that there is no place in the brain where all this information comes together, the problem arises as to just how the resulting conscious experience is unified. What mechanisms allow us to experience the world in such a unified way? What happens when this unity breaks down, as in various pathological cases?

As was seen earlier, some attempts to solve the binding problem have just as much to do with trying to isolate the precise brain mechanisms responsible for consciousness. For example, Crick and Koch's (1990) idea that synchronous neural firings are (at least) necessary for consciousness can be viewed as an attempt to explain how disparate neural networks bind together separate pieces of information to produce unified subjective conscious experience. Perhaps the binding problem and the hard problem of consciousness are very closely connected in the end. If the binding problem can be solved, then we arguably have identified the elusive neural correlate of consciousness and have, therefore, perhaps also solved the hard problem. This exciting area of inquiry is central to some of the deepest questions in the philosophical and scientific exploration of consciousness.

With respect to binding, there are several accounts in the extant literature. For example, Humphreys (2003) offers evidence that binding is not a unitary process but instead involves multiple stages that can become dissociated from each other as a result of brain injury. For example, he explains that people with achromatopsia (loss of color vision) and visual agnosia (loss of ability to recognize or name objects while the visual sense itself is not defective) give us reason to believe that "visual processing is fractionated at a neural level, with different regions specialized for coding color, motion, form, and location information" (Humphreys 2003, 115). A subject with achromatopsia can have selective loss of color vision without impairment in motion vision. Likewise, patients with integrative agnosia, among other things, show that we bind locally oriented elements into edges before binding edge elements into holistic shapes.

In addition to Crick and Koch's temporal synchrony account, perhaps the best-known attempt to explain binding is Anne Treisman's (1993, 2003) theory that actually distinguishes three forms of binding: properties, parts, and perceptual grouping. Attention also plays a critical role in her theory. Her influential "feature integration theory" (FIT) emphasizes the way that spatial attention selects the appropriate features to be bound. Treisman points out that her theory is consistent with the temporal synchrony account, but that

> the binding problem is really two separate problems: how do we select the correct combinations of features to bind, and how are their conjunctions encoded and maintained once they have been bound? The spatial attention account offered by FIT answers the first, whereas the synchronized firing account deals with the second.
>
> (Treisman 2003, 104–105)

Binding is essential for conscious experience, but it is important to be clear about the way Treisman uses the term "attention." For example, she does not require personal-level conscious attention.

It is always interesting to examine what happens in cases where unity breaks down, as we'll also see in Chapter 4. Young (2003), for example, discusses prosopagnosia, the inability to recognize familiar faces overtly, and the Capgras delusion, the belief that other people, usually close relatives, have been replaced by imposters. There is an abundance of empirical data showing that prosopagnosics exhibit some covert recognition of familiar faces. Young observes that "the Capgras delusion might form a kind of mirror image of prosopagnosia. In prosopagnosia, overt recognition is impaired but emotional orientating responses may be relatively preserved. In Capgras delusion, overt recognition is relatively preserved but emotional orientating responses are lost" (Young 2003, 243). There are many different pathologies which result from a breakdown of unity, such as "split-brain" or commissurotomy cases, dissociative identity disorder (formerly called multiple personality disorder), and schizophrenia. Patients with Balint's syndrome (or simultanagnosia) see only one object at a time located at one "place" in the visual field. Subjects seem not to be aware of even two items or objects in a single overall conscious state. I will return to these and other psychopathologies in Chapter 4.

Bayne and Chalmers (2003) attempt to clarify what is meant by the unity of consciousness and identify a number of important interconnected theses, which are also clearly relevant to the binding problem. Perhaps most central is what they call the "unity thesis," according to which "necessarily, any set of conscious states of a subject at a time is unified" (Bayne and Chalmers 2003, 24). Bayne and Chalmers also describe "objectual unity" as follows: "Two states of consciousness are *objectually unified* when they are directed at the same object" (2003, 24). The earlier case of seeing a single moving blue ball would be an example. It would seem that such binding takes place unconsciously and is simply presupposed in the resulting experience of an object. A somewhat different notion of unity arises when we consider whether a *conjunction* of conscious states yields a *further* conscious state. This is closer to what Bayne and Chalmers call "subsumptive unity": "Two conscious states are *subsumptively unified* when they are both subsumed by a single state of consciousness" (2003, 27). For example, we might suppose that auditory and visual conscious states can combine into a single overall conscious perceptual state. The result is that the subject experiences the conjunction of the states, such as hearing and seeing a band at a concert, or feeling and hearing a wave crashing onto the beach, and so on. In terms of the underlying neural realization of subsumptive and conjunctive unity, there at least are some "convergence zones" where more than one conscious state may be "tied together" in some way. But it seems unreasonable to insist that there must be a place in the brain where a conjunctive state comes together *in addition to* the neural activity in different brain areas. This would especially seem unlikely when a conscious state is multimodal. Indeed, even *within*, say, the visual cortex there is little reason to suppose that there is a *separate* conjunctive state for motion, color, and shape. Once again, this is primarily what generates the binding problem in the first place. This issue will reappear in Chapter 4 with respect to synesthesia.

2.6 Three alternative theories of consciousness

Three other theories which have gained significant attention in recent years are also worth considering here. The first posits that consciousness has more to do with information integration than with its neural realization, the second looks deeper than the neural level to quantum mechanics to try to explain consciousness, and the third challenges the very notion that conscious mental states are generated by brain activity (or at least brain activity alone) in the sense that consciousness is instead a capacity of the whole organism.

2.6.1 Integrated information theory

Information integration is often seen as an important aspect or function of consciousness. However, neuroscientist Giulio Tononi (2004, 2008) identifies consciousness with integrated information and holds that having the right kind of information integration is both necessary and sufficient for consciousness, regardless of whether it is realized in something neural or biological. Some of the mathematical details are very technical but basically, according to Tononi's integrated information theory (IIT), consciousness is a purely information-theoretic property of systems. He uses a mathematical measure "φ" (phi, pronounced "fi") that measures not only the information in the parts of a given system but also the information in the organization of the entire system. The entire system can contain many overlapping complexes and the complex with the highest φ value will be conscious according to IIT. Consciousness varies in quantity and comes in many degrees which correspond to φ values. The quantity of consciousness generated is directly proportional to the degree of information integration in a system. As Tononi recognizes, IIT might seem to imply a form of panpsychism. According to IIT, the quality of consciousness is determined by the internal informational relations within the system. Here is a representative quote:

> (i) the quantity of consciousness corresponds to the amount of integrated information generated by a complex of elements; (ii) the quality of experience is specified by the set of informational relationships generated within that complex. Integrated information (φ) is defined as the amount of information generated by a complex of elements, above and beyond the information generated by its parts. Qualia space (Q) is a space where each axis represents a possible state of the complex, each point is a probability distribution of its states, and arrows between points represent the informational relationships among its elements generated by causal mechanisms (connections). Together, the set of informational relationships within a complex constitute a shape in Q that completely and univocally specifies a particular experience.
>
> (Tononi 2008, 216)

Other neuroscientists, notably Christof Koch, have recently endorsed the IIT approach and even expressed sympathy for panpsychism (Koch 2012, chapter eight). Koch adopts a kind of functionalism: "It is not the nature of the stuff that the brain is made out of that matters for mind, it is rather the organization of that stuff – the way the parts of the system are hooked up . . . consciousness is substrate-independent" (Koch 2012, 120–121). To my mind, this is a rather radical departure from Koch's previous neural-based reductionist approaches to consciousness. Koch even goes so far as to say that "consciousness is a fundamental . . . property of living matter" and, as Leibniz says, "it is a simple substance" (119). However, Leibniz's "monads" (the simplest substances) are not meant to be physical in the sense that Koch seems to require for what might realize the IIT. Further, Leibnizian monads do not have parts and do not even causally interact with each other. Perhaps even more surprising is that Koch still dismisses the hard problem: "don't be taken in by philosophical grandstanding and proclamations that the hard problem of consciousness will always be with us" (Koch 2012, 137). This is rather odd considering that Koch seems now to concede that consciousness cannot really be reduced to anything physical. He seems to have given up on the hard problem rather than offered a solution or reply. The question seems to remain: Why or how does consciousness arise from integrated information?

Other questions arise: Exactly why aren't sophisticated and complex information-processing robots conscious? Wouldn't Deep Blue or some other chess-playing machine meet a minimal level of φ to be conscious? What about Watson which defeated a number of Jeopardy champions in that well-known game show? What about single cells, blades of grass, or bacteria? Doesn't integrated information, even very sophisticated integration, occur without consciousness in various unconscious processing subsystems in the brain? It is difficult to see why some systems in our brains, such as those which involve our ability to move and act in various ways (e.g. the cerebellum), have so much less information integration than the conscious subsystems (see Graziano 2013, chapter eleven). Yet Koch and Tononi elsewhere and together (Tononi and Koch 2015) argue that IIT does have the resources to explain why some integrated systems would not be conscious due to a much lower level of φ. To be fair, Tononi often emphasizes the graded nature of consciousness; that is, consciousness comes in degrees. Still, it is not easy to have it both ways; that is, seemingly endorse a form of panpsychism but then insist that IIT does not really imply that consciousness is everywhere.

Tononi explains it thus:

> How close is this position to panpsychism, which holds that everything in the universe has some kind of consciousness? Certainly, the IIT implies that many entities, as long as they include some functional mechanisms that can make choices between alternatives, have some degree of consciousness. Unlike traditional panpsychism, however, the IIT does not attribute consciousness indiscriminately to all things. For example, if there are no interactions, there is no consciousness whatsoever. For the IIT, a camera sensor as such is completely unconscious.
>
> (Tononi 2008, 236)

As was briefly noted in the previous chapter, Chalmers (1995, 1996) is also sympathetic to the notion that information is the key to consciousness. Although he is a property dualist, Chalmers also flirts with panpsychism in presenting his "naturalistic dualism." He suggests that consciousness might be an absolutely fundamental feature of the universe and uses what he calls "the principle of organizational invariance" which says that "any two systems with the same fine-grained functional organization will have qualitatively identical experiences" (1995, 19; see also Chalmers 1996, chapter seven). Chalmers has in mind the system of input–output relations of the functional units of the brain. But, as we've seen in the previous chapter, it is not clear how property dualism or panpsychism explain consciousness either.

2.6.2 Quantum approaches to consciousness

Some scientists look deeper than the neural level to quantum mechanics, which is the study of subatomic particles, to try to explain consciousness. Some background first: Max Planck (1848–1957) is often considered the father of quantum theory. The bizarre and apparently indeterministic world of quantum physics is very different from the deterministic world of classical physics. Quantum events most certainly occur in the brain just as they do elsewhere in the physical world, but whether these events are somehow correlated with conscious events is very controversial. The typical physicalist (say, identity theorist) can at least point to current successes in learning about specific brain functions as some evidence that we are on the right track by focusing at the neural level.

The term "quantum" refers to a discrete element of energy in a system, such as the energy of a particle, with this energy being related to a fundamental frequency of its oscillation. Neither the term "particle" nor the word "wave" really describes the nature of a quantum entity but both are useful for our purposes. Needless to say, some of the details required by quantum theory are very technical. But one key aspect of quantum theory is that subatomic particles and electromagnetic waves are neither simply particles nor waves but have certain properties of each. This originated the concept of "wave-particle duality" whereby particles are understood as discrete packets of energy with wave-like properties. Therefore, a particle's quantum state can be represented as a wave of arbitrary shape and extending over space as a wave function. The "uncertainty principle" states that position and momentum cannot simultaneously be measured with complete precision. However, one can measure the position alone of a moving free particle, creating an *eigenstate* of position with a very large wave function at a particular position x, and zero everywhere else. If one performs a position measurement on such a wave function, the resultant x will be obtained with 100% probability (that is, with complete precision). This is called an *eigenstate* of position. If the particle is in an eigenstate of position, then its momentum is completely unknown. On the other hand, if the particle is in an eigenstate of momentum, then its position is completely unknown. Quantum randomness is observed in processes such as spontaneous emission of light and in radioactive decay, and is usually considered a fundamental feature of nature, independent of our knowledge. In the quantum world, the two possibilities can exist at the same time but, in the classical (macro) world, one or the other must be the case. When we make an observation at the quantum level, the two ("superposed") states have to collapse into one or the other, which is known as the "collapse of the wave function."

There are a number of quantum approaches which aim to explain the nature of consciousness (Marshall and Zohar 1990; Silberstein 1998, 2001; Stapp 1999; Beck and Eccles 1992). Perhaps it is to be expected that these theories are somewhat more speculative than many others. Further, some authors, such as Beck and Eccles, advocate dualism in the traditional sense of non-physical (or at least non-material) events causing material changes in the brain. But I'll focus here on a quantum consciousness proposal from Roger Penrose and Stuart Hameroff, which they call "Orch OR" for "orchestrated objective reduction" (Hameroff and Penrose 1996, 2014). The theory explicitly refers to a subcellular neural structure.

The basic idea is that consciousness arises through quantum effects occurring in subcellular neural structures known as "microtubules" which are structural proteins in cell walls. The lowest neurophysiological level at which quantum processes have been proposed as a NCC is the level at which the interior of single neurons is considered; that is, the cytoskeleton. It consists of protein networks made up of two kinds of structures, neurofilaments and microtubuli, which are essential for transport processes within neurons (and other cells). Microtubuli are cylindrical polymers arranged in a tubular array with an outside diameter of about 25 nanometers (nm $= 10^{-9}$ meter). The tubulins in microtubuli are the substrate used to realize Penrose's theoretical framework neurophysiologically. The main idea is that the collapse of such coherent tubulin states corresponds to elementary acts of consciousness.

According to this view, then, consciousness depends on biologically "orchestrated" coherent quantum processes in the microtubules within brain neurons. These quantum processes correlate with neuronal synaptic and membrane activity, and the process ends with the specific "objective reduction" ("OR") of the quantum state. This orchestrated OR activity ("Orch OR") results in moments of conscious awareness. The Orch OR is related to the fundamentals of quantum mechanics and space–time geometry, which suggests that there may even be a connection between the brain's biomolecular processes and the basic structure of the universe.

In the background is Penrose's view that elementary acts of consciousness are non-algorithmic; that is, non-computable (Penrose 1989, 1994). The emergence of a conscious act is a process that cannot be described algorithmically and so cannot be computed. With his background as an anesthesiologist, Hameroff suggested microtubules as a place where reductions of quantum states can take place (Hameroff and Penrose 1996). The respective quantum states are assumed to be coherent superpositions of tubulin states that extend over many neurons. Their simultaneous gravitation-induced collapse is interpreted as an individual elementary act of consciousness. Hameroff (personal communication) holds that Orch OR should be thought of as an alternative identity theory, such that conscious events are *identical to* collapses of the wave function, as opposed to the idea that conscious events *cause* the collapse.

Given the puzzling and often very counterintuitive nature of quantum physics, the jury is certainly still out on whether quantum approaches will be a scientifically valuable method in explaining consciousness. One concern is simply that these authors are trying to explain one somewhat puzzling phenomenon (consciousness) in terms of another mysterious phenomenon (quantum effects). Thus, the thinking seems to go, perhaps the two are essentially related somehow and so other physicalistic accounts are just looking in the wrong place or at the wrong level of neural activity. It is also much less clear just how quantum theories could empirically be falsified. Of course, this doesn't automatically mean that some such theory isn't correct. One exciting aspect of this approach is the resulting interdisciplinary interest it has generated among physicists and other scientists in the problem of consciousness.

Many philosophers will of course also raise some of the same philosophical doubts about the other theories explored thus far, such as how they could solve the hard problem or respond to conceivability arguments. For example, one might ask how or why a conscious event occurs when a wave function collapses. And surely it is *conceivable* that consciousness is not tied to microtubules and wave function collapses. It is also perhaps less clear just how quantum brain events can explain the numerous kinds of qualia which we experience regularly. It is difficult to see how quantum events could explain the *variety* of qualitative experiences we can have; that is, various emotions and perceptual experiences.

2.6.3 The enactive (or sensorimotor) theory of consciousness

I close this chapter with a radically different physicalist take on the relationship between consciousness and the brain. This view explicitly rejects the notion that consciousness can be explained by brain activity and even that conscious states arise from brain states alone. Some cite psychologist J. J. Gibson (1979) and philosopher Maurice Merleau-Ponty (1945) as early inspirations for this account. Among philosophers, a related recent idea goes back to Clark and Chalmers (1998) who argued for the "extended-mind" thesis whereby mental states are not "in the head" (see also Clark 2008; Hutto and Myin 2012). However, they mainly had intentional states and memory in mind, such as the way we might think of a diary or electronic storage device, not necessarily conscious states.

In recent years, there has certainly been increased attention to what is called an "embodied approach" to cognition (including consciousness) which focuses on the importance of bodily interactions with the world. Part of the reason for this is the emphasis in cognitive science on building practical mobile robots which can successfully interact with the environment. With regard to consciousness, however, this "enactive" or "sensorimotor" theory holds that conscious experiences are inseparable from bodily activities and sensorimotor expectations (O'Regan and Noë 2001). On this view, what we feel and experience is determined by what we do and what we know how to do. Perceptual experience should be seen mainly as a way of interacting with the environment; that is, *developing a skill* for interacting with visual input and manipulating some aspect of the world. What distinguishes perceptual experiences is the different ways in which a perceiver perceptually engages with the environment. What differentiates hearing from seeing, for example, are the differences between the patterns of auditory versus visual engaging with the world. Similarly, within a single (sub-) modality such as color vision, what sets apart an experience of red from an experience of green are also the differences in the modes of interaction with the environment that are involved. When we move our bodies and interact with the environment, the ways we hear sounds and see colors vary. In addition and perhaps more radically, instead of aiming to find NCCs or the neural basis for phenomenal states, we need to look to the overall interactions between an organism and its environment.

To be clear, we might think of the extended-mind hypothesis as a consequence of thinking about embodied cognition. If we have some reason to think that we need to include the body to understand the mind (or consciousness), then we should also include outside tools or objects as partly constitutive of mental states. One reason to include the body to understand conscious experience is that we can enjoy the "perceptual presence" of objects even when we cannot attend to some of their features. How exactly this is possible is what Noë (2004, 59–65) calls the "problem of perceptual presence." For example, how can we sense the perceptual presence of the whole cat when parts of the cat are, say, literally out of view behind a picket fence? Similarly, if a parked car is partly hidden from view by a tree, we still sense the presence of that part of the car which we cannot see. Even more generally, we experience outer objects as three-dimensional and with an unseen backside even when we often only actually see them, strictly speaking, as two-dimensional. Noë argues that we don't merely *think* or *believe* that the hidden features are present but rather that they are present *phenomenologically*. According to sensorimotor theory, this is because we implicitly grasp that we could, for example, walk around and perceive the object from other perspectives. According to the sensorimotor theory, the cat is still perceptually *accessible* to us, which is best explained by our possession of sensorimotor skills and the expectation that we can perceive different parts of the cat by moving our bodies in certain ways. Much the same goes for the other sensory modalities, such as touch. When you hold a bottle in your hands with your eyes closed, you still have a sense of the presence of a whole bottle, even though you only make tactile contact with parts of the bottle.

Although clearly still a physicalist view, sensorimotor theory rejects the notion that conscious states are *generated* by brain activity. Consciousness is instead a capacity of the whole organism. We need to "go beyond the notion of a skull-centered correlate of consciousness to consider the multifarious ways in which brain processes are part of organismic cycles that generate the somatic, environmental, and social dimensions of our experience" (Varela and Thompson 2003, 282). If these authors are correct, then the search for necessary conditions of consciousness in the brain *that are jointly sufficient* is doomed to failure because they would not account for other essential contributions of an animal's body and environment. The fundamental point is that "no neural process *per se* can be 'the place where consciousness happens' because conscious experience occurs only at the level of the whole embodied and situated agent. Neurons and [even] neural assemblies are not conscious subjects; persons and animals are" (Varela and Thompson 2003, 281). Of course, we might wonder if they are conflating conscious *states* with conscious *creatures*.

So where does the mind start and the rest of the world begin? It is important to distinguish between the *content* of a mental state and the *state* or *vehicle* that has the content. This is the difference between what is represented, or what the state is about, and what is doing the representing. So an identity theorist would hold that the vehicle of a conscious state is in the brain for many of the reasons we have seen throughout. So a conscious desire for some cold water is about the water but the desire itself is a brain state. It is important to notice that, on the sensorimotor view, it is not merely a mental state's *content* or *meaning* that is external to the brain or skull (which is a much more widely held view) but that the *vehicle* itself, or at least part of it, is also outside the head. This is also what Hurley calls "the insight of *vehicle externalism*" (2003, 81). Noë also says that he is defending "externalism about the vehicles of content of experience" (2004, 221). It is this latter claim which many, including myself, find very puzzling and unclear at times. It is one thing to say that the content of a belief or desire is outside the skull but quite another to hold that the tastes, pains, and visual experiences themselves are not in the head. It is also relatively unproblematic (among realists at least) to say that outer objects can *cause* the existence of a conscious state, such as a perception of a red apple. It is unproblematic to hold that one's bodily actions can have an *effect* on one's consciousness experience but it doesn't follow that one's experience *is* the bodily activity. Stepping on hot coal will *cause* me to be in pain but this activity doesn't *constitute* the pain. Proper heart and lung functioning is *necessary* for consciousness but they are not the *vehicles* of consciousness.

Indeed, I am still not quite sure what it means to say things like "conscious experiences occur at the level of the entire organism" or that "conscious mental states occur (partly? fully?) outside the skull." To be sure, the *content* and *causal interaction* of conscious states will frequently involve reference to bodily and motor elements, but that is still not to say that consciousness, or the vehicle of consciousness, is literally partly located outside the skull. Yet Noë says things like "The taste of licorice is not something that happens in brains" (Noë 2009, 8).

It seems to me that there may be significant confusion or conflation between "content," "cause," and "identity" (or "constitution"). What exactly is the view? Sometimes it is unclear. On the one hand, it often sounds like a strong identity or constitutive claim is being made about the relationship between sensorimotor skills and consciousness. "Perceptual experience . . . *is* an activity of exploring the environment drawing on knowledge of sensorimotor dependencies and thought" (Noë 2004, 228) and "perceptual experience *just is* a mode of skillful exploration of the world (Noë 2004, 194). Again: "Visual experience is simply not generated [in the brain] *at all*. Experience is not the end product of some kind of neural processing" (O'Regan 2011, 65). On the other hand, there are many examples of a much more modest causal or dependency claim. "I have been arguing that, *for at least some experiences*, the physical substrate [vehicle] of the experience *may* cross boundaries, implicating neural, bodily, and environmental features" (Noë 2004, 221) and "experiencing a raw feel *involves* engaging with the real world" (O'Regan 2011, 112).

Further, as others have argued, it is very difficult to make sense of dreams and hallucinations on this view (Block 2005, 263–265; Revonsuo 2010, 182–183) since bodily action seems irrelevant or totally absent. The same goes for when direct brain stimulation causes specific conscious states. It would also still seem possible to doubt the consciousness, the subjective life, of a futuristic robot which can successfully interact with the environment as well as we do. Perhaps it is just a non-biological version of a zombie. To be fair, sensorimotor theorists do offer some replies to these objections (Noë 2004, 210–215; O'Regan 2011, 65–66), but I will not pursue the matter here.

Perhaps somewhat like an eliminativist or even a behaviorist, the sensorimotor approach denies that there is a hard problem of consciousness because experience does not really derive from brain activity. But, of course, we might still wonder why or how "experience" results from bodily interaction with the environment. Unless they are committed to an untenable and extreme form of behaviorism, it seems that they have simply changed the subject and now use the terms "experience" and "consciousness" to refer to objective bodily behavior and even the outside world.

Chapter summary

In this chapter, we discussed a number of theories of consciousness which explicitly reference neuroscience in one way or another. For example, after some background on the brain and the search for the so-called "neural correlates of consciousness" (NCCs), we briefly presented Crick and Koch's neurobiological temporal synchrony theory, Edelman and Tononi's dynamic core hypothesis, Lamme's recurrent processing theory, and Prinz's attended intermediate-level representation theory. We then delved into the question of exactly how attention and consciousness are related with the help of some experimental results and such phenomena as inattentional and change blindness. The so-called "binding problem" was also introduced along with several key notions of the "unity of consciousness." This chapter ended with critical discussion of a few intriguing, and radically different, alternative theories of consciousness, including information integration theory (IIT), quantum theories of consciousness, and the enactive or sensorimotor theory.

Further reading

For additional reading on NCCs and the binding problem, see the numerous papers in Metzinger 2000, Baars, Banks, and Newman 2003, and Cleeremans 2003. See Stapp 2007 for a critical review of quantum approaches including Orch OR. For more on the enactive or sensorimotor approach, see Block's 2005 review of Noë 2004, as well as Varela and Thompson 2003, Noë 2004, Noë and Thompson 2004, O'Regan 2011, and Hutto and Myin 2012. There is also a special issue of the *Journal of Consciousness Studies* 11 (1) (2004), under the title "Are There Neural Correlates of Consciousness?", with a target article by Noë and Thompson, followed by commentaries and author response.

Notes

1 For more on this line of argument and also much more on the knowledge argument, see Prinz (2012, chapter ten).

2 Mole, Smithies, and Wu 2011, Mole 2008, 2011, Wu 2014, and Montemayor and Haladjian 2015.

3 For much more discussion of Prinz's view and these cases, see Barrett 2014 and Wu 2014, 150–152, 183–186.

4 See also Phillips 2011 and Wu 2014, 187–190 for further critical discussion of Block's view.

3

REPRESENTATIONAL AND COGNITIVE THEORIES OF CONSCIOUSNESS

An important question that should be answered by any theory of consciousness is: What makes a mental state a conscious mental state? In the previous chapter we examined several theories including some that attempt to reduce consciousness to neural states. The primary focus of this chapter will be on "representational theories of consciousness" which attempt to reduce consciousness to "mental representations" rather than directly to neural or other physical states. This approach has been quite popular over the past few decades. Examples include first-order representationalism (FOR) which attempts to explain conscious experience primarily in terms of world-directed (or first-order) intentional states, and higher-order representationalism (HOR) which holds that what makes a mental state M conscious is that a HOR is directed at M. In addition, so-called "self-representationalism" is also critically discussed in this chapter. As we shall see, there are some similarities between HOR and self-representationalism. Two other cognitive theories of consciousness,

Daniel Dennett's multiple drafts theory and Bernard Baars' global work-space theory, are also introduced in this chapter.

3.1 Representational theories of consciousness

Unlike the theories explored in the previous chapter, many current theories attempt to reduce consciousness in *mentalistic terms* such as "thoughts" and "awareness." One approach along these lines is to reduce consciousness to mental representations of some kind. The notion of a "representation" is of course very general and can be applied to photographs, signs, and various natural objects, such as the rings inside a tree. Indeed, this is part of the appeal of representational theories since much of what goes on in the brain might also be understood in a representational way. Neuronal representations are often understood on the model of maps which are types of representations often used in neuroscientific research. Further, mental events are thought to represent outer objects partly because they are caused by such objects in, say, cases of veridical visual perception. Philosophers often call these mental states "intentional states" which have representational content; that is, mental states which are "about something" or "directed at something" such as when one has a thought about a house or a perception of a tree. Although intentional states, such as beliefs and thoughts, are sometimes contrasted with phenomenal states, such as pains and color experiences, it is clear that many conscious states have both phenomenal and intentional properties, such as in visual perceptions.

The general view that we can explain conscious mental states in terms of representational or intentional states is called "representationalism." Although not automatically reductionist in spirit, most versions do attempt such a reduction. Most representationalists believe that there is still room for a second-step reduction to be filled in later by neuroscience. Another related motivation for representational theories of consciousness is the belief that an account of intentionality can more easily be given in natural-istic terms, such as in causal theories whereby mental states are understood as representing outer objects in virtue of some reliable causal connection. The idea, then, is that if consciousness can be explained in representational terms and representation can be understood in purely physical terms, then there is the promise of a naturalistic theory of consciousness. Most generally, however, representationalism can be defined as the view that the phenomenal properties of experience (that is, the "qualia" or "what it is like of experience" or "phenomenal character") can be explained in terms of the experiences' representational properties. Alternatively, we might say that conscious mental states have no mental properties other than their representational properties. For example, when I look at the blue sky, what it is like for me to have a conscious experience of the sky is simply identical to my experience's representation of the blue sky, and the property of "being blue" is a property of the representational object of experience.

3.1.1 Consciousness and intentionality

It is worth mentioning that the precise relationship between intentionality and consciousness is itself a major ongoing area of research with some arguing that genuine intentionality actually presupposes consciousness in some way (Searle 1992; Siewart 1998; Horgan and Tienson 2002). If this is correct, then it wouldn't be possible to *reduce* consciousness to intentionality as representationalists desire to do. But, as we shall see below, most representationalists insist that intentionality is explanatorily prior to consciousness (Gennaro 1995; Gennaro 2012, chapter two). Indeed, representationalists typically argue that consciousness requires intentionality, but not vice versa. Of course, unlike Descartes, few if any today hold that all intentional states are conscious. Descartes' view was that mental states are *essentially* conscious and there are no unconscious mental states at all.

However, a more modest but still controversial claim has been made, for example, by John Searle (1992, 132) and is called the "Connection Principle":

(CP) Every unconscious intentional state is at least potentially conscious.

Searle thinks that the "notion of an unconscious mental state implies accessibility to consciousness" (1992, 152). Searle's argument for CP rests on the notion that every intentional state has "aspectual shape" which can only ultimately be accounted for via consciousness. The idea is that *genuine* (as opposed to "as-if") intentional content must ultimately "seem" a certain way to a creature and so presupposes a conscious first-person point of view. But a number of serious, and perhaps decisive, objections to CP have been raised over the years. I mention only three here:

First, the notion of "potential" at work in CP cannot be logical or metaphysical possibility since that would surely be too strong. Thus, something more like "psychologically possible" seems more reasonable. But then if we take CP literally, Searle faces the problem that it mistakenly rules out a host of actual abnormal psychological phenomena, such as deeply repressed states or any unconscious state that merely could not in fact become conscious due to brain lesions (Rosenthal 1990).

Second, there seems to be no way for CP to acknowledge intentional states that occur via some forms of unconscious perceptual processing. For example, there seem to be two visual pathways in the brain (Milner and Goodale 1995). Visual processing along the *ventral stream* pathway is conscious. But visual processing also occurs along the *dorsal stream* visual pathway, which generates representations not accessible to consciousness. The dorsal stream functions more like an unconscious (and very fast) visual motor system that causes the relevant behavior due to systematic tracking relations with the environment. Searle might of course deny that dorsal stream representations are genuinely intentional and it is somewhat controversial that the states employed in motor-control are genuine representations (as opposed to mere trackers of environmental objects or properties).

Third, CP would automatically rule out the possibility of organisms (past and perhaps present) who have at least some intentional states but who are not conscious. Given the evolutionary process, it seems reasonable to suppose that some genuine intentional states could be present, say in insects or some small fish, prior to the emergence of consciousness. This is the problem with CP that Shani calls a denial of "gradualism" whereby converging lines of empirical evidence show that "the evolution of subjectivity is a gradual process manifesting various levels of ascending complexity, each serving as a platform for the emergence of . . . subjective existence" (Shani 2007, 59; Shani 2008). Perhaps there are lower animals (even lizards and rodents) that only have some very basic beliefs and desires. This seems likely on at least *some* level of evolutionary development. It is difficult to see why such animals *cannot* have any genuine intentional states (including perceptual states) unless those states could also be conscious. At the least, it seems *possible* for such an organism to exist and we should resist attempts to rule it out *a priori*.

However, Horgan and Tienson (2002) reject what they call *separatism* which is the reductive representationalist view that intentionality is separable from consciousness. They argue for what is called "phenomenal intentionality" (Kriegel 2013) or "cognitive phenomenology" (Chundoff 2015). One rationale for separatism is to make a reductionist explanation of consciousness possible. But if intentionality is deeply intertwined with consciousness, then a reductionist explanation would be difficult or perhaps even impossible to obtain. Some similarly argue that beliefs, desires, and other intentional states themselves have phenomenology. Horgan and Tienson distinguish the Intentionality of Phenomenology (IP) from the Phenomenology of Intentionality (PI). They state PI as follows:

(PI) "Mental states of the sort commonly cited as *paradigmatically intentional . . . when conscious*, have phenomenal character that is inseparable from their intentional content" (2002, 520, italics mine).

In addition, they advocate the claim that "there is a *kind* of intentionality, pervasive in *human* mental life, that is constitutively determined by phenomenology alone" (2002, 520, italics mine). However, the problem is their starting point; that is, the first-person *human* point of view. They have in mind paradigmatic human cases of intentional states, which they argue involve phenomenology. But what about the possibility of attributing only intentional states to animals and even to robots? It at least seems *possible* for a creature or robot to have some intentional states without consciousness.

Overall, however, we should keep in mind that explaining the nature of "mind" might be distinguishable, at least to some extent, from the problem of explaining consciousness. That is, if one accepts the existence of unconscious mental states, then one might suppose that giving an account of "mentality" need not necessarily require explaining consciousness. Further, one might suppose that an organism or robot could possess only unconscious mental states. As we saw in Chapter 1, for example, one might argue that mental states can be understood functionally or as neural states but many have countered that consciousness cannot also be understood in the same way (perhaps as evidenced by the absent qualia problem and the hard problem). Nonetheless, as we also saw in Chapter 1, the so-called "mind–body" problem is often inextricably intertwined with the problem of consciousness. In addition, some authors who acknowledge the existence of unconscious mental states (Searle, Horgan, and Tienson) argue that they ultimately entail the presence of consciousness.

3.2 First-order representationalism

A first-order representational (FOR) theory of consciousness is one that attempts to explain and reduce conscious experience primarily in terms of world-directed (or first-order) intentional states. The two most-cited FOR theories are those of Fred Dretske (1995) and Michael Tye (1995, 2000) though there are many others as well. Tye's theory will be the focus of this section. Like other FOR theorists, Tye holds that the representational content of my conscious experience (that is, what my experience is about or directed at) is identical to the phenomenal properties of experience. Tye and other representationalists often use the notion of the "transparency of experience" in support for their view (Harman 1990). This is an argument based on the phenomenological first-person observation that when one turns one's attention away from, say, the blue sky and onto one's experience itself, one is still only aware of the blueness of the sky (Moore 1903). The experience *itself* is not blue but rather one "sees right through" one's experience to its representational properties, and there is nothing else to the experience over and above such properties.

Whatever the exact nature of the argument from transparency (Kind 2003), it is clear that not all mental representations are conscious, and so the key question remains: What exactly distinguishes conscious from unconscious mental states (or representations)? What makes an unconscious mental state a conscious mental state? Here Tye defends what he calls "PANIC theory." The acronym "PANIC" stands for poised, abstract, nonconceptual, intentional content. Without probing into every aspect of PANIC theory, Tye holds that at least some of the representational content in question is nonconceptual (N), which is to say that the subject can lack the concept for the properties represented by the experience in question, such as an experience of a certain shade of red that one has never seen before. The exact nature or even existence of nonconceptual content of experience is itself a highly debated and difficult issue in philosophy of mind (Gunther 2003; Gennaro 2012, chapter six). But conscious states clearly must have "intentional content" (IC) for any representationalist. Tye also asserts that such content is "abstract" (A) and so not necessarily about particular concrete objects. This qualification is needed to handle cases of hallucinations where there are no concrete objects at all. Perhaps most important for mental states to be conscious, however, is that its content must be "poised" (P), which is an importantly functional notion. Tye explains that the

> key idea is that experiences and feelings . . . stand ready and available to make a direct impact on beliefs and/or desires. For example . . . feeling hungry . . . has an immediate cognitive effect, namely, the desire to eat. . . . States with nonconceptual content that are not so poised lack phenomenal character [because] . . . they arise too early, as it were, in the information processing.
>
> (Tye 2000, 62)

A common objection to any FOR account is that it cannot explain all conscious states. Some conscious states do not seem to be "about" or "directed at" anything, such as pains, anxiety, or after-images, and so they would be nonrepresentational conscious states. If so, then conscious states cannot generally be explained in terms of representational properties (Block 1996). Tye responds that pains and itches do represent in the sense that they represent parts of the body. After-images and hallucinations either misrepresent (which is still a kind of representation) or the conscious subject still takes them to have representational properties from the first-person point of view. Indeed, Tye (2000) goes to great lengths to respond to a whole host of alleged counterexamples to FOR. For example, with regard to conscious emotions, he says that they "are frequently localized in particular parts of the body. . . . For example, if one feels sudden jealousy, one is likely to feel one's stomach sink . . . [or] one's blood pressure increase" (2000, 51). Tye believes that something similar is true for fear or anger. Moods, however, are quite different and not usually localizable in the same way. But if one feels, say, elated, then one's overall conscious experience is changed.[1]

Some have invoked hypothetical cases of inverted qualia against HOR. Recall from Chapter 1 that these are hypothetical cases where behaviorally indistinguishable individuals have inverted color perceptions of objects, such as person A visually experiences a lemon in the same the way that person B experiences a ripe tomato, and likewise for all yellow and red objects. If it is possible that there are two individuals whose color experiences are inverted with respect to the objects of perception, we would have a case of *different* phenomenal experiences with the *same* represented properties. A somewhat different twist on the inverted spectrum problem is Block's (1990) Inverted Earth case. On Inverted Earth every object has the complementary color to the one it has here, but we are asked to imagine that a person is equipped with color-inverting lenses and then sent to Inverted Earth completely ignorant of those facts. Since the color inversions cancel out, the phenomenal experiences remain the same, yet there certainly seem to be different representational properties of objects involved. The strategy on the part of critics, in short, is to think of counterexamples (either actual or hypothetical) where there is a difference between the phenomenal properties in experience and the relevant representational properties in the world. These objections can, perhaps, be answered by Tye and others in various ways, but significant debate continues (MacPherson 2005). Moreover, "intuitions" dramatically differ as to the very plausibility and value of such thought experiments.

Perhaps a more serious objection to Tye's theory is that what seems to be doing most of the work on his PANIC account is the extremely functional-sounding "poised" notion, and so he is not really explaining phenomenal consciousness in *entirely* representational terms (Kriegel 2002). It is also unclear how a disposition can confer *actual* consciousness on an otherwise unconscious mental state. Peter Carruthers similarly asks: "How can the mere fact that an [unconscious state] is now in a position to have an impact upon the . . . decision-making process [or beliefs and desires] confer on it the subjective properties of feel and 'what-it-is-likeness' distinctive of phenomenal consciousness?" (2000, 170). This is indeed a difficult question to answer.

3.3 Higher-order representationalism

3.3.1 Higher-order thought (HOT) theories

As we have seen, one question that should be answered by any theory of consciousness is: What makes a mental state a *conscious* mental state? There is also a long tradition that has attempted to understand consciousness in terms of some kind of higher-order awareness. For example, John Locke (1689/1975) once said that "consciousness is the perception of what passes in a man's own mind." However, this intuition has been revived by a number of contemporary philosophers (Armstrong 1981; Rosenthal 1986, 2005; Lycan 1996).[2] In general, the idea is that what makes a mental state conscious is that it is the object of some kind of higher-order representation (HOR). A mental state M becomes conscious when there is a HOR of M. A HOR is a "meta-psychological" or "meta-cognitive" state; that is, a mental state directed at another mental state. So, for example, my desire to write a good book becomes conscious when I am (non-inferentially) "aware" of the desire. Intuitively, it seems that conscious states, as opposed to unconscious ones, are mental states that I am "aware of" in some sense. So conscious mental states arise when two (unconscious) mental states are related in a certain specific way, namely that one of them (the HOR) is directed at the other (M).

This is sometimes referred to as the Transitivity Principle (TP):

(TP) A conscious state is a state whose subject is, in some way, aware of being in it.

Conversely, the idea that I could be having a conscious state while totally unaware of being in that state seems very odd (if not an outright contradiction). A mental state of which the subject is completely unaware is clearly an unconscious state. For example, I would not be aware of having a subliminal perception, and thus it is an unconscious perception.[3] Any theory which attempts to explain consciousness in terms of higher-order states is known as a higher-order representational theory of consciousness. It is best initially to use the more neutral term "representation" because there are many flavors of higher-order theory, depending upon how one characterizes the HOR in question. Higher-order theorists are united in the belief that their approach can better explain consciousness than any purely FOR theory which has significant difficulty in explaining the difference between unconscious and conscious mental states.

The most common division of HOR theories is between higher-order thought (HOT) theories and higher-order perception (HOP) theories. HOT theorists, such as David Rosenthal, think it is better to understand the HOR as a thought containing concepts. HOTs are treated as cognitive states involving some kind of conceptual component. HOP theorists urge that the HOR is a perceptual or experiential state of some kind (Lycan 1996) which does not require the kind of conceptual content invoked by HOT theorists. Although HOT and HOP theorists agree on the need for a HOR theory of consciousness, they do sometimes argue for the superiority of their respective positions (Rosenthal 2004; Lycan 2004). I personally favor a version of the HOT theory of consciousness for the reasons discussed in this chapter and elsewhere (Gennaro 1996, 2012). I think that HOT theory is plausibly motivated by the Transitivity Principle and offers a reasoned way to differentiate conscious and unconscious mental states. I do not think that directly reducing consciousness to neurophysiology is currently the best strategy to take, but this is not because of the typical objections to materialism discussed in Chapter 1 (section 1.7).

One can also find something like TP in premise 1 of Lycan's (2001) general argument for HOR. The entire argument runs as follows:

(1) A conscious state is a mental state whose subject is aware of being in it.
(2) The "of" in (1) is the "of" of intentionality; what one is aware of is an intentional object of the awareness.
(3) Intentionality is representational; a state has a thing as its intentional object only if it represents that thing.
Therefore, (4) Awareness of a mental state is a representation of that state. (From 2, 3)
Therefore, (5) A conscious state is a state that is itself represented by another of the subject's mental states. (1, 4)

The intuitive appeal of premise 1 leads fairly naturally to the final conclusion – (5) – which is just another way of stating HOR. Another compelling rationale for HOR, and HOT theory in particular, is as follows (based on Rosenthal 2004, 24): A non-HOT theorist might still agree with HOT theory as an account of introspection or reflection, namely that it involves a conscious thought about a mental state (Block 1995). This seems to be a fairly common-sense definition of introspection that includes the notion that introspection involves conceptual activity. It also seems reasonable for anyone to hold that when a mental state is unconscious, there is no HOT at all. But then it stands to reason that there should be something "in between" those two cases; that is, when one has a first-order conscious state. So what is in between no HOT at all and a conscious HOT? The answer is an unconscious HOT, which is precisely what HOT theory says. Moreover, this nicely explains what happens when there is a transition from a first-order conscious state to an introspective state: an unconscious HOT becomes conscious.

HOT theorists further agree that one must become aware of the lower-order (LO) state noninferentially. We might suppose, say, that the HOT must be caused noninferentially by the LO state to make it conscious. The point of this condition is mainly to rule out alleged counterexamples to HOT theory, such as cases where I become aware of my unconscious desire to kill my boss because I have consciously inferred it from a session with a psychiatrist, or where my envy becomes conscious after making inferences based on my own behavior. The characteristic *feel* of such a conscious desire or envy may be absent in these cases, but since awareness of them arose via conscious inference, the HOT theorist accounts for them by adding this noninferential condition.

A common initial objection to HOR theories is that they are circular and lead to an infinite regress. It might seem that the HOT theory results in circularity by defining consciousness in terms of HOTs; that is, we shouldn't explain or define a concept by using that very same concept. It also might seem that an infinite regress results because a conscious mental state must be accompanied by a HOT, which, in turn, must be accompanied by another HOT *ad infinitum*. However, the standard reply is that when a conscious mental state is a first-order world-directed state, the HOT is not itself conscious; otherwise, circularity and an infinite regress would follow. When the HOT is itself conscious, there is a yet higher-order (or third-order) thought directed at the second-order state. In this case, we have *introspection* which involves a conscious HOT directed at an inner mental state. When one introspects, one's attention is directed back into one's mind. For example, what makes my desire to write a good book a conscious first-order desire is that there is an unconscious HOT directed at the desire. In this case, my conscious focus is directed at the book and my computer screen, so I am not consciously aware of having the HOT from the first-person point of view. When I *introspect* that desire, however, I then have a conscious HOT (accompanied by a yet higher, third-order, HOT) directed at the desire itself (see Rosenthal 1986, 1997, and Figure 3.1).

It is worth discussing several other objections to HOT theories: First, some argue that various animals (and even infants) are not likely to have the conceptual sophistication required for HOTs, and so that would render animal (and infant) consciousness very unlikely (Dretske 1995; Seager 2004). Are cats and dogs capable of having complex HOTs such as "I am in mental state M"? Although most who bring forth this objection are not HOT theorists, Peter Carruthers (1989) is one HOT theorist who actually embraces the conclusion that (most) animals do not have phenomenal

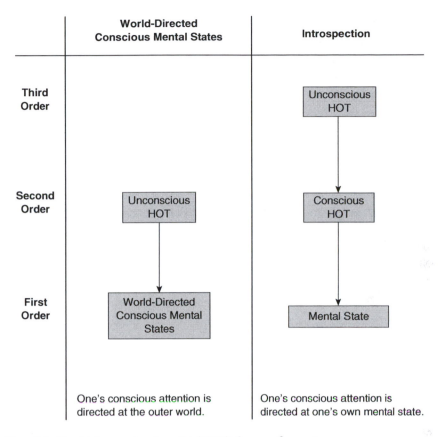

Figure 3.1 The higher-order thought (HOT) theory of consciousness

consciousness. I (Gennaro 1993, 1996) have replied to Carruthers on this point; for example, it is argued that the HOTs need not be as sophisticated as it might initially appear and there is ample comparative neurophysiological evidence supporting the conclusion that animals have conscious mental states. Most HOT theorists do not wish to accept the absence of animal or infant consciousness as a consequence of holding the theory.

The debate has continued over the past two decades[4] but to give just one example which seems to favor my view, Clayton and Dickinson and their colleagues have reported ingenious and convincing demonstrations of memory for time in scrub jays (Clayton, Bussey, and Dickinson 2003). Scrub jays are food-caching birds, and when they have food they cannot eat, they hide it and recover it later. Because some of the food is preferred but perishable (such as crickets), it must be eaten within a few days, while other food (such as nuts) is less preferred but does not perish as quickly. In cleverly designed experiments using these facts, scrub jays are shown, even days after caching, to know not only *what* kind of food was *where* but also *when* they had cached it (see also Clayton, Emery, and Dickinson 2006). This strongly suggests that the birds have some degree of self-concept or "I-concept" which can figure into HOTs. That is, such experimental results seem to show that scrub jays have episodic memory which involves a sense of self over time. Further, many crows and scrub jays return alone to caches they had hidden in the presence of others and recache them in new places (Emery and Clayton 2001). This suggests that they know that *others* know where the food is cached, and thus, to avoid having their food stolen, they recache the food. This strongly suggests that these birds can have some mental concepts, not only about their own minds but even of other minds. I will return to animal consciousness in Chapter 5.

A second objection has been referred to as the "problem of the rock" (Stubenberg 1998) and the "generality problem" (Van Gulick 2004) but it is originally due to Alvin Goldman (Goldman 1993). When I have a thought about a rock, it is certainly not true that the rock becomes conscious. So why should I suppose that a mental state becomes conscious when I think about it? This objection forces HOT theorists to explain just how adding a HOT changes an unconscious state into a conscious one. There have been, however, a number of responses to this kind of objection (Rosenthal 1997; Van Gulick 2000, 2004; Gennaro 2005, 2012, chapter four). A common theme is that there is a principled difference in the *objects* of the thoughts in question. For one thing, rocks and similar objects are not mental states in the first place, and so HOT theorists are first and foremost trying to explain how a *mental state* becomes conscious. The objects of the HOTs must be "in the head."

Third, the above leads somewhat naturally to an objection related to Chalmers' hard problem. It might be asked just how exactly any HOR theory really explains the subjective or phenomenal aspect of conscious experience. How or why does a mental state come to have a first-person qualitative "what it is like" aspect by virtue of the presence of a HOR directed at it? HOR theorists have been slow to address this problem but a number of responses have emerged. Some argue that this objection misconstrues the main and more modest purpose of (at least, their) HOT theories.

The claim is that HOT theories are theories of consciousness only in the sense that they are attempting to explain what differentiates conscious from unconscious states; that is, in terms of a higher-order awareness of some kind. A full account of "qualitative properties" or "sensory qualities" (which can themselves be unconscious) can be found elsewhere in their work, but is independent of their theory of consciousness (Rosenthal 1991, 2005; Lycan 1996). Thus, a full explanation of phenomenal consciousness does require more than a HOR theory, but that is no objection to HOR theories as such.

Another response is that proponents of the hard problem unjustly raise the bar as to what would count as a viable explanation of consciousness so that any reductionist attempt would inevitably fall short (Carruthers 2000; Gennaro 2012). Part of the problem may be a lack of clarity about what would even count as an explanation of consciousness (Van Gulick 1995c). Once this is clarified, however, the hard problem can indeed be solved.

My own response to how HOTs explain conscious states has more to do with the rather Kantian idea that the concepts that figure into the HOTs are necessarily presupposed in conscious experience (Gennaro 2012, chapter four, 2005). To briefly summarize and in a Kantian spirit, the idea is that first we receive information via our senses or the "faculty of sensibility." Some of this information will then rise to the level of unconscious mental states but these mental states do not become conscious until the more cognitive "faculty of understanding" operates on them via the application of concepts. We can arguably understand such concept application in terms of HOTs directed at first-order states. Thus, I consciously experience (and recognize) the brown tree as a brown tree partly because I apply the concepts "brown" and "tree" (in my HOTs) to my basic perceptual states. If there is a real hard problem here, I have argued that it has much more to do with explaining concept acquisition (Gennaro 2012, chapters six and seven).

Notice that this solution is unlike reductionist accounts in non-mentalistic terms and so is immune to Chalmers' criticism about the plausibility of those theories. There is no problem about how a specific brain activity "produces" conscious experience, nor is there an issue about any *a priori* or *a posteriori* relation between brains and consciousness. The issue instead is how HOT theory is realized in our brains for which there seems to be some evidence thus far (Gennaro 2012, chapters four and nine). Like so-called "zombies," though, perhaps we should still admit the *conceivability* of consciousness without HOTs (or vice versa). But, to reiterate from Chapter 1, much the same would seem to apply to Chalmers' own view; that is, surely it is not self-contradictory to suppose that, for example, consciousness is not a fundamental ontological feature of the world.

A fourth and very important objection to HO (higher-order) approaches is the question of how any of these theories can explain cases where the HO state might *misrepresent* the LO mental state (Byrne 1997; Neander 1998; Levine 2001; Block 2011). After all, if we have a representational relation between two states, it seems possible for misrepresentation or malfunction to occur. If it does, then what explanation can be offered by the HOT theorist? If my LO state registers a *red* percept and my HO state registers a thought about something *green* due, say, to some neural misfiring, then what happens? It seems that problems loom for any answer given by a HOT theorist. For example, if a HOT theorist takes the option that the resulting conscious experience is reddish, then it seems that the HOT plays no role in determining the qualitative character of the experience. On the other hand, if the resulting experience is greenish, then the LO state seems irrelevant. Rosenthal and Weisberg hold that the HO state determines the qualitative properties even when there is no LO state at all which are called "targetless" or "empty" HOT cases (Rosenthal 2005, 2011; Weisberg 2008, 2011). My own view (Gennaro 2012, 2013) is that no conscious experience results in such cases, for how can a sole (unconscious) HOT result in a conscious state at all? I think there must be a conceptual match, complete or partial, between the LO and HO state for a conscious state to exist in the first place. Weisberg and Rosenthal argue that what really matters is how things seem to the subject and, if we can explain that, we've explained all that we need to. But somehow the HOT *alone* is now all that matters. Wouldn't this defeat the purpose of HOT theory which is supposed to explain state consciousness in terms of the *relation* between *two states*? Moreover, HOT theory is supposed to be a theory of (intransitive) state consciousness; that is, the *lower-order state* is supposed to be the conscious one.

In the end, I argue for the much more nuanced claim that:

> Whenever a subject S has a HOT directed at experience e, the content c of S's HOT determines the way that S experiences e (provided that there is a *full or partial* conceptual match with the lower-order state, *or* when the HO state contains more specific or fine-grained concepts than the

LO state has, *or* when the LO state contains more specific or fine-grained concepts than the HO state has, *or* when the HO concepts can combine to match the LO concept).

(Gennaro 2012, 180)

The reasons for the above qualifications are discussed at length in Gennaro (2012, chapter six) but they basically attempt to explain what happens in some abnormal cases (such as visual agnosia) and in some other atypical contexts (e.g. perceiving ambiguous figures such as the vase–two faces) where mismatches might occur between the HOT and LO state. For example, visual agnosia, or more specifically *associative agnosia*, seems to be a case where a subject has a conscious experience of an object without any conceptualization of the incoming visual information. There appears to be a first-order perception of an object without the accompanying concept of that object (either first- or second-order, for that matter). Thus its "meaning" is gone and the object is not recognized. In short, it seems that there clearly can be conscious perceptions of objects without the application of concepts; that is, without recognition or identification of those objects. But we might instead hold that associative agnosia is simply an unusual case where the typical HOT does not fully match up with the first-order visual input. That is, we might view associative agnosia as a case where the "normal," or most general, object concept in the HOT does not accompany the input received through the visual modality. There is a *partial match* instead. A HOT might *partially recognize* the LO state. So associative agnosia would be a case where the LO state *could* still register a percept of an object O (because the subject still has that concept), but the HO state is limited to some features of O. Bare visual perception remains intact in the LO state but is confused and ambiguous, and thus the agnosic's conscious experience of O "loses meaning," resulting in a different phenomenological experience. When, for example, the agnosic does not (visually) recognize a whistle, perhaps only the concepts "silver," "roundish," and "object" are applied to the object. But as long as that is how the agnosic *experiences* the object, then HOT theory is left unthreatened.

In any case, I hold that misrepresentations cannot occur between M and HOT *and* still result in a conscious state (Gennaro 2012, 2013). Misrepresentations cannot occur between M and HOT *and* result in a conscious experience reflecting mismatched and incompatible concepts.

Once again, and especially with respect to targetless HOTs, it is difficult to see how an *unconscious* HOT *alone* results in a conscious mental state. This important objection forces HOT theorists to be clearer about just how to view the relationship between the LO and HO states.[5]

3.3.2 Dispositional HOT theory

Peter Carruthers (2000) thinks that it is better for various reasons to think of HOTs as dispositional states instead of the standard view that the HOTs are actual, though he also understands his "dispositional HOT theory" to be a form of HOP theory (Carruthers 2004). The basic idea is that the consciousness of an experience is due to its *availability* to higher-order thought. So "conscious experience occurs when perceptual contents are fed into a special short-term buffer memory store, whose function is to make those contents available to cause HOTs about themselves" (Carruthers 2000, 228). Some first-order perceptual contents are available to a higher-order "theory of mind mechanism," which transforms those representational contents into conscious contents. Thus, no actual HOT occurs. Instead, according to Carruthers, some perceptual states acquire a dual intentional content; for example, a conscious experience of red not only has a first-order content of "red," but also has the higher-order content "seems red" or "experience of red." Thus, he calls his theory "dual-content theory." Carruthers makes interesting use of so-called "consumer semantics" to fill out his theory of phenomenal consciousness. The content of a mental state depends, in part, on the powers of the organisms which "consume" that state; for example, the kinds of inferences which the organism can make when it is in that state.

Carruthers' dispositional theory is often criticized by those who, among other things, do not see how the mere disposition toward a mental state can render it conscious (Rosenthal 2004; Gennaro 2004b, 2012). Recall that a key motivation for HOT theory is the Transitivity Principle (TP). But the TP clearly lends itself to an *actualist* HOT theory interpretation, namely that we *are* aware of our conscious states and not aware of our unconscious states. As Rosenthal puts it, "being disposed to have a thought about something doesn't make one conscious of that thing, but only potentially conscious of it" (2004, 28). Thus it is natural to wonder just how dual-content theory *explains* phenomenal consciousness. It is difficult to understand how a *dispositional* HOT can render, say, a perceptual state *actually* conscious.

To be sure, Carruthers is well aware of this objection and attempts to address it in some places (such as Carruthers 2005, 55–60). He again relies on consumer semantics in an attempt to show that changes in consumer systems can transform perceptual contents. But the central and most serious problem remains: that is, dual-content theory is vulnerable to the same objection raised by Carruthers against FOR. On both views, it is difficult to understand how the functional or dispositional aspects of the respective theories can yield actual conscious states. This point is made most forcefully by Jehle and Kriegel (2006). They point out that dual-content theory "falls prey to the same problem that bedevils FOR: It attempts to account for the difference between conscious and [un]conscious . . . mental states purely in terms of the functional roles of those states" (Jehle and Kriegel 2006, 468). It does indeed seem that if we accept Carruthers' argument against FOR, then it also undermines his own dual-content theory. After all, it is clear that Carruthers intends functional-role semantics to play an essential role in his theory, such that a mental state's content is determined by its functional role in a person's mental life.

3.3.3 Higher-order perception (HOP) theory

David Armstrong (1968, 1981) and William Lycan (1996, 2004) have been the leading HOP theorists in recent years. Unlike HOTs, HOPs are not thoughts and can have at least some nonconceptual content. HOPs are understood as analogous to outer perception. One standard objection to HOP theory, however, is that unlike outer perception, there is no obvious distinct sense organ or scanning mechanism responsible for HOPs. Similarly, no distinctive sensory quality or phenomenology is involved in having HOPs whereas outer perception always involves some sensory quality. Lycan concedes the disanalogy but argues that it does not outweigh other considerations favoring HOP theory (Lycan 1996, 28–29, 2004, 100). Lycan's reply might be understandable, but the objection remains an obvious and serious one nonetheless. I do not think that this disanalogy can be overstated. After all, this represents a major difference between normal outer perception and any alleged inner perception, which arguably involves the most central characteristic of perception.

Lycan (2004, 101–110) offers several other reasons to prefer HOP theory to HOT theory. For example, he urges that consciousness, and especially active introspection, of our mental states is much more like perception than thought in so far as perception allows for a greater degree of voluntary control over what areas of our phenomenal field to make conscious. I have argued against Lycan's claim that HOP theory is superior to HOT theory because, by analogy to outer perception, there is actually an important *nonvoluntary* or *passive* aspect to perception not found in thought (2012, chapter three). The perceptions in HOPs are *too* passive to account for the interrelation between HORs and first-order states. Thus, HOTs are preferable. While it is true that many thoughts do occur nonvoluntarily and somewhat spontaneously, introspective thoughts (i.e. conscious HOTs) can also be controlled voluntarily at least as well as conscious HOPs. We often actively search our minds for information, memories, and other mental items. Recall the way it was put in Kantian terms: we can distinguish between the faculties of *sensibility* and *understanding*, which must work together to make experience possible. What is most relevant here is how the passive nature of the sensibility (through which outer objects are given to us) stands in contrast to the active and more cognitive nature of the understanding which thinks about that which enters via the sensibility. In any case, what ultimately justifies treating HORs as thoughts is the application of concepts to first-order states (Gennaro 1996, 101, 2012, chapter four).

In recent years, however, Lycan has changed his mind and no longer holds HOP theory, mainly because he thinks that *attention* to first-order states is sufficient for an account of conscious states and there is little reason to view the relevant attentional mechanism as *intentional* or as *representing* first-order states (Sauret and Lycan 2014). Armstrong and Lycan had indeed previously often spoken of HOP "monitors" or "scanners" as a kind of attentional mechanism but now it seems that "leading contemporary cognitive and neurological theories of attention are unanimous in suggesting that attention is not intentional" (Sauret and Lycan 2014, 365). They cite Prinz (2012), for example, who holds that attention is a psychological process that connects first-order states with working memory (as we saw in Chapter 2). Sauret and Lycan explain that "attention is the mechanism that enables subjects to become aware of their mental states" (2014, 367) and yet this "awareness of" or "directness" is a non-intentional selection of mental states. Thus, Sauret and Lycan (2014) find that Lycan's (2001) argument, discussed above, goes wrong at premise 2, namely that the "of" mentioned in premise 1 is the "of" of intentionality. Instead, the "of" is, for example, perhaps more of an "acquaintance relation" which is presumably non-intentional. Although Sauret and Lycan do not present a theory of "acquaintance," let alone one with the level of detail offered by HOT theory, they do briefly reference a couple of "candidates" in the literature.

For my own part, I doubt that the acquaintance strategy is a better alternative (see Gennaro 2015a). Such acquaintance relations would presumably be understood as somehow "closer" than the representational relation. But this strategy is at best trading one difficult problem for an even deeper puzzle, namely just how to understand the allegedly intimate and nonrepresentational "awareness of" relation between HORs and first-order states. It is also more difficult to understand such "acquaintance relations" within the context of a reductionist approach. Indeed, acquaintance is often taken to be unanalyzable and simple, in which case it is difficult to see how it could usefully explain anything, let alone the nature of conscious states. Zahavi (2007), no friend of HOT or HOP theory, also recognizes how unsatisfying invoking "acquaintance" can be. He explains that advocates of this approach

> never offer a more detailed analysis of this complex structure. That is, when it comes to a positive description of the structure of original pre-reflective self-awareness [or, acquaintance with a mental state] they are remarkably silent, either claiming in turn that it is unanalysable, or that the unity of its complex structure is incomprehensible. This is hardly satisfactory.
>
> (Zahavi 2007, 281)

It seems to me that we still do not have a good sense of what this acquaintance relation is.

3.3.4 Consciousness and conceptualism

Let us return to the claim that HOT theory can help to explain how one's conceptual repertoire can transform our phenomenological experience. Concepts, at minimum, involve recognizing and understanding objects and properties. Having a concept C should also give the concept possessor the ability to discriminate instances of C and non-C's. For example, if I have the concept "lion" I should be able to identify lions and distinguish them from other even fairly similar land animals. Rosenthal invokes the idea that concepts can change one's conscious experience with the help of several nice examples (2005, 187–188). For example, acquiring various concepts from a wine-tasting course will lead to different experiences from those enjoyed before the course. I acquire more fine-grained wine-related concepts, such as "dry" and "heavy," which in turn can figure into my HOTs and thus alter my conscious experiences. As is widely held, I will literally have different qualia due to the change in my conceptual repertoire. As we learn more concepts, we have more fine-grained experiences and thus we will experience more qualitative complexities. A botanist will likely have somewhat different perceptual experiences than I do while walking through a forest. Conversely, those with a more limited conceptual repertoire, such as infants and animals, will have a more coarse-grained set of experiences. Much the same goes for the way I experience a painting after learning more about artwork and color. The notion of "seeing-as" ("hearing-as" and so on) is often invoked and depending upon the concepts I possess, my conscious experience will literally allow me to experience the world differently. Susanna Siegel (2010) similarly argues that acquisition of certain conceptual abilities can make some things, such as Russian sentences and pine trees, phenomenally look different. After one learns Russian (or Cyrillic), there is a phenomenal difference between looking at a written page in that language. The increased understanding of a language causes a phenomenal shift in the experience. Much the same seems true once one has learned how to recognize pine trees in a grove containing many different kinds of trees. These considerations do not of course, by themselves, prove that newly acquired concepts are *constitutive* parts of the resulting conscious states as opposed merely to having a *causal* impact on those states.

In any case, Chuard (2007) defines conceptualism as the claim that "the representational content of a perceptual experience is fully conceptual in the sense that what the experience represents (and how it represents it) is entirely determined by the conceptual capacities the perceiver brings to bear in her experience" (Chuard 2007, 25). We might similarly define conceptualism as follows:

(CON) Whenever a subject S has a perceptual experience e, the content c (of e) is fully specifiable in terms of the concepts possessed by S.

Thus the central philosophical issue is whether one can have contentful conscious experiences of objects (or properties or relations) without having the corresponding concepts. The basic idea is that, just like beliefs and thoughts, perceptual experiences also have conceptual content, contrary to what many seem to think. This position has some affinity to Sellars' "myth of the given" warning against the possibility of unconceptualized experiences "given" in perception (Sellars 1956). In a somewhat Kantian manner, we might say that all conscious experience presupposes the application of concepts, or, even stronger, the way that one experiences the world is *entirely* determined by the concepts one possesses. Indeed, Gunther (2003, 1) initially uses Kant's famous slogan that "thoughts without content are empty, intuitions [= sensory experiences] without concepts are blind" to sum up conceptualism (Kant 1781/1965, A51/B75).

In Gennaro 2012, chapter six, I connect HOT theory and conceptualism via the following "HOT-CON Argument" which argues from HOT theory to conceptualism:

(1) Whenever a subject S has a conscious perceptual experience *e*, one has a HOT directed at *e*.

(2) Whenever a subject S has a HOT directed at *e*, the content *c* of S's HOT determines the way that S experiences *e* (provided there is a match with the lower-order state).

(3) Whenever there is a content *c* of S's HOT determining the way that S experiences *e*, the content *c* (of *e*) is fully specifiable in terms of concepts possessed by S.

Therefore, (4) Whenever a subject S has a conscious perceptual experience *e*, the content *c* (of *e*) is fully specifiable in terms of concepts possessed by S.

The above is somewhat oversimplified, especially with regard to premise (2), but I argue that there is a very close and natural connection between HOT theory and conceptualism.

Leaving aside HOT theory, however, nonconceptualists reject conceptualism for a variety of reasons. For example, one attempt to support nonconceptualism begins with the premise that many perceptual experiences are extremely rich in content. It seems, for example, that we can *simultaneously* experience a complex visual scene, such as a landscape, and it is implausible to suppose that the subject deploys concepts for every object (and property and relation) that the experience represents. Numerous objects, shapes, and colors are represented, not to mention the relations between them. Unlike beliefs and thoughts, which solely have conceptual content, perceptual experiences represent in a way that goes well beyond one's conceptual capacities. In short, we can have perceptual experiences that outrun our conceptual capacities.

A conceptualist can respond to the richness argument in a number of ways. She might initially challenge the central premise that conscious experience is very rich. The claim is that, contrary to initial intuitions, we really do not consciously experience very much at any given time. The rationale for this strategy comes from several different and, in my view, compelling sources such as "filling-in," inattentional blindness, and change blindness. Recall the discussion from the previous chapter on these phenomena which suggests that we at most seem to consciously experience in detail what is in our focal visual field. I am sympathetic to the notion that our perceptual experiences are not as rich as they might seem.

It is also often argued that conscious perceptual experience, whether rich or not, is much more *fine grained* than the concepts one possesses. In other words, it seems that one can experience an object or property without having the concept of that specific object or property. For example, a subject could experience a shade of red or a new shape without having the corresponding concept, and the same can presumably be said for auditory and other experiences. Thus, one seems to be able to have conscious experiences with nonconceptual content; that is, perceptual states that represent the world in novel ways that do not reflect the concepts possessed by a subject. It would seem that I can perceptually discriminate and experience many more colors and shapes than I have concepts for. A number of authors have raised this argument against conceptualism.[6] Along the same lines, Evans asks rhetorically: "Do we really understand the proposal that we have as many color concepts as there are shades of color that we can sensibly discriminate?" (Evans 1982, 229).

The main initial conceptualist reply comes from McDowell (1994), who argues that we can form *demonstrative concepts*, such as "that shade of red" or "is colored thus" for each specific shade of color that is experienced (cf. Brewer 1999, 170–174). We therefore do in fact have enough fine-grained concepts to account for the perceptions in question, though they are special demonstrative concepts rather than the typical "general" concept. This has been called the "demonstrative strategy" (Chuard 2006), but nonconceptualists argue that demonstrative concepts are not really concepts because they do not allow for re-identification of objects, which is essential for concept possession. Not all conceptualists are satisfied by this response (Gennaro 2012, 175–180), but I will drop the matter here.

3.4 Hybrid and self-representational accounts

A final cluster of related representationalist views holds that the HOR in question should be understood as *intrinsic* to (or part of) an overall complex conscious state. This stands in contrast to the standard view that the HOT is *extrinsic* to (that is, entirely distinct from) its target mental state. The assumption, made by Rosenthal for example, about the extrinsic nature of the HOR has come under attack and thus various hybrid representational theories can be found in the literature. One motivation for this movement is some dissatisfaction with standard HOR theory's ability to handle some of the objections addressed above. Another reason is renewed interest in a view somewhat closer to the one held by Franz Brentano (1874/1973) and others, normally associated with the phenomenological tradition (Husserl 1913/1931; Sartre 1956; Smith 2004; Textor 2006). To varying degrees, these related theories have in common the idea that conscious mental states, in some sense, represent *themselves*, which still involves having a thought about a mental state, just not a distinct or separate mental state. Thus, when one has a conscious desire for a beer, one is also aware that one is in that very state. The conscious desire both represents the beer and itself. It is this "self-representing" which makes the state conscious.

These theories are known by various names. For example, I have argued that, when one has a first-order conscious state, the (unconscious) HOT is better viewed as intrinsic to the target state, so that we have a complex conscious state with parts (Gennaro 1996, 2006, 2012). I call this the "wide intrinsicality view" (WIV) and argue, for example, that Jean-Paul Sartre's theory of consciousness can be understood in this way (Gennaro 2002, 2015a). On the WIV, first-order conscious states are complex states with a world-directed part and a meta-psychological component. Conscious mental states can be understood as brain states which are combinations of passively received perceptual input and presupposed higher-order conceptual activity directed at that input. Concepts in HOTs are presupposed in having first-order conscious states. Robert Van Gulick (2000, 2004, 2006) has also explored the related alternative that the higher-order state is part of an overall global conscious state. He calls such states "HOGS" (higher-order global states) whereby a lower-order unconscious state is "recruited" into a larger state, which becomes conscious partly due to the implicit self-awareness that one is in the lower-order state.

This general approach is also forcefully advocated by Uriah Kriegel in a series of papers (beginning with Kriegel 2003a, 2003b and culminating in Kriegel 2009; cf. Kriegel and Williford 2006). Kriegel has used several different names for his "neo-Brentanian theory," but most recently calls it the "self-representational theory of consciousness." To be sure, the notion of a mental state representing itself or a mental state with one part representing another part is in need of further explanation. Nonetheless, there is agreement among these authors that conscious mental states are, in some important sense, reflexive or self-directed.

Kriegel (2006, 2009) has tried to cash out TP in terms of a ubiquitous (conscious) "peripheral" self-awareness which accompanies all of our first-order focal conscious states. Not all conscious "directedness" is attentive and so perhaps we should not restrict conscious directedness to that which we are consciously focused on. If this is right, then a first-order conscious state can be both attentively outer-directed and inattentively inner-directed. I have argued against this view at length (Gennaro 2008a; Gennaro 2012, chapter five). For example, although it is surely true that there are degrees of conscious attention, the clearest example of genuine "inattentive" consciousness is outer-directed awareness in one's peripheral visual field. But this obviously does not show that any such inattentional consciousness is *self-directed* when there is outer-directed consciousness, let alone at the very same time. Also, what is the evidence for such self-directed inattentional consciousness? It is presumably based on phenomenological considerations but I confess that I do not find such ubiquitous inattentive self-directed "consciousness" in my experience, which should presumably show up in a clear Nagelian sense if it is based on phenomenological observation. Except when I am introspecting, conscious experience is so completely outer-directed that I deny we have such peripheral self-directed consciousness when in first-order conscious states. It does not seem to me that I am consciously aware (in any sense) of my own *experience* when I am, say, consciously attending to a movie or to the task of building a bookcase. Even some who are otherwise very sympathetic to Kriegel's phenomenological approach find it difficult to believe that "pre-reflective" (inattentional) self-awareness accompanies conscious states (Siewart 1998; Zahavi 2004) or at least that *all* conscious states involve such self-awareness (Smith 2004). None of these authors are otherwise sympathetic to HOT theory or reductionist approaches to consciousness.

Interestingly, Kriegel has said for example that "the mental state yielded by that integration may not actually represent itself. . . . At most, we can say that one part of it represents another part" (Kriegel 2005, 48). Thus, Kriegel later explains that only an *indirect* self-representation is applicable to conscious states (2009, 215–226). This comes in the context of his attempt to make sense of a self-representational view within a naturalistic framework, but it is also more like the WIV in structure, the main difference being that Kriegel thinks that pre-reflective self-awareness is itself (peripherally) conscious.

One point of emphasis in recent years has been on attempts to identify just how HOR and self-representationalism can be realized in the brain. After all, most representationalists tend to think that their accounts of the structure of conscious states are realized in the brain (though it may take some time to identify all the main neural structures). One issue is sometimes framed as the question: "How global is HOT theory?" That is, do conscious mental states require widespread brain activation or can at least some be fairly localized in narrower areas of the brain? Perhaps most interesting is whether the prefrontal cortex (PFC) is required for having conscious states (Gennaro 2012, chapter nine). I disagree with Kriegel (2007, 2009 chapter seven) and Block (2007) that, according to higher-order and self-representational views, the PFC is required for most conscious states. However, it may very well be that the PFC is required for more sophisticated *introspective* states or conscious HOTs, but this wouldn't be a problem for HOT theory because it does not require introspection for first-order conscious states.

Is there evidence of conscious states without PFC activity? For example, Rafael Malach and colleagues show that when subjects are engaged in a perceptual task or absorbed in watching a movie, there is widespread neural activation but little PFC activity (Grill-Spector and Malach 2004; Goldberg, Harel, and Malach 2006). Although some other studies do show PFC activation, this is mainly because of the need for subjects to *report* their experiences. Also, basic conscious experience is not decreased entirely even when there is extensive bilateral PFC damage or lobotomies (Pollen 1999, 2003). This line of argument is also relevant to the issue of animal and infant consciousness.

It seems to me that this is an advantage for HOT theory with regard to the oft-cited problem of animal and infant consciousness. If any theory requires PFC activity for *all* conscious states whereas HOT theory does not, then HOT theory is actually in a better position to account for animal and infant consciousness since it is doubtful that infants and most animals have the requisite PFC activity.

But one might also ask: Why think that unconscious HOTs can occur outside the PFC? What is the positive evidence for this? If we grant that unconscious HOTs can be regarded as a kind of "pre-reflective self-consciousness," then we can for example look to Newen and Vogeley (2003) for some answers. They distinguish five levels of self-consciousness ranging from "phenomenal self-acquaintance" and "conceptual self-consciousness" up to "iterative meta-representational self-consciousness." The majority of their paper is explicitly about the neural correlates of consciousness (NCCs) of what they call the "first-person perspective" and the "egocentric reference frame." Citing numerous experiments, they point to various "neural signatures" of self-consciousness. The PFC is rarely mentioned and then usually only with regard to more sophisticated forms of self-consciousness. Other brain areas are much more prominently identified, such as the medial and inferior parietal cortices, the temporoparietal cortex, the posterior cingulate cortex, and the anterior cingulate cortex.[7]

3.5 Two other cognitive theories of consciousness

Aside from the explicitly representational approaches discussed above, there are also related attempts to explain consciousness in cognitive and somewhat functionalist terms. The two most prominent such theories are worth describing here.

3.5.1 The multiple drafts model of consciousness

As we saw in Chapter 1, Daniel Dennett (1988, 1991) has some sympathy for eliminative materialism. He also rejects the very assumption that there is a clear line between conscious and unconscious mental states, especially in terms of the problematic notion of "qualia." He is perhaps most concerned that materialists avoid falling prey to what he calls the "myth of the Cartesian theater," the notion that there is some privileged

place in the brain where everything comes together to produce conscious experience. He explains:

> Let's call the idea of such a centered locus in the brain *Cartesian mat-
> erialism*, since it's the view you arrive at when you discard Descartes's
> dualism but fail to discard the imagery of a central (but material)
> Theatre where "it all comes together." . . . Cartesian materialism is the
> view that there is a crucial finish line or boundary somewhere in the
> brain, marking a place where the order of arrival equals the order of
> "presentation" in experience because *what happens there* is what you
> are conscious of.
>
> (Dennett 1991, 107)

Dennett (1991, 2005) has also put forth what he calls the multiple drafts
model (MDM) of consciousness. Although similar in some ways to representationalism, the MDM holds that all kinds of cognitive activity occur
in the brain via parallel processes of *interpretation* which are under frequent
revision. The MDM rejects the idea of a "self" as an inner observer; that is,
the "self" as a fictional subject. The self is rather the *product* or *construction* of
a narrative that emerges over time, which Dennett (2005) calls the "center
of narrative gravity." Various streams of information compete for "fame in
the brain" and the winner simply gets expressed via behavioral outputs and
verbal reports. But there is no internal phenomenal self; we mistakenly infer
that there is a *center* of narrative gravity. Part of the problem is also that if we
posit a homunculus (= "little man") in the brain which observes a stream
of qualia, then we would have to posit yet another smaller homunculus in it
to observe the former homunculus' stream of qualia, and so on *ad infinitum*.
Instead we really just have numerous parallel information streams in our
brains and we weave a tale about who we are and our past.

Dennett rejects a strong emphasis on any phenomenological or first-
person approach to investigating consciousness, advocating instead what
he calls "heterophenomenology" according to which we should follow a
more neutral path "leading from objective physical science and its insist-
ence on the third person point of view, to a method of phenomenological
description that can (in principle) do justice to the most private and inef-
fable subjective experiences" (1991, 72). First-person reports cannot
really be trusted at all. Consciousness is just objective physical information
expressed in verbal and non-verbal behavior. We might think of Dennett's

view as stating, in Block's terms, that there really is no phenomenal consciousness (at least as it is often defined) and it is all access consciousness.[8]

Dennett is often accused of *explaining away* consciousness rather than really explaining the very first-person subjective experience that almost everyone else believes needs explaining. He comes close to endorsing behaviorism in so far as all that matters is the third-person verifiable behavioral evidence of a system. Explaining human consciousness is not very different in principle to explaining the complex behavior of a robot. Overall, it seems fair to say that Dennett's view of the self, though perhaps also somewhat radical, is more plausible than his theory (or elimination) of consciousness.

Metzinger's (2003, 2011) "self-model theory (SMT) of subjectivity" also has some affinities to Dennett's view, especially in terms of thinking of a self as a kind of "narrative." There is no such ontological entity as "the" self; rather, there is a self-model and a world-model. What we folk-psychologically refer to as "the self" is not a model of a thing, but is instead an ongoing process. Pliushch and Metzinger (2015) apply SMT to the rather puzzling and thorny phenomenon of self-deception.[9]

3.5.2 Global workspace theory of consciousness

Bernard Baars' global workspace theory (GWT) of consciousness is probably the most influential theory proposed among psychologists (Baars 1988, 1997). The basic idea and metaphor is that we should think of the entire cognitive system as built on a "blackboard architecture" which is a kind of global workspace. According to the GWT, unconscious processes and mental states compete for the spotlight of attention, from which information is "broadcast globally" throughout the system. Consciousness consists in such global broadcasting and therefore also has, according to Baars, an important functional and biological adaptation (*contra* epiphenomenalism). We might say that a conscious state is created by a kind of global access to select bits of information in the brain and nervous system. We experience a conscious state precisely when such information is globally available. The information or "messages" that are globally broadcast become conscious and are available to the organism for verbal report or voluntary action. The winning message is like an actor on stage in the spotlight selected via attention. In comparison to the very few items available in consciousness at a given time, there so many more neural processes which are not conscious. The brain is structured to be able to handle only a handful of items at a time, commonly associated with the limits of attention and working memory. As we saw in the previous chapter, the notions of attention and information also play prominent roles in Prinz's theory and Tononi's information integration theory.

Despite Baars' frequent use of "theater" and "spotlight" metaphors, he argues that his view does not entail the presence of the material Cartesian theater that Dennett is so concerned to avoid. The spotlight on stage is surrounded by either vague (peripheral) consciousness or the "unconscious audience" who, although in the dark, still receive information from the spotlight. There is no homunculus in the brain which observes a stream of qualia but there may be neural convergence zones where some elements of conscious experience are tied together. It is, in any case, an empirical matter just how the brain performs the functions Baars describes, such as detecting mechanisms of attention and working memory.

Stanislas Dehaene (2014, especially chapter five) and other collaborators have endorsed and further developed GWT, especially in terms of its neural realization (Dehaene and Naccache 2001; Dehaene and Changeux 2011), which has come to be known as the "neuronal global workspace" (NGW). We can think of GWT in neural terms as "cortical" or "neuronal" workspaces which can encompass widespread neural connections, such as in feedback loops (as was also described in the previous chapter). In some cases, these connections may involve the prefrontal cortex but they can also involve other areas, such as the temporal and parietal brain areas. There are "major hubs" which are the brain's main interconnection centers. In this way, Dehaene and Baars are both content to borrow from the neural theories of consciousness described in the last chapter (e.g. Lamme), depending on just what the latest brain research shows. According to Dehaene, consciousness is "just brain-wide information sharing [which] we may use . . . in whatever way we please" (2014, 165). With regard to Dennett's homunculus worry, Dehaene explains that "there is no 'I' who looks inside us. The stage itself is the 'I'. . . . The audience of the global workspace is not a little man in the head but a collection of other unconscious processors that receive a broadcast message and act upon it" (2014, 166). To use a computer or artificial intelligence analogy, Dehaene tells us that "subprograms would exchange data via a shared 'blackboard,' a common data structure similar to the 'clipboard' in a personal computer. The conscious workspace is the clipboard of the mind" (2014, 166).

With regard to the hard problem, for example, Dehaene says:

> My opinion is that Chalmers swapped the labels: it is the "easy" problem that is hard, while the hard problem just seems hard because it engages ill-defined intuitions. Once our intuition is educated by cognitive neuroscience and computer simulations, Chalmers's hard problem will evaporate . . . much like vitalism – the misguided nineteenth-century thought that, however much detail we gather about the chemical mechanisms of living organisms, we will never account for the unique qualities of life.
>
> (Dehaene 2014, 262)

In any case, there is little reason to revisit all of the materialist replies again here. In the next chapter, we will further explore the fascinating and sometimes disturbing world of consciousness and psychopathology.

Chapter summary

The primary focus of the chapter was on representational theories of consciousness which attempt to reduce consciousness to mental representations rather than directly to neural states. Examples of this popular approach are first-order representationalism (FOR), which attempts to explain conscious experience primarily in terms of world-directed (or first-order) intentional states, and higher-order representationalism (HOR) which holds that what makes a mental state M conscious is that it is the object of some kind of HOR directed at M. Objections to each view were raised and potential responses offered. In addition, some hybrid and self-representational approaches were also critically discussed. The overall question that should be answered by any of these theories is: What makes a mental state a conscious mental state? One importantly related question is just how one's conscious experience is shaped by one's possessed concepts. Two other cognitive theories of consciousness, Daniel Dennett's multiple drafts model and Bernie Baars' global workspace theory, were also explained and some objections were raised.

Further reading

See Gennaro 2012, chapter two, Chudnoff 2015, and the essays in Bayne and Montague 2011 and Kriegel 2013 for much more on the relationship between intentionality and consciousness. For other versions of FOR, see Harman 1990, Kirk 1994, Byrne 2001, and Droege 2003. See Chalmers 2004 for an excellent discussion of the dizzying array of possible representationalist positions. For some other variations on HOT theory, see Rolls 2004, Picciuto 2011, and Coleman 2015. For others who hold some form of the self-representational view, see Caston 2002, Williford 2006, and Janzen 2008; even Carruthers' 2000 theory can be viewed in this light since he contends that conscious states have two representational contents. Some authors (such as Gennaro 2012) view their hybrid positions to be a modified version of HOT theory and Rosenthal 2004 has called it "intrinsic higher-order theory."

Notes

1 For a recent exchange on the representational content of moods, see Kind 2014 and Mandelovici 2014.
2 See also Armstrong 1968, Rosenthal 1997, Lycan 2001, and Gennaro 1996, 2012.
3 I view the TP primarily as an *a priori* or conceptual truth about the nature of conscious states (Gennaro 2012, 28–29).
4 See Carruthers 2000, 2005, 2008, Gennaro 2004b, 2009, 2012, chapters seven and eight.
5 For an attempt to bring together HOT theory and Orch OR quantum theory, see Hameroff, Pylkkanen, and Gennaro 2014. A HOT theorist should at least be open to the possibility that HOT theory might be best realized at a deeper sub-neuronal level; hence, "deeper-order thought" (DOT) theory.
6 Evans 1982, Peacocke 2001, Heck 2000, Kelly 2001a, 2001b, Tye 2006, and Schmidt 2015.
7 See Kozuch (2014) for a very nice discussion of the PFC in relation to higher-order theories.
8 Dennett (2005, chapters one and three) rejects the possibility of zombies and dismisses the hard problem given his type-A materialism. He also responds at length to the knowledge argument (2005, chapter five).

9 This denial of a "self" might remind some readers of various mystical and Eastern (especially Indian) views, such as the Buddhist "not-self" (*anattā* or *anātman*) doctrine which is perhaps analogous to Hume's view on persons (Siderits, Thompson, and Zahavi 2011). But, of course, this is an entirely separate metaphysical issue which does not rule out having "I-thoughts" or applying the "I" concept to one's own everyday experiences in general. It may be that the word "I" doesn't really *refer* to what many people believe it refers to (e.g. an enduring substance of some kind) given a sophisticated metaphysical view about the nature of persons. But that is not to say that we don't often think about ourselves or our mental states in a less rigorous sense and use such a concept from moment to moment. Indeed, one often finds such linguistic expressions and concepts in Buddhist writings (such as *ahamkāra* and *asmīti*).

4

CONSCIOUSNESS AND PSYCHOPATHOLOGY

This chapter outlines the growing and cutting-edge interdisciplinary field sometimes called "philosophical psychopathology" (Graham and Stephens 1994) along with the related "philosophy of psychiatry" area which covers the topics of mental illness, psychopathy, and moral responsibility. Various cognitive deficits are explained with the focus on how they negatively impact and distort conscious experience, such as phantom limb pain, amnesia, split-brain cases, somatoparaphrenia, schizophrenia, visual agnosia, and dissociative identity disorder (DID). Many of these disorders force one to take up the related philosophical problem of personal identity as well as the problem of free will and moral responsibility (especially for psychopathy). A number of psychopathologies are commonly viewed as pathologies of self- or body-awareness in some way. In addition to the work of numerous philosophers, the recent explosion of interest is also due to the provocative and accessible writings of neurologists, most notably Oliver Sacks (starting with his 1987 book), Todd Feinberg (2001, 2009), and V. S. Ramachandran (2004). One of the exciting results is the important interdisciplinary interest that has been generated among philosophers, psychologists, and scientists.[1]

Let's begin with a disorder which challenges our sense of personal identity and calls into question the unity of consciousness.

4.1 Dissociative identity disorder (DID) and amnesia

Philosophers have of course always been intrigued by disorders of consciousness. Part of the interest is presumably that if we can understand how consciousness goes wrong, then we can better theorize about the normal functioning mind. Going back at least as far as Locke (1689/1975), there has been some discussion about the philosophical implications of multiple personality disorder (MPD) which is now called "dissociative identity disorder" (DID). Questions abound: could there be two centers of consciousness in one body? What makes a person the same person over time? These questions are closely linked to the traditional philosophical problem of personal identity. Much the same can be said for memory disorders, such as various forms of amnesia. Does consciousness require some kind of autobiographical memory or psychological continuity?

DID is a condition in which a person displays multiple distinct identities (known as "alters") with each perceiving and interacting with the environment in its own way. At various times, one of the alters is in charge of the subject's behavior. Each alter has a very specific pattern of behaving, perceiving, thinking, and speaking. The alters seem to emerge involuntarily and not all alters are even known to the subject. Thus, there is significant amnesia on the subject's part for periods of time when an alter was in control. This would seem to imply that there are really two (or even more) persons and one body, at least at different times, especially if Locke's view is correct. Locke's account of personal identity through time famously appealed to consciousness and memory. On his view, a later person (P2) is identical to an earlier person (P1) just in case P2's consciousness "can be extended backwards" to P1. This is taken to mean that P2 consciously remembers P1's thoughts and experiences, which is often called the "psychological account of personal identity." My personhood goes with my mind and especially with my consciousness and memory, not necessarily with my body. So a case of DID would seem to be a case where a single body houses two distinct personalities, often with profoundly different character traits and desires. It would seem that cases of DID show that a single conscious subject is not required to have identity of consciousness.

Further, even Locke recognized that if they are really two different persons, then it is difficult to make sense of holding one morally responsible for another's actions. Thus, as we shall see below, there is an often-cited link between personal identity and moral responsibility (Kennett and Matthews 2002). After all, it would seem to be wrong to punish or blame (or praise, for that matter) one person for the actions (or thoughts) of another person. We are justified in holding a person responsible for some past action only if the person is identical to the person who performed that action. Locke argues that one is justifiably held accountable only for those actions performed by a person to whom one's present consciousness extends. This would apply not only to a person whose alter had committed crimes but perhaps also to an elderly inmate who has lost all memory of committing a crime simply due to long-term aging. One might also think of the well-known Dr. Jekyll and Mr. Hyde tale of two persons, one good and one evil, inhabiting the same body (from the Robert Louis Stevenson 1886 classic novel).

However, in some circles, DID has been a very controversial diagnosis. Back when it was called multiple personality disorder (MPD), there was a clear problem of over-diagnosis, especially in the 1980s, perhaps stemming from the publication of the book Sybil which, along with the subsequent film, had a great impact on the popular culture of the time. Even in the psychiatric community there has been a great deal of disagreement about the causes, and even existence, of DID. Some argue that DID (and MPD previously) does not really exist at all and point to cases of irresponsible therapists who encouraged their patients to believe that they had been abused as children or who were accused of implanting such memories in patients via hypnosis. Significant controversy still surrounds the diagnosis of DID but it remains as a category in the American Psychiatric Association's Diagnostic and Statistical Manual of Mental Disorders, or DSM. Most today hold that DID results from repeated childhood abuse and that dissociating is a way to cope with and distance oneself from traumatic experiences.

Recall from Chapter 3 that Dennett (1991) doubts that there is really some "self" in each of us in the way that is normally understood, and so he views DID as further evidence of how our philosophical "intuitions" about the "self" can go wrong. Instead, there are multiple drafts which create a "center of narrative gravity" or a biography with which one can identify. The mind is a collection of unintelligent subcomponents without an overall executive control center. So if there really isn't one "self" in the normal case, then there won't really be two or more selves in a case of DID. Instead, as was discussed in the previous chapter, we each tell a tale to ourselves which is mostly fairly consistent but, perhaps due to traumatic experiences, we sometimes need to create multiple narratives to function and survive in different environments.[2]

As we saw above, the link between personal identity and memory is a close one, at least according to one prominent theory. This is one reason why many think it is appropriate to speak of multiple people in cases of DID. But what about cases where we clearly have a single person but her consciousness is negatively affected by severe memory loss? Amnesia is a condition in which one's memory is lost. *Anterograde* amnesia is the loss of short-term memory: the loss or impairment of the ability to form new memories through memorization. *Retrograde* amnesia is the loss of pre-existing memories to conscious recollection, beyond an ordinary degree of forgetfulness. The person may be able to memorize new things that occur after the onset of amnesia (unlike in anterograde amnesia), but be unable to recall some or all of their life prior to the onset.

Sacks' (1987) patient Jimmie G., for example, didn't even recognize himself in the mirror because he thought he was twenty years younger, having no memory of those intervening years. He didn't recognize the doctor each time he came in to see him. He had Korsakoff's syndrome due to long-term heavy drinking. Nonetheless, Jimmie G. retained much of his procedural memory; that is, memory for how to do certain things or display various skills. This is an example of a "dissociation" between two cognitive abilities; that is, cases where one cognitive function, x, is preserved but another, y, is damaged. In Jimmie G. and other similar cases, procedural learning can not only remain undamaged (such as typing or riding a bicycle), but the patient can also learn new skills (such as following a moving target with a point) without having any conscious memory of the previous learning episodes. A "double dissociation" is found when x and y can each function independently of the other.

It is worth mentioning that neither the dualist nor the materialist can easily explain what happens in DID. For example, if we take DID to show that there can be more than one conscious mind associated with a body, then, for example, a substance dualist would be hard pressed to explain how more than one non-physical mind comes to be causally connected to a single body. On the other hand, materialists have the difficulty of explaining how two people, often exhibiting very different personalities and behaviors, can co-exist in a single brain. Thus far at least, brain imaging tools do not yield very much of an explanation.

4.2 Split-brain cases

Another frequently discussed abnormality of self and consciousness comes from patients who have undergone a commissurotomy or a "brain bisection" operation (Nagel 1971; Sperry 1984). They were performed decades ago as a last resort to relieve the seizure symptoms of severe epilepsy when all else fails. During the procedure, the nerve fibers connecting the two brain hemispheres (the corpus callosum) are cut, resulting in so-called "split-brain" patients. So "split-brain cases" are those patients where severing the corpus callosum blocks the inter-hemispheric transfer of, for example, perceptual and motor information.

These patients eventually show little effect of the operation in everyday life. The consciousness of their world and themselves appears to remain as unified as it was prior to the operation. Perhaps this is because patients can of course normally move their heads and eyes in such a way as to get information to both hemispheres. But more interesting for our purposes is that, under certain laboratory conditions, these patients behave as though two "centers of consciousness" have been created. The original unity seems to be gone and two centers of unified consciousness seem to have replaced it, each associated with one of the two cerebral hemispheres. However, Gazzaniga (1992) had initially urged that the left hemisphere is the real "interpreter" and is the dominant conscious hemisphere because our language centers are usually in the left hemisphere.

Here are some further details: The human retina functions in such a way that the left half of each retina is primarily connected to the left hemisphere of the brain and the right half of each retina is primarily hooked up to the right hemisphere of the brain. The human visual system takes information from the left visual field of both eyes to the right hemisphere and information from the right visual field of both eyes to the left hemisphere. Given the crossing over of fibers in the optic chiasm, the effect is that the two sides of the brain reflect opposite sides of the outer world.

Some puzzling results were found in carefully controlled laboratory presentations where patients were forced to look straight ahead without being able to move their heads as usual. Differing stimuli were shown to patients' left and right visual fields, revealing striking dissociations of consciousness and behavior. Their left hands literally did not know what their right hands were doing. Shown one stimulus on the left and a different one on the right, each hand will respond appropriately to its respective stimulus but not to the other. Moreover, patients typically showed verbal knowledge only of the stimuli shown to their right field and not to those in their left field, even though their left hand is able to respond appropriately to the left field stimuli. Given the typical location of primary language function in the left hemisphere, the right hemisphere, which receives visual input from the left visual field, remains unable to verbally describe what it sees.

One example of the odd behavior is the following: During an object recognition task, a subject might report seeing a bottle, due to the left hemisphere, while his left hand (controlled by his right hemisphere) was searching to find a hammer from a group of objects. Patients would report seeing one thing but some of their bodily behavior would indicate that they saw something else.

Notice that split-brain cases often have more to do with "synchronic identity"; that is, how many selves are present *at a given time*, as opposed to DID where "diachronic identity" is the main issue; that is, how many selves are present *over time*. Nonetheless, even for split-brain cases, Bayne (2010) argues for a "rapid-switching model" in which two selves alternate in existence. Only one self exists at a given time although which one of them exists may switch rapidly and repeatedly over short intervals of time. The rapid-switching hypothesis seems to have the advantage of a kind of "unity thesis" such that all the experiences had by a given patient at a given time would remain phenomenally unified.

But, again, one issue is that split-brain patients sometimes reach for or identify different objects with their left and right hands at the same time. A second issue is whether the switch hypothesis can accommodate split-brain patients' strong sense of having a single unified stream of consciousness over time without any breaks. If the switch hypothesis were true, it seems reasonable to think there would be breaks in the continuity of one's consciousness when the switches occur. But a brain-bisected person continues to believe not just that *something* persists across time in both everyday life and in the lab, but that she does too.[3]

When it comes to some disorders, perhaps it is better to think of them in terms of *degrees of integration*. That is, normal consciousness is unified and strongly integrated in ways that are familiar to us and meet the definitions above. However, instead of debating whether there are one, two, three, or more "persons" in these odd cases (and others below), perhaps it's best to put it in terms of degrees of lack of integration such that one's consciousness is more or less "fragmented" depending upon one's deficit.

Van Gulick (2015) explains how integration and unity play an important role in several current theories of consciousness such as Baars's global workspace theory, Tononi's integrated information theory (IIT), Jesse Prinz's attended intermediate-level representation (AIR) theory, Bayne's phenomenal unity thesis, and the combination of Van Gulick's own higher-order global states (HOGS) model with what he calls "virtual self realism" (VSR). Van Gulick explains that on the VSR, "the self is not a distinct entity, nor is it a special subsystem of the mind or brain . . . [but] treats that virtual self in a more realistic way . . . as a structure defined by the combined contents of experience" (Van Gulick 2015, 234).

Normal consciousness is unified in a variety of ways but disorders of disunity can also disrupt the unity of consciousness. Van Gulick discusses various senses of "conscious unity" and several specific pathologies of disunity – dissociative identity disorder, split-brains, neglect and extinction – and each is considered in relation to the integration-based theories of consciousness listed above. He favors an explanation offered by his own HOGS view:

> Thus, from the perspective of HOGS and VSR, multiplicity appears theoretically possible, but only if the human brain can support two or more simultaneous [global] states, each defining a distinct, unified point of view and associated virtual self. However, HOGS and VSR would seem to exclude genuine multiplicity in the context of a single [global] state.
>
> (Van Gulick 2015, 243)

But Van Gulick also explains how other integration theories might account for the psychopathologies in question. For example,

> from the perspective of IIT, whether multiple centers of consciousness could exist within a single brain would depend entirely on whether the structure and organization of that brain was segregated into two nonoverlapping

high-information systems, each of which is highly integrated internally but not integrated with the other. If the φ values of two such systems are higher than any of their subsystems, as well as higher than any larger system of which they are parts, then each would be a conscious subject or self according to IIT.

(2015, 240)[4]

4.3 Somatoparaphrenia, anosognosia, and delusions

Somatoparaphrenia is a bizarre type of body delusion where one denies ownership of a limb or an entire side of one's body. It is sometimes called a "depersonalization disorder." Relatedly, anosognosia is a condition in which a person who suffers from a disability seems unaware of the existence of the disability. A person whose limbs are paralyzed will insist that his limbs are moving and will become furious when family and caregivers say that they are not. Somatoparaphrenia is usually caused by extensive right-hemisphere lesions. Lesions in the temporoparietal junction are common in somatoparaphrenia, but deep cortical regions (for example, the posterior insula) and subcortical regions (for example, the basal ganglia) are also sometimes implicated (Valler and Ronchi 2009). Anton's syndrome is a form of anosognosia in which a person with partial or total blindness denies being visually impaired, despite medical evidence to the contrary. The patient typically confabulates; that is, makes up excuses for the inability to see, rationalizing what would seem to be delusional behavior. Thus, the blind person will insist that she can see and stumble around a room bumping into things. Patients with somatoparaphrenia utter some rather stunning statements, such as "parts of my body feel as if they didn't belong to me" (Sierra and Berrios 2000, 160) and "when a part of my body hurts, I feel so detached from the pain that it feels as if it were somebody else's pain" (Sierra and Berrios 2000, 163). It is difficult to grasp what having these conscious thoughts and experiences is like.

Higher-order thought (HOT) theory has been critically examined in light of some psychopathologies because, according to HOT theory, what makes a mental state conscious is a HOT of the form that "I am in mental state M." The requirement of an I-reference leads some to think that HOT theory cannot explain or account for some of these "depersonalization" pathologies. There would seem to be cases where I can have a conscious state and not attribute it to myself but rather to someone else. Liang and Lane (2009) initially argued that somatoparaphrenia threatens HOT theory because it contradicts the accompanying HOT that "I am in mental state M." The "I" is not only importantly *self-referential* but essential in tying the conscious state to *oneself* and, thus, to one's *ownership* of M.

Rosenthal (2010) basically responds that one can be aware of bodily sensations in two ways that, normally at least, go together: (1) aware of a bodily sensation *as one's own*, and (2) aware of a bodily sensation *as having some bodily location*, like a hand or foot. Patients with somatoparaphrenia still experience the sensation as their own but also as having a mistaken bodily location (perhaps somewhat analogous to phantom limb pain where patients experience pain in missing limbs). Such patients still do have the awareness in (1), which is the main issue at hand, but they have the strange awareness in (2). So somatoparaphrenia leads some people to misidentify the bodily location of a sensation as someone else's, but the awareness of the sensation itself remains one's own. Lane and Liang (2010) are not satisfied and, among other things, counter that Rosenthal's analogy to phantom limbs is faulty, and that he has still not explained why the identification of the *bearer* of the pain cannot also go astray.

Among other things, I have replied (in Gennaro 2015c, 57–58) first that we must remember that many of these patients often deny feeling *anything* in the limb in question (Bottini et al. 2002). As Liang and Lane point out, patient FB (Bottini et al. 2002), while blindfolded, feels "no tactile sensation" (2009, 664) when the examiner would in fact touch the dorsal surface of FB's hand. In these cases, it is therefore difficult to see what the problem is for HOT theory at all. But when there really is a bodily sensation of some kind, a HOT theorist might also argue that there are really two conscious states that seem to be at odds (Gennaro 2015c). There is a conscious feeling in a limb but also the (conscious) attribution of the limb to someone else. It is also crucial to emphasize that somatoparaphrenia is often characterized as a *delusion of belief*, often under the broader category of anosognosia, a condition in which a person who suffers from a disability seems unaware of the existence of the disability (Breen et al. 2000; de Vignemont 2010; Feinberg 2011). A delusion is often defined as a false belief that is held based on an incorrect (and probably unconscious) *inference* about external reality or oneself that is firmly sustained despite what almost everyone else believes and despite what constitutes incontrovertible and obvious proof or evidence to the contrary (Radden 2010; Bortolotti 2013). In some cases, delusions seriously inhibit normal day-to-day functioning. This "doxastic" conception of delusion is common among psychologists and psychiatrists (Bayne and Pacherie 2005; Bortolotti 2009). Beliefs, generally speaking, are themselves often taken to be intentional states integrated with other beliefs. They are typically understood as caused by perceptions or experiences that then lead to action or behavior. Thus, somatoparaphrenia is, in some ways, closer to self-deception and involves frequent confabulation. If this is a reasonable interpretation of the data, then a HOT theorist can argue that the patient has the following two conscious states:

S1: a conscious *feeling* (i.e., a tactile sensation) in the limb in question, and

S2: a conscious *belief* that the limb (and thus sensation) belongs to someone else.

Having both S1 and S2 simultaneously, especially if both are conscious at any given time, is indeed strange and perhaps even self-contradictory in some sense, but the puzzlement has nothing to do with HOT theory.

A similar critique of self-representationalism (Kriegel 2009) based on somatoparaphrenia might also be posed to what Billon and Kriegel (2015) call "subjectivity theories" which says that "there is something it is like for a subject to have mental state M only if M is characterized by a certain mine-ness or for-me-ness. Such theories appear to face certain psychopathological counterexamples: patients appear to report conscious experiences that lack this subjective element" (Billon and Kriegel 2015, 29). Patients with somatoparaphrenia seem to be cases where one has a conscious state without the "for-me-ness" aspect and thus not experienced as one's own. However, Billon and Kriegel counter that

> none of the patients that we know of claim feeling *sensations that are not theirs*. Rather, they say that they feel touch in someone else's limb. This does not yet imply that they feel sensations that are not their own – unless it is analytic that one cannot feel one's sensations but in one's own body, which we have phenomenological and empirical reasons to deny.
>
> (Billon and Kriegel 2015, 37)[5]

Many disorders, including somatoparaphrenia, involve delusion or self-deception. A delusion is distinct from a belief based on incorrect or incomplete information, poor memory, illusion, or other effects of perception. Self-deception is a process of denying or rationalizing away the relevance, significance, or importance of opposing evidence and logical argument. Self-deception involves convincing oneself of a truth (or lack of truth) so that one does not reveal any self-knowledge of the deception. Delusions have certainly received extensive treatment from philosophers in recent years, sometimes in connection with self-deception.[6]

4.4 Phantom limb pain and other bodily disorders

Phantom limb pain involves sensations (such as cramping pain) described as perceptions that an individual experiences relating to a limb or an organ that is no longer physically part of the body. These sensations are seen most frequently following the amputation of an arm or a leg, but may also occur following the removal of other body parts or even an internal organ. Part of the reason is that the brain area representing that part of the body becomes starved of input which then results in excessive neural activity. A materialist might take phantom limb pain as some support for her position in the sense that the pain is obviously not in the missing body part so it must instead be in the brain.

In a clever effort to help ease phantom limb pain (especially in the hands), Ramachandran devised a therapy based on a "mirror box." When an existing hand of a patient is put inside, the mirror makes it appear to the patient that the missing hand is also present. By moving and stretching out the existing hand, it appears that the other hand is trying to relieve some of the painful symptoms in the missing hand. For a significant percentage of amputees, the visual input tricks the brain into thinking that there is a real hand which can stretch and uncramp, relieving much of the phantom pain.

There are a few other abnormal phenomena having to do with the body or bodily perception. Anarchic hand syndrome is a neurological disorder caused by brain lesion in which individuals frequently perform seemingly voluntary movements that they do not consciously intend and cannot directly inhibit. Some hand movements occur without the normal conscious intention to do so which must surely be very odd from the first-person conscious point of view. The body swap illusion occurs when volunteers are tricked into the false perception of owning another body (an actual person or mannequin). The illusion is carried out by altering the perspective of a volunteer with a video camera connected to someone else usually several feet away. This can make people feel that the other body is really theirs. It is as if one's consciousness is centered in the other body. Mirror self-misidentification occurs when one believes that one's reflection in a mirror is some other person.

4.5 Agnosia

Agnosia is the loss of ability to recognize objects, persons, sounds, shapes, or smells while the specific sense itself is not defective and there is no significant memory loss. Focusing on visual agnosia, it is known to come in two types: *apperceptive* visual agnosia, cases where "recognition of an object fails because of an impairment in visual perception," and *associative* visual agnosia, cases "in which perception seems adequate to allow recognition, and yet recognition cannot take place" (Farah 2004, 4). The latter is far more interesting to philosophers since it appears to be an instance of having a "normal percept stripped of its meaning" (Teuber 1968). So, recall from Chapter 3, a patient may be unable to name or recognize a whistle. Associative agnosics are not blind and do not have damage to the relevant areas of the visual cortex. In addition, associative agnosics tend to have difficulty in naming tasks and with grouping objects together. Unlike in apperceptive agnosia, there seems to be intact basic visual perception; for example, patients can copy objects or drawings that they cannot recognize, albeit very slowly. But the deficit in associative agnosics is more cognitive than in patients with apperceptive agnosia. Patients will also often see the details or parts of an object, but not the "whole" of the object at a glance. The main point is that the very phenomenal experience of associative agnosics has changed in a way that corresponds to a lack of conceptual deployment. It is, however, important to recognize that associative agnosics still do have the relevant correct concept because they can apply it to *other* modalities. For example, a patient might easily identify a whistle by sound instead of sight. Like other disorders, the lack of unity in consciousness is striking for those who suffer from agnosia. Their conscious experience is not typically imbued with the usual meaning or understanding of objects in the world. Their conscious experience lacks the kind of holistic grasp of objects enjoyed by the rest of us.

There are other similar psychopathologies with devastating effects on consciousness. Prosopagnosia, also known as "faceblindness" and "facial agnosia," occurs when patients cannot consciously recognize very familiar faces, sometimes even including their own. They do not get any sense of familiarity when looking at another's face but can sometimes make inferences via auditory or other visual cues (e.g. clothes, hair) to compensate. However, skin conductance responses show that there is some kind of emotional arousal when in the presence of a known person. Akinetopsia is the loss of motion perception or visual animation, sometimes called "motion blindness." The visual world seems to come to a standstill or appears more like a sequence of frozen snapshots such that objects don't really move but appear to "jump" from one place to another. One's visual consciousness is distorted both with respect to temporal sequence and the unity of consciousness. Simultanagnosia occurs when patients can recognize objects in their visual field but only one at a time. They cannot make out the full scene they belong to or make a whole image out of the details. They literally "cannot see the forest for the trees." Outside of a narrow area in the visual field, these patients say they see nothing but an undifferentiated mess. One's visual consciousness is thus distorted with respect to the unity of consciousness. Alexithymia is a deficiency in understanding, processing, or describing emotions. It is common to many on the autism spectrum and can be difficult to distinguish from agnosia.

4.6 Neglect and blindsight

As we saw briefly in Chapter 2, hemispatial neglect (also called hemiagnosia and hemineglect) is a neuropsychological condition in which there is a deficit in attention to and awareness of one side of space. There is typically damage to the right posterior parietal lobe. It is defined by the inability for a person to process and perceive stimuli on one side of the body or environment that is not due to a lack of sensation. In hemineglect, one loses all sense of one side of one's body or sometimes one half (divided vertically) of everything spatial in one's experience. Whatever is going on in hemineglect, unified consciousness seems to remain. It is just that its "range" has been bizarrely circumscribed. It encompasses an experience of only half the body or half of objects seen, not of the whole body or whole objects. Where we expect perception and proprioception of the whole body and whole objects, these patients perceive only one half of the body or objects in general.

As we have also seen, an additional launching point for some work in abnormal psychology came from the discovery of the phenomenon known as "blindsight" (Weiskrantz 1986) which is very frequently discussed in the philosophical literature regarding its implications for consciousness and unconscious visual processing. Blindsight patients are blind in a well-defined part of the visual field (due to specific cortical damage), but yet, when forced, can guess the location or orientation of an object in the blind field with a much higher than expected degree of accuracy (even up to 95 percent of the time). For example, patients can correctly guess the orientation of lines in circles filled with vertical or horizontal shapes in their blind field. The same goes for some shapes, such as an "X" or "O." The patient is surprised by her success since she tends to think that she is purely guessing without gaining any conscious visual information at all.

4.7 Autism

Autism is a disorder characterized by impaired social interaction and communication, and by restricted and repetitive behavior. It is a developmental disorder that affects a child's ability to develop social skills and engage in social activities. It is sometimes thought of as a more serious version of a spectrum of cases called Asperger's syndrome. Researchers largely agree that autistic humans have a number of clear deficits, such as impaired empathizing skills and deception detection. Autistics also exhibit a lack of imagination and an inability to pretend. There is typically a lack of normal eye contact and gaze monitoring, along with a lack of normal social awareness and responsiveness, such as would normally occur when one is embarrassed or sympathetic to another's embarrassment (Hillier and Allinson 2002). So, for example, Baron-Cohen (1995) argues that various mechanisms are impaired in the mind of autistic humans, such as major impairment of what he calls the "Shared Attention Mechanism." Thus, it seems clear that autistic humans have particular difficulty with understanding other minds (Baron-Cohen 1995; Frith and Hill 2003; Nichols and Stich 2003).

Some, however, have claimed that individuals with autism are "mind-blind" in more significant ways and are virtually incapable of mindreading and perhaps even metacognition or at least some form of self-consciousness

(Carruthers 1996; Frith and Happé 1999). "Mindreading" is a technical term used in the literature to refer to a set of abilities to discern other people's mental states from their behaviors and from contextual factors. It does not refer to supernatural abilities or telepathy. Given his parallel arguments regarding animals and infants based on HOT theory, Carruthers seems committed to the equally startling view that autistic children lack conscious states. He reasons that if autistic subjects lack self-awareness, then autistic individuals should be "as blind to their own mental states as they are to the mental states of others" (Carruthers 1996, 262), and "they lack phenomenally conscious mental states" (Carruthers 2000, 202).

Here I make one further observation (based on Gennaro 2012, 257–262): There seem to be numerous cases where autistic subjects engage in deep meditation and prolonged focusing of attention on inner feelings or images (Frith and Happé 1999, 14–16; Ridge 2001, 331–333). Thus, we have examples where introspective ability is sometimes even *greater* than normal, not to mention the admittedly unusual case of Temple Grandin who holds a Ph.D. and is a professor of animal science. So we might argue that instead of a lack of mindreading skills negatively impacting one's metacognitive ability, such intense self-awareness might cause subjects to lack the typical awareness of others. That is, the self-preoccupation of some autistic individuals might even explain their lack of mindreading skills. Many of the main deficits in question, such as impaired empathizing skills, lack of imagination, and difficulties with joint attention, might result from a *heightened* sense of introspection.

Hirstein (2015) argues that recent evidence points to widespread underconnectivity in autistic brains due to deviant white matter connections (the same goes for some other psychopathologies). Specifically, there is prefrontal–parietal underconnectivity and underconnectivity of the default mode network in autistic subjects. These phenomena along with similar data from other psychopathologies may help shed light on the current debate in the consciousness literature about whether conscious states require prefrontal and parietal or temporal connectivity (cf. Chapter 3 on HOT theory). If it can be shown that people with autism (or any other psychopathology) have conscious states despite such underconnectivity, this would certainly constitute an argument for the claim that conscious states in the posterior cortex do not require associated prefrontal activity.

4.8 Synesthesia

Synesthesia is literally a "union of the senses" whereby two or more of the five senses that are normally experienced separately are involuntarily and automatically joined together in experience (Ramachandran and Hubbard 2001; Cytowic 2003). For example, some synesthetes experience a color when they hear a sound or see a letter. Some instances of synesthesia do occur entirely within the visual sense. For example, "grapheme-color synesthesia" involves experiencing (black) letters or numbers as inherently colored. For example, one might always experience the letter "R" or the number "2" as red, or the letter "N" and the number "8" as purple. All letters and numbers are experienced as having clearly distinct and regular colors. A more specific example of grapheme-color synesthesia might have "A" experienced as blue, "B" as green, "C" as yellow, and so on. This is perhaps the most common form of synesthesia.

Others experience tastes, smells, shapes, or touches in almost any combination. These sensations are automatic and cannot be turned on or off. Motion-sound synesthesia involves hearing sounds in response to visual motion and flickers (Saenz and Koch 2008). Saenz and Koch report evidence that, for at least four synesthetes, seeing visual motion or non-moving visual flashes automatically causes the perception of sound. These synesthetes outperformed control subjects on a difficult visual task involving rhythmic temporal patterns; for example, judging whether two successive sequences (either both auditory or both visual) were the same or different. This is presumably because these synesthetes not only see but also hear the patterns. Unlike many other abnormal psychological phenomena, however, synesthesia is not a disease or illness and is not harmful. In fact, the vast majority of synesthetes prefer to have synesthesia and could not imagine life without it. Synesthesia can, for example, aid one's memory of names and phone numbers and can be an asset for creative art. Still, what "it is like to be" a synesthete must be quite different from normal conscious experiences. In a sense, we might say that they experience an enhanced form of conscious experience as opposed to the typical disorder; that is, something is added to conscious experience instead of the more typical subtraction.

One explanation for this kind of synesthesia is that there is "cross-activation" or "cross-wiring" of adjacent brain regions (Ramachandran and Hubbard 2001). The idea is that the brain representation involves more neural integration than is typical between the brain areas responsible for the two contents. The normal lack of overlap between the brain regions is absent:

> The fusiform gyrus [in the temporal lobes] contains the color area V4 . . . which processes color information, but . . . the number area of the brain, which represents visual numbers . . . , is right next to it . . . [and] imaging experiments on people with synesthesia suggest that showing black and white numbers to a synesthete produces activation in the color area.
>
> (Ramachandran 2004, 65)

There is thus a kind of brain "hyperconnectivity" in these synesthetes not found in other people. Other related neural explanations appeal to "disinhibited cortical feedback" between brain areas such that information is processed in a bottom-up fashion but later-stage brain activation feeds back to activate earlier stages. It is this abnormal feedback that causes the unusual synesthetic experiences (Grossenbacher and Lovelace 2001).

The kind of unity described above seems closest to what Tye calls "neurophysiological unity" such that "conscious states may be said to be neurophysiologically unified if and only if they are realized in a single neural region or via a single neurological mechanism" (Tye 2003, 12). Of course, one difficult question is just how to individuate neural states, which Tye never really addresses at length. Perhaps we ought to individuate the neural representation of synesthete experiences rather widely in all cases, including the cross-modal cases. One might again suppose that feedback loops and top-down integration of brain activity are necessary for having any kind of conscious state (Gennaro 2012). For example, the brain structures involved in feedback loops seem to resemble the structure of at least some form of HOT theory where lower-order and higher-order states combine to produce conscious states. Edelman and Tononi (2000b) also emphasize the more global nature of conscious states and it is reasonable to interpret this as the view that conscious states are anchored in multiple interconnected brain areas. In cases of cross-modal synesthesia, then, we should also similarly look for multiple overlapping brain areas as the vehicle (including in motion-sound cases). Of course, even assuming that Ramachandran and Hubbard's (2001) view of intra-modal cases (or something like it) is right, that doesn't by itself establish that it applies to cross-modal cases. Nonetheless, it seems to be a fairly reasonable inference or, at least, it makes for a testable hypothesis.

In any case, let us turn our attention to the nature of mental illness and to topics in philosophy of psychiatry.

4.9 Philosophy of psychiatry and the nature of mental illness

Some of the interdisciplinary work in what is often termed "philosophy of psychiatry" centers around the nature of mental illness and how to classify and explain it. Some argue that our current diagnostic categories, as found in the *Diagnostic and Statistical Manual of Mental Disorders*, the DSM-5 (American Psychiatric Association 2013), are faulty because, among other things, they are derived only from symptoms rather than underlying physical pathologies (Murphy 2009; Poland 2014). Genuine mental illnesses are not just some symptoms but destructive pathological processes which occur in biological systems. So some have doubted the very existence of mental illnesses as they are often understood (Szasz 1974). Szasz contends that belief in mental illness by psychiatrists is the result of dogmatism and a pseudoscientific approach. He argues that by definition "disease" means "bodily disease" and so is a concept that really shouldn't be applied to the mind given that the mind is not literally part of the body. Szasz thinks that adopting the concept of a physical illness into the realm of mental is incompatible with human agency. One reason is that mental illnesses, unlike physical ones, are not typically reducible to biophysical causes. The physical world is deterministic but the mental world must necessarily be free.

Szasz's view has been criticized as a misguided appeal to dualism and libertarian free will. Many already think that mental illnesses have been (or will be) reduced to neurological or neurochemical dysfunction, such as in depression. They argue that advances in neuroscience give us good reason for thinking that there are neurological or neurochemical correlates for at least some mental illnesses (Bentall 2004). Perhaps this will even help to alleviate, for example, various types of addiction, although it is perhaps not quite as simple as it might seem (Graham 2013, chapter seven). In any case, if identity theory is true, then mental states are just brain states and so dualism is false. Brain damage to very specific areas seems also to support the notion that psychopathologies are due to abnormally functioning or damaged brains. As we saw in Chapter 1, an identity theorist is also not committed to the rejection of mental states (or illness) altogether; rather, this would be more of an eliminativist position.

In spite of the debate over how to define mental illness and even its existence, it is generally accepted that mental illnesses are real and involve serious disturbances of conscious experience which cause significant impairment in people, even sometimes leading to self-destructive behavior and suicide. The most serious mental illnesses, such as schizophrenia, bipolar disorder, major depression, and schizoaffective disorder, are often chronic and can cause serious disability. There have of course also been major (largely past) controversies about the existence of some particular "mental illnesses," such as homosexuality, hysteria, and premenstrual dysphoric disorder.

Several authors have offered a more nuanced "realist" view of mental disorder or illness. For example, Zachar (2014) believes that psychiatric disorders are real but argues for a somewhat middle ground position between a "relativistic" (or anti-realist) view and a strong form of realism such that there are entirely objective "essential" natures to such disorders which form "natural kinds." He calls his view the "imperfect community model" which "refers to the fact that the various symptom configurations that are classified by psychiatrists resemble each other in a number of ways, but there is no property or group of properties that all of them share in common as a class" (Zachar 2014, 19). Various positions on how we should classify psychopathologies are also explored at length in Kincaid and Sullivan (2014) who point out that "the view adopted most often in this volume allows for natural kinds without a single set of necessary and sufficient conditions but instead with multiple different property combinations with family resemblance similarity relations" (Kincaid and Sullivan 2014, 3).[7]

As we shall see, related to all of these areas of inquiry one can find interesting work on overlapping ethical issues. For example, if mental illnesses or serious abnormalities, such as psychopathy and schizophrenia, undermine rational agency, then questions arise about the degree to which the mentally ill (or those with psychopathologies) are capable of making genuinely "free" or "voluntary" decisions. This bears on central questions regarding the degree of moral and legal responsibility that those afflicted with various psychopathologies can be assigned. Further, the relevance of some neuroscientific evidence to ethical and legal questions has also spurred interest in recent years.

So let us first look more closely at two further disorders which also raise questions about moral responsibility and free will, namely schizophrenia and psychopathy.

4.10 Schizophrenia

Schizophrenia is a mental disorder characterized by disintegration of thought processes and of emotional responsiveness. It most commonly manifests itself as auditory hallucinations, paranoid or bizarre delusions, or disorganized speech and thinking, and it is accompanied by significant social or occupational dysfunction. Thought insertion, a common symptom of schizophrenia, is the delusion that some thoughts are not one's own and are somehow being inserted into one's mind. In some particularly severe forms of schizophrenia, the victim seems to lose the ability to have an integrated or "unified" experience of her world and self. The person often speaks in an incoherent fashion, doesn't even complete sentences, and is unable to act on simple plans of action. Once again, it is difficult to understand fully what it is like to consciously experience the world in this way.

Graham and Stephens (2000) suggest that thought insertion should be understood as alienated self-consciousness or meta-representation.[8] Kircher and Leube (2003) claim to show that a deficient self-monitoring system underlies some of the hallucinations and thought disorders in schizophrenia. Graham and Stephens (2000) think that schizophrenics make introspective inferential mistakes about the source of inserted thoughts based on delusional background beliefs. Some bodily movements can of course be movements of my limbs without counting as actions of mine or as caused by me. Perhaps someone else is controlling my movements or they are entirely involuntary such as the physical (motor) tics and vocalizations in Tourette's syndrome or in anarchic hand syndrome. But in these cases the bodily movements are still self-attributed to the person with the disorder, so something else must be going on to explain attributions to others in thought insertion. If a song spontaneously runs through my mind, I still think of it as an episode in my mind. But it does not count as my mental activity in the same way as when I am thinking through a math problem or trying to plan a trip counts as mine. The latter, but not the former, involves intentional thought that expresses my agency. There seems to be something special going on when I consciously engage in some activity which involves mental effort and voluntariness. Graham and Stephens (2000, 152) call the feeling of *having* a mental state the "sense of subjectivity" and the feeling of *causing* my mental state the "sense of agency." They urge that these two can come apart in unusual cases, so that thought insertion involves the sense of subjectivity without the sense of agency, which also accounts for the curious "passivity experience" of schizophrenics. So attributing thoughts to someone else makes sense because they still must be caused by something or someone.

Gallagher (2000, 2004) makes the similar distinction between a "sense of ownership" and a "sense of agency" but, in contrast to Graham and Stephens's (2000) "top-down" approach, argues instead that the primary deficit regarding thought insertion is more of a "bottom-up" problem with the first-person experience itself rather than a self-monitoring abnormality. What happens at the introspective level is not erroneous but rather a correct report of what the schizophrenic actually experiences; that is, thoughts that feel different and externally caused. Gallagher also points to some preliminary neurological evidence which indicates abnormalities in the right inferior parietal cortex for delusions of control.

The issue here is perhaps somewhat analogous to what we saw with respect to somatoparaphrenia in section 4.3. Just as we might distinguish between experiencing a sensation as one's own as opposed to its *bodily location* in patients with somatoparaphrenia, so we might distinguish between experiencing a thought as one's own as opposed to its *origin* in patients with schizophrenia.

It is important, however, to remember that the vast majority of schizophrenics are nonviolent, though some paranoid schizophrenics are prone to violence. One interesting issue is: Does violence or psychopathology have a genetic component that can be passed down to one's descendants? Scientists have not of course found, say, a "violence gene" or a "schizophrenia gene" *automatically* dooming its unlucky owners to a life of crime. Instead, they are attempting to tease out the complex interactions among genetic (and environmental) influences and violence. The idea at best is that certain genetic traits, when combined with certain repeated life experiences (such as childhood abuse), can propel a person toward a life of crime or mental instability. Even if there is a genetic "component" predisposing one to violence or depression, this would seem to be far different from, say, a gene for one's eye color. In the latter case, the resulting trait is *guaranteed* to follow from having the requisite gene. This is not the case for violence or schizophrenia, which suggests that environmental factors also play a part in its development in particular cases. Some genes also regulate the production of important neurotransmitters which, in turn, may cause abnormal symptoms later in life.

There is also the possibility that personality type plays an indirect role in one's subsequent behavior; that is, one's personality may make manifesting certain psychopathologies more likely. For example, a generally more aggressive person may be more likely to succeed in business and achieve one's life goals but may also be more prone to violence depending on upbringing. Personality traits, such as irritability, impulsivity, and risk-taking, lead one to be crime-prone but one's environment can either dampen or aggravate violent impulses and genetic predispositions. Some recent work on the extent to which crime is inherited comes from twin studies, adoption studies, and molecular genetic studies. There is some data to suggest that there is "more crime among adopted children whose biological parents are criminal than among adopted children whose biological parents are not criminal" (Cullen and Agnew 2011, 34). Interestingly, the correlation of schizophrenia between identical twins, who have identical genomes, is about one half (48 percent). Although this is quite high compared to the general population, it again indicates that schizophrenia cannot be *entirely* a genetic disease (like, say, Down's syndrome).

4.11 Psychopathy

Psychopathy is a mental disorder characterized by a lack of empathy and remorse, shallow emotions, egocentricity, and deceptiveness. These abnormalities certainly seem to include deficits of consciousness, such as the inability to show empathy to others or to experience some deep emotional connection to others. Psychopathy is sometimes accompanied by narcissistic personality disorder which results in a pattern of grandiosity and need for admiration, along with a lack of empathy. Psychopaths are unable to feel distress by the perception of others in pain. Although the degree to which someone has the capacity for empathic distress can obviously vary, psychopaths are very different from other people.

Psychopaths also have difficulty distinguishing between different types of norms, such as the difference between a violation of *moral* norms or rules and a violation of *conventional* norms (Dolan and Fullam 2010). Normal people tend to characterize moral norms as very serious and generalizable beyond their present context whereas conventional norms are thought of as dependent on context and authority. Even children begin to grasp the distinction between moral and conventional norms at around two years of age. Psychopaths, on the other hand, fail to consistently grasp the differences between them and tend to treat all norms as norms of convention. Non-psychopaths, on the other hand, understand the difference, say, between punching someone (a moral norm violation) and failing to respond in the third person to a formal invitation (a conventional norm violation). It is not even clear that psychopaths fully grasp moral concepts.

Psychopaths are often diagnosed using the revised version of the "Psychopathy Checklist" (PCL-R) which includes such personality traits as a lack of remorse or guilt, shallow affect, grandiose sense of self-worth, and socially deviant lifestyle (Hare 2003; Malatesti and McMillan 2010). However, the very category of psychopathy is somewhat controversial within psychiatry. The DSM treats the diagnosis as "antisocial personality disorder" which includes such symptoms as destructive and criminal behavior. For this reason, there is of course the worry that the diagnosis will be used to excuse such behavior. The philosophical literature on the moral responsibility of psychopaths is enormous (beginning with Murphy 1972). But it is worth noting that some psychopaths are even considered "successful" in the sense that they avoid criminal behavior. They can be found in corporate and other respected institutional settings, such as the academic, legal, and medical professions (Babiak, Neumann, and Hare 2010). In these contexts, some psychopathic personality traits can even be seen as virtues (Anton 2013). Psychopaths are often intelligent and calculating but they can also be impulsive and pay little attention to their own long-term interests.

Nichols (2004) argues that psychopaths are *amoral* in the sense that they do not care about moral standards or perhaps cannot even understand moral standards, as opposed to *immoral* in the sense of regularly acting immorally while able to take moral considerations into account. Still, psychopaths seem otherwise to be fully rational agents. Nichols therefore argues that the flaws of psychopaths are traceable to emotional deficits rather than to reason. Maibom (2005), however, makes the case that psychopaths do in fact suffer from impairments of rationality. For example, they often have trouble learning from experience and in long-term planning. Still, psychopaths seem normal when it comes to general intelligence so perhaps their deficits are somewhat restricted to moral reasoning. It may also be that psychopathy involves both emotional and rational deficits caused by abnormal neuropsychological development.

One curious fact is that, despite a lack of empathy and the inability to identify with others' sensory experiences, psychopaths are clearly very good at understanding other minds, especially in more cognitive aspects. After all, psychopaths are often very good at deceiving and manipulating others which most certainly requires some mindreading skills. Some serial killers and child molesters can be cunning and patient to gain a victim's trust. Of course, having abnormal mindreading skills does not automatically lead to psychopathy. As we saw in section 4.7, autistic people also have mindreading difficulties but they do not share the other characteristics of psychopaths.

4.12 Psychopathy, free will, and moral responsibility

When there is a mass school shooting or similar horrible crime, we often wonder about a suspect's mental health and whether it should excuse them from responsibility. One of the boys responsible for the Columbine High School massacre (Eric Harris) was sometimes called a psychopath. One reason why discussions like these occur is probably because of the effects that mental illness might have on moral responsibility attributions, especially in the case of psychopaths. Another reason is obviously to try to help us prevent similar crimes by looking for key "warning signs." But this line of thought also leads some to think that

> [t]o diagnose someone as mentally ill is to declare that the person is entitled to adopt the sick role and that we should respond as though the person is a passive victim of the condition. Thus, the distinguishing features of dysfunction that we should look for are not a universally consistent set of exclusive qualities, but things that provide the grounds for the normative claim made by applying the label "mental illness."
>
> (Edwards 2009, 80)

As we will see, a careful analysis of the relationship between mental illness and theories of moral responsibility indicates that several factors seem to matter when it comes to holding a mentally ill person responsible for what he or she has done. Much the same comes into play in the portrayal of serial killers, such as Ted Bundy and Jeffrey Dahmer, in documentaries, television shows, and more academic settings.

As we saw in Chapter 1, libertarians believe that the core ideas of "could have done otherwise" and "control" over actions are essential for free will and for holding someone morally responsible for an action. If one really couldn't do otherwise, then how could we blame, punish, or otherwise hold that person morally responsible? The idea, for example, is that if a man were to rob an elderly lady, then he was compelled to do so given his state of mind at that time. But if he really *couldn't* have done otherwise, how can we really hold him morally responsible for the action? Recall from Chapter 1, however, that compatibilists do believe that one can still be morally responsible for an action that one could not avoid at that time (Frankfurt 1969, 1971). They think that the so-called "principle of alternative possibilities" (PAP) is false:

(PAP) A person is morally responsible for what she does do only if she can do otherwise.

Nonetheless, even a compatibilist believes that there are some situations in which one is *not* morally responsible for an action, such as when one is externally coerced or when one desires to behave in ways that run counter to one's "true self" or motives. At least some cases of mental illness may fall into this group, such as in obsessive compulsive disorder (OCD) and various addictions. For example, I may strongly desire to take various drugs or drink alcohol but yet wish that I did not have that desire.

Does any of this mean that, say, a psychopathic serial killer shouldn't be punished? If determinism is true, then it may be that we should no longer think of punishment as some kind of retribution based on libertarian free will. Perhaps we should simply focus on deterring others (and the criminals themselves) from committing future crimes. Most people in a society will wish to avoid incarceration and will behave accordingly. But for those who still do harm others, incarceration is at least a way to keep them from harming others in the general population. By analogy, we normally don't think that wild animals have libertarian free will but it doesn't follow that we should allow them to live among us to wreak havoc. Maybe serial killers and pedophiles really can't help what they do and really aren't morally responsible, but that doesn't mean that we should invite them to a family gathering or let them all out of prison.

It is also important to note that to say that a psychopathic murderer is determined does not necessarily mean that he is "legally insane," which is a far narrower notion. In the United States at least, to be legally insane has more to do with "not understanding the difference between right and wrong" or "not understanding the consequences of one's actions" which is a very high hurdle for the defense to prove. Simply taking steps to avoid getting caught seems to indicate that a criminal recognizes the immorality, or at least illegality, of an action (see Morse 2010 for a nice discussion of the legal issues and history).

Theories of moral responsibility in philosophical circles normally focus on "attribution" and "accountability" (Watson 1996). Attribution refers to what capacities must be present to be responsible. For example, one basic condition might be an action is attributable to a person if it stems from her (conscious) "will" or "agency" in the right sort of way. Tremors from Parkinson's disease, for example, are not typically attributed to an agent's will. But we can also ask about how we should treat a person when an action is correctly attributed to someone. This has more to do with accountability. It is one thing to conclude that I said something nasty to my boss or girlfriend but another to decide what should be done to me as a result.

In terms of consciousness, it is with respect to emotions where there is significant focus on theories of moral responsibility (Wallace 1996; Fischer and Ravizza 1998; Brink and Nelkin 2013). So-called "reactive attitude theories" give moral emotions a key role in both attribution and accountability. The term "reactive attitude" was originally coined by Peter Strawson as a way to refer to the emotional responses that arise when we respond to what people do (Strawson 1962). Reactive attitudes are often intense conscious emotional states such as resentment, indignation, disgust, guilt, hatred, love, and shame. On this view, to respond to a person's action with one of these reactive attitudes is to simultaneously hold him accountable, which would also imply attributability. If I punch you in the face, you are likely to react angrily and thereby hold me accountable. If I am kidnapped and beaten for days before escaping, I am likely to feel absolute disgust and hatred toward my kidnapper. However, genuinely legitimate excuses for such behavior might cause us eventually to change our reactive responses. Suppose that I am attacked by my kidnapper but then learn that he suffers from psychotic delusions due to paranoid schizophrenia and he really believed that I was going to kill his family. A person whose agency is damaged by such delusions is arguably not a deserving target for our reactive attitudes and should be exempt from accountability. Still, it might be very difficult as a practical matter to detach oneself entirely in this way from another's behavior under some circumstances. Even a sympathetic psychiatrist might get angry if a patient suddenly attacks her, not to mention the fact that any parent would likely be outraged and disgusted if one of her children were about to be assaulted by a pedophile (even if the parent is similarly enlightened). It is perhaps due to the reactive attitudes that we might also, paradoxically perhaps, just find it psychologically impossible to try to "sympathize with" or "understand" a psychopathic killer's point of view, especially when a victim is a family member or close friend. Even if we are viewing such a scenario entirely from the outside (such as watching a television documentary on a serial killer), if we are going to expend mental energy and invest emotionally in such cases, we would likely normally direct it at the victim and victim's family.

Some think that a responsible agent must have conscious access to moral reasons along with the ability to understand how such reasons fit together (Fischer and Ravizza 1998). Psychopaths are puzzling for many reasons; for example, they seem to be rational in one sense but also mentally ill at the same time. Reactive attitude theorists have thus argued that psychopaths should be excused from moral responsibility. Given their difficulty in distinguishing between moral and conventional norms, many reactive attitude theorists conclude that psychopaths are not properly sensitive to moral reasons and so should not be held accountable (Fischer and Ravizza 1998; Russell 2004). It would therefore be inappropriate to express reactive attitudes toward psychopaths, perhaps analogous to getting angry at a lion for killing someone after escaping from the zoo.

However, others do think that psychopaths can be held accountable for their actions. Shoemaker (2011) for example, has argued that:

> [a]s long as [the psychopath] has sufficient cognitive development to come to an abstract understanding of what the laws are and what the penalties are for violating them, it seems clear that he could arrive at the conclusion that [criminal] actions are not worth pursuing for purely prudential reasons, say. And with this capacity in place, he is eligible for criminal responsibility.
>
> (Shoemaker 2011, 119)

Shoemaker's view may be correct if we have *legal* responsibility in mind, but the real problem is whether psychopaths are *morally* responsible for their actions. After all, if moral responsibility requires understanding *moral* reasons, then psychopaths arguably should be excused. Perhaps criminal or legal responsibility is possible without full-blown moral responsibility. According to Fischer and Ravizza (1998, 79), "[c]ertain psychopaths . . . are not capable of recognizing . . . that there are moral reasons . . . this sort of individual is not appropriately receptive to reasons, on our account, and thus is not a morally responsible agent." Others argue that psychopaths literally have a form of moral disability which should at least lessen their responsibility to some extent (Greenspan 2003). Some brain abnormalities and genetic factors associated with psychopathic traits also appear to justify the claim that psychopaths cannot be morally responsible for their behavior. According to Glannon (2008), the impairments of the psychopath justify mitigated responsibility but not a full excuse. Still, psychopaths are capable of practical reasoning in achieving their goals which suggests that they have some capacity to respond to moral reasons against performing harmful acts and refrain from performing them.[9] No one of course argues that psychopaths are not conscious at all, but it seems clear that their own conscious experience, perhaps especially with respect to conscious awareness of moral norms and another's suffering, is greatly affected.

But if we are all determined to act the way we do, then the question becomes: what is so special about psychopaths or those with mental illnesses which warrants treating them differently than others in terms of moral responsibility? Perhaps the answer is nothing, or perhaps it is simply distinguishing the different ways that their actions are caused.

4.13 Consciousness and moral responsibility

Finally, it is worth pointing out that some philosophers believe that moral responsibility (and free will for that matter) requires consciousness of at least some kind. Given the close connection between acting freely and making conscious decisions, it is not surprising that one might, in turn, hold that consciousness of some kind is necessary for moral responsibility as well.

Levy (2014) defends what he calls the consciousness thesis; that is, "consciousness of some of the facts that give our actions their moral significance is a necessary condition for moral responsibility" (Levy 2014, 1). Levy is somewhat unusual in that he continues to maintain that no one is really ever morally responsible, for reasons he offers elsewhere (in Levy 2011). However, he notes that whether consciousness is a necessary condition for moral responsibility is still an interesting and important question. Levy (2014) argues that only when agents satisfy the consciousness thesis do their actions express their personal-level attitudes and so they are capable of exercising "reason-responsiveness." Levy recognizes that reasoning and problem solving, for example, often do occur in the absence of conscious choice and guidance. Some conclude that this poses a serious threat to some theories of moral responsibility since they indicate that we often lack consciousness of the facts that give our actions their moral significance. Others argue that we need not be conscious of these facts to be responsible and thus there are a number of philosophers who reject the consciousness thesis (Arpaly 2002; Sher 2009). Levy also maintains that the work of Libet (1999) and Wegner (2002) is irrelevant to moral responsibility since "it makes no difference whether or not consciousness has the powers they contend it lacks" (Levy 2014, vii). Recall from Chapter 1 that Libet's pioneering work into the timing of conscious intentions and Wegner's work on the illusion of conscious will are often interpreted as showing that consciousness is epiphenomenal; that is, lacking any causal role in producing action.

Interestingly, Levy invokes Baars's global workspace theory (GWT) to help spell out the functional role of awareness (Baars 1988, 1997). According to Levy, since consciousness plays the role of integrating representations, and behavior driven by non-conscious representations is inflexible and stereotyped, only when a representation is conscious "can it interact with the full range of the agent's personal-level propositional attitudes" (Levy 2014, vii). Levy argues that this shows that consciousness of key features of our actions is a necessary (though not sufficient) condition for moral responsibility since consciousness of the morally significant facts to which we respond is required for these facts to be expressive of the agent herself. He tells us that "[t]he integration of information that consciousness provides allows for the flexible, reasons-responsive, online adjustment of behavior" (Levy 2014, 39). Without this integration, "behaviors are stimulus driven rather than intelligent responses to situations, and their repertoire of responsiveness to further information is extremely limited" (Levy 2014, 39).

With respect to, for example, Fischer and Ravizza's (1998) control-based account of moral responsibility, Levy explains that control theorists hold that "an agent is (directly) morally responsible for those actions over which he or she exercises the capacity for (sufficient) control" (Levy 2014, 109). Fischer and Ravizza specifically argue that responsibility does not require *regulative* control, or actual access to alternative possibilities, but rather only *guidance* control. And "roughly speaking, we exercise guidance control over our actions if we would recognize reasons, including moral reasons, as reasons to do otherwise, and we would actually do otherwise in response to some such reason in a counterfactual scenario" (Levy 2014, 109). Levy insists that guidance control (like other control-based accounts) requires satisfaction of the consciousness thesis. In any case, the consciousness thesis is the claim that an agent must be able to access conscious of (what she takes to be) the facts concerning her action. According to the consciousness thesis, then, if an action is morally wrong, the agent must be conscious of (some of) the aspects that make it wrong to be blameworthy for the action.[10]

Chapter summary

This chapter explored the growing and cutting-edge interdisciplinary field called "philosophical psychopathology" along with the related "philosophy of psychiatry" which covers the overlapping topics of mental illness, psychopathy, and moral responsibility. Numerous abnormal phenomena were explained with the focus on how they negatively impact consciousness, such as phantom limb pain, split-brain cases, somatoparaphrenia, visual agnosia, and dissociative identity disorder (DID). For example, a number of psychopathologies are commonly viewed as pathologies of self- or body-awareness in some way. Many of these disorders forced us to discuss the importantly related philosophical problems of personal identity, the unity of consciousness, and free will and moral responsibility (especially with respect to psychopathy and schizophrenia). Two controversial claims are that psychopaths are not morally responsible for their actions and that moral responsibility requires consciousness of some kind.

Further reading

For more on various psychopathologies, see Sacks 1987, Ramachandran 2004, Ramachandran and Blakeslee 1998, Radden 2004, Stephens and Graham 2000, Frith and Hill 2003, Farah 2004, Hirstein 2005, Feinberg and Keenan 2005, Bortolotti 2009, Bayne and Fernandez 2009, Bayne 2010, Radden 2010, Feinberg 2011, Graham 2013, and Gennaro 2015b.

For much more on mental illness and philosophy of psychiatry, see Radden 2004, Maibom 2005, Hirstein 2005, Fulford, Thornton, and Graham 2006, Cooper 2007, Glannon 2008, Graham 2013, Murphy 2013, Blaney, Krueger, and Millon 2014, Zachar 2014, Kincaid and Sullivan 2014, and Schramme 2014.

For more on split-brain cases, see Nagel 1971, Puccetti 1973, 1981, Marks 1981, Sperry 1984, and Gazzaniga 2000. For more recent philosophical discussion, see Tye 2003, chapter five, Cleeremans 2003, Dainton 2008, and Bayne 2008, 2010, chapter nine.

On synesthesia, see Ramachandran 2004, chapter four, Robertson and Sagiv 2005, Simner and Hubbard 2013, and Bennett and Hill 2014.

For much more on compatibilist views of free will, see McKenna and Coates 2015 and Dennett 2003. For more on free will, consciousness, and moral responsibility, see Waller 2015 and the 2015 *Journal of Consciousness Studies* (vol. 22 (7–8)) book symposium on Levy 2014. For more on consciousness and free will, see Baumeister, Mele, and Vohs 2010, Caruso 2012, and Hodgson 2012. See Sinnott-Armstrong and Nadel 2011 for much more on Libet's experiments, and Pockett, Banks, and Gallagher 2009, Clark, Kiverstein, and Vierkant 2013, and Sinnott-Armstrong 2014 for more on the sense of agency and free will.

Journals such as *Philosophy, Psychiatry, and Psychology*, *Cognitive Neuropsychiatry*, and *NeuroEthics* have also helped to foster interdisciplinary work on psychopathologies and mental illness (see also Farah 2010 and Illes and Sahakian 2011 on neuroethics). In addition to MIT Press's *Philosophical Psychopathology* book series, Oxford University Press's *International Perspectives in Philosophy and Psychiatry* series and the *Oxford Series in Neuroscience, Law, and Philosophy* are invaluable (such as Malatesti and McMillan 2010, Fulford et al. 2013, Vincent 2013, Nadelhoffer 2013, and Kiehl and Sinnott-Armstrong 2013). For some further discussion of neuroscience, evolution, and morality, see P. S. Churchland 2011, 2013.

Notes

1 Such as Stephens and Graham 2000, Farah 2004, Feinberg and Keenan 2005, Graham 2013, and Gennaro 2015b.

2 See Radden 1996 for a book-length study of DID with an emphasis on ethical issues and personal responsibility.

3 See also Schechter 2010, 2012 and Brook 2015 for further critical discussion of Bayne's view.

4 The reader will likely have noticed that the notion of time or temporality is often integral to understanding disorders of consciousness as well as being an important feature of normal consciousness, such as memory and personal identity. Some fascinating questions arise in this context as well. For example, do we experience the present moment as an instant or as a "specious" present? How does the brain process the incoming temporal information from various modalities to produce unified experience? For more on temporal consciousness and the experience of time, see Dainton 2010 and Le Poidevin 2000 and the references therein. Historically, such major figures as Kant, Husserl, and William James have all viewed time as a central aspect of consciousness (see also Andersen and Grush 2009). As we saw in Chapter 1, temporal synchrony in neural firing rates is sometimes offered as important for binding and experiencing a unity of consciousness. However, see Dennett and Kinsbourne 1992 for a more skeptical view of ascertaining precise temporal measurements in the brain. See Fuchs 2013 for the importance of temporality in accounting for some psychopathologies, especially schizophrenia and depression. Other psychopathologies also clearly involve a damaged temporal component, such as in *akinetopsia*, which is the loss of motion perception or visual animation, and *simultanagnosia* where patients can recognize objects in their visual field only one at a time.

5 Lane 2015 replies not only to Gennaro and Billon and Kriegel, but also clarifies and further develops some of his influential previous work in this area. He also replies to Mylopoulos 2015 who discusses the phenomenon of "action consciousness" and its breakdowns in pathological conditions. Mylopoulos introduces a novel framework which parallels one that is used to discuss state consciousness. In particular, she distinguishes between first-order and higher-order theories of action consciousness, where the former deny but the latter affirm the claim that an action is conscious

only if one is aware of it in some suitable way. Mylopoulos argues that higher-order theories of action consciousness enjoy significant advantages when it comes to making progress on understanding pathological cases in which action consciousness is impaired or disrupted. She focuses on anarchic hand syndrome, utilization behavior, and delusions of control in schizophrenia.

6 Hirstein 2005, Bayne and Fernandez 2009, Bortolotti 2009, Radden 2010, Droege 2015, and Pliushch and Metzinger 2015. There are also numerous other very strange delusions discussed in the literature, such as Cotard syndrome which is a rare neuropsychiatric disorder in which people hold a delusional belief that they are dead (either figuratively or literally), do not exist, are putrefying, or have lost their blood or internal organs, Capgras syndrome which is a disorder in which a person holds a delusion that a friend, spouse, parent, or other close family member has been replaced by an identical-looking impostor, and Fregoli Delusion, the belief that different people met by the deluded believer are actually the same person in disguise.

7 See also Graham 2013, chapters two through six, for an excellent overview and discussion on these matters.

8 See also Frith 1992, Sabanz and Prinz 2006, Bortolotti and Broome 2009, Parnas and Sass 2011, and Graham 2013, 254–261.

9 For a number of additional essays on psychopathy and moral capacities (and incapacities), see Schramme 2014.

10 For one view in opposition to Levy's position, see Sher 2009 but also see Levy's reply to Sher in Levy 2014, 121–129.

5

ANIMAL AND MACHINE CONSCIOUSNESS

This chapter will address the extent to which nonhuman animals are conscious and whether or not machines could be conscious. This importantly extends the overall problem of consciousness beyond human consciousness to two major areas in contemporary consciousness studies. Regarding animals, most important perhaps is what criteria should be used when inferring that an animal is conscious. We have also come a long way from the Cartesian view that animals are mere "automata" and do not even have conscious experience. In addition to the obviously significant behavioral similarities between humans and many animals, much more is known today about our neurophysiological similarities.

The possibility of machine (or robot) consciousness has also intrigued philosophers and non-philosophers alike for decades, including in science fiction books and movies. Could a machine really think or be conscious? Could a robot really subjectively experience the smelling of a rose or the feeling of pain? One important early launching point was a well-known paper by the mathematician Alan Turing (1950) which proposed what has come to be known as the "Turing test" for machine intelligence and thought (and perhaps consciousness as well). Another much-discussed argument is John Searle's (1980) famous Chinese room argument, which has spawned an enormous amount of literature since its original publication. Searle is concerned to reject what he calls "strong AI" which is the view that suitably programmed computers literally have minds. The similarities and differences between human brains and computer programs (and robots) are also assessed and the nature of "connectionist" networks and artificial intelligence is described.

Let's begin with animal consciousness.

5.1 Animals and the problem of other minds

It is clear that we have come a long way from the Cartesian view that animals are mere "automata," that is, beings governed exclusively by the mechanistic laws, and that they do not even have conscious experience (perhaps partly because they do not have immortal souls). Other major figures in the early modern period, such as Leibniz, also struggled with the question of animal (or "brute") consciousness (Gennaro 1999). In addition to the obvious behavioral similarities between humans and many animals, much more is known today about other physiological similarities such as brain and DNA structures. To be sure, there are important differences as well and there are, no doubt, some genuinely difficult "grey areas" where one might have legitimate doubts about some animal or organism consciousness. Nonetheless, it seems fair to say that most philosophers today accept the fact that a significant portion of the animal kingdom is capable of having conscious mental states. Of course, this is not to say that various animals can have all of the same kinds of sophisticated conscious states enjoyed by human beings, such as reflecting on philosophical and mathematical problems, enjoying artworks, thinking about the vast universe or the distant past, and so on. However, it still seems reasonable to believe that animals can have at least some conscious states from rudimentary pains to various perceptual states and perhaps even to some level of self-consciousness.

One way to approach this topic is via the traditional "problem of other minds"; that is, how can one know that others have conscious mental states, especially given the less direct access we have compared to knowing our own minds? Although there is no generally accepted solution to this problem, most people are in practice willing to take for granted that other human beings have mental states similar to theirs. However, knowledge of animal minds seems to present some difficulties. Nonhuman animals cannot describe their mental states using language. Although there have been attempts to teach human-like languages to members of other species, none can do so in a way that would easily solve this problem. Instead, it would seem that despite the similarities between our behavior and those of other animals, any such knowledge of their minds would have to be somewhat less certain than immediate knowledge of our own minds. Nonetheless, a strong inductive rationale for animal consciousness seems sufficient to establish a reasonable belief that (most) animals have conscious mental states. Sometimes, this takes the form of an argument by analogy such that, for example, we know how we feel when we exhibit the behavior of someone in fear or in pain and so it seems reasonable to think that the same conscious states are present when a dog or lion displays the same behavior. It is still unlikely that we consciously make such inferences when we observe animal behavior; rather, we most likely simply take it for granted.

But let's look further at what evidence we might use to make such inferences. Although many different criteria might be put forth (Baars 2005), most will fall under one or more of the following headings:

(1)   Non-verbal or non-vocal behavioral evidence
(2)   Ability to use language and/or to communicate
(3)   Ability to learn, solve problems, and be creative
(4)   Similarity of brain structure

Rocks and tables display none of the above criteria and we don't think they are conscious (*pace* panpsychists). Trees and plants are alive but also do not meet any of the above criteria; for example, they don't jump away or scream when approached with a chainsaw or lawnmower. At the other extreme, humans normally seem to meet all four criteria. However, when we look at the animal kingdom we find a wide variety of evidence that is somewhat mixed. Some animals may only meet two or three criteria whereas others might only meet one. What should we make of these cases? At the least, we might suppose that the more criteria met, the more likely an animal is conscious. As we'll see, however, none of the above criteria is conclusively necessary or sufficient. Of course, it may also depend upon the *degree* to which a given animal can meet a particular criterion.

With regard to criterion (1), non-verbal or non-vocal behavioral evidence, such as behavioral reactions to stimuli or bodily movements: If a dog moves in a way similar to us when someone steps on my leg, this seems to be some evidence that the dog is conscious. If, as we have supposed in earlier chapters, that mental states cause bodily movements, then it seems reasonable to infer that the mental state (pain, suffering) is present when the typical bodily effect is observed. This is the familiar argument by analogy often presented in favor of animal consciousness.

With regard to criterion (2), the ability to use language and/or to communicate, we obviously communicate with each other via a common language and thus take for granted that there is conscious thought behind linguistic utterances. But even though many animals cannot communicate with us in the same way, it is clear that they communicate with each other, such as in the fairly sophisticated whale, chimp, and bird vocalizations.

With regard to criterion (3), the ability to learn, solve problems, and be creative, the fact that a human student or an animal can learn from a teacher provides some evidence that they have conscious minds. Conscious memory and thought seem necessary for at least some kinds of learning. Further, if an animal is able to solve a somewhat novel practical problem, then it seems that reasoning is required. Many animals are able to "figure out" what to do when confronted with a challenging or unexpected situation, such as making a tool to acquire some food. In some cases, this involves what appears to be a creative solution to a problem. Humans are clearly also able to be creative in a number of ways. Rocks and tables, on the other extreme, do not learn or solve problems.

Further, to follow up on the above criteria, some will use "behavioral versatility" or "stimulus independence" as good evidence in support of animal consciousness (Griffin and Speck 2004; Newen and Bartels 2007). If an animal adjusts its behavior appropriately in response to novel and unpredictable challenges, it seems more likely that it is consciously thinking about its situation than when it responds uniformly. Fixed and rigid responses to stimuli seem to indicate a lack of conceptual representation whereas behavioral versatility indicates an ability to think about a given stimulus and act in a much more context-dependent fashion. When one has concepts, one is thus able to form thoughts that contain those concepts.

With regard to criterion (4), similarity of brain structure, we might now use comparative neurophysiological evidence to help us to determine animal consciousness. For example, numerous animals, including some non-mammals, have some form of thalamo-cortical structure that seems to be a locus of some conscious experience in humans. In addition, most animals share with us some rather primitive areas of the brain, such as the amygdala in the limbic system, responsible for emotions such as fear. This is of course one way that discovering specific neural correlates of consciousness (NCCs) in humans might in turn shed light on animal consciousness, especially given our common evolutionary history. To the extent that animals do lack some of our brain structures which are responsible for more sophisticated mental capacities (such as the prefrontal cortex), it seems reasonable to suppose that they are not capable of having these kinds of mental states.

Unfortunately, for each of our four criteria there appear to be some problematic cases which show that none of the criteria individually are *sufficient* for inferring animal consciousness. Present-day robots and machines, not to mention future ones, are capable of some communication and language use (as well as some appropriate behavioral responses to stimuli). But it is unclear that either suffices for establishing robot consciousness. Bees, for example, are well known to communicate to other bees where honey can be found through a series of rather complicated "dances." Perhaps bees are conscious but it is at least not as obvious as some other animals. The case is perhaps even weaker for various insects, such as ants and moths, which nonetheless display "avoidance behavior" that allow them to survive. Weaker still would be the behavior of bacteria and single-celled organisms, although the behavior in question tends to be more rigidly fixed. There is also nothing remotely like a "brain" in bacteria and not much of a brain in tiny insects. What about creativity? Well, defining creativity is a very difficult task but someone might suppose that spiders creatively make their webs, some of which are very complex. Further, we can program computers to solve chess and mathematical problems but again this hardly seems to be enough for consciousness. Perhaps there could also be an animal capable of reasoning through and solving a practical problem who is not even conscious at all.

It may also be that each one of the four criteria is not *necessary* for consciousness, depending on unusual circumstances or one's metaphysical views. For example, someone who is paralyzed and cannot behave or communicate may of course still be conscious. And maybe some primitive organisms can be conscious without having any of the abilities mentioned in criterion (3). More controversially, some dualists and panpsychists don't believe that the brain is necessary at all for consciousness, as we saw in Chapter 1.

Nonetheless, it seems that one can reach a reasonable inductive inference in favor of consciousness the more criteria that are met (e.g. higher mammals) and a reasonable inductive inference against consciousness when, say, fewer than two criteria are met (some insects). It is important to emphasize that satisfying each criterion can come in very different degrees; for example, compare the behavior of an ape with the behavior of a lizard. Further, the matter can even become very complex within a single species, such as if one restricted one's attention to consciousness and fish (Allen 2013)!

My own view is that when there is a difficult borderline case, we should mainly go with what shared brain structures the animal or organism has in comparison to humans. Thus, I am rather skeptical of consciousness in many insects though I confess to being unsure what to say about some other species with very limited brain structures. In some instances, of course, it may even be difficult to know whether *another human* is conscious, such as in some coma cases and in persistent vegetative states (PVS), both of which also raise significant ethical problems. However, the existence of some borderline cases in which we do not quite know what to say does not imply that there aren't other clear cases of presence and absence of consciousness.

5.2 Animals, metacognition, and mental time travel

Numerous experiments are thought to show that animals perhaps have "metacognitive" states or some form of self-consciousness. A number of key areas are under continuing investigation. For example, to what extent can animals recognize themselves, such as in a mirror, to demonstrate some level of self-awareness? To what extent can animals deceive or empathize with other animals, either of which would indicate awareness of the minds of others? Can animals know that others have mental states? Can animals think about their past selves via episodic memory? These and other important questions are at the center of much current theorizing about animal cognition (Bekoff, Allen, and Burghardt 2002; Keenan, Gallup and Falk 2003; Lurz 2009). Further, as we saw in Chapter 3, the higher-order thought (HOT) theory of consciousness *requires* having at least some metacognitive or meta-psychological thoughts. Thus, it is particularly important to examine the experimental results since one major philosophical theory of consciousness might entail a lack of animal consciousness unless there are self-concepts (or I-thoughts) and mental concepts present (recall from Chapter 3 the disagreement between myself and Carruthers on HOT theory). Of course, a HOT is a kind of metacognitive or meta-psychological state, which is of the form "I am in mental state M now." The allegation, however, is that HOT theory rules out animal consciousness because animals (or at least most animals) do not possess such sophisticated I-concepts and mental concepts.

I-thoughts are thoughts about one's own mental states or about "oneself" in some sense. Whether animals have I-thoughts has become a central topic of empirical investigation. As we have seen, I-thoughts are closely linked to what psychologists call "metacognition"; that is, mental states about mental states, or "cognitions" about other mental representations (Koriat 2007; Beran et al. 2012; Proust 2013). Although some reject the notion that most nonhuman animals have I-thoughts, the evidence seems to be growing that many animals are capable of having I-thoughts and even have some ability to understand the mental states of others (Terrace and Metcalfe 2005; Hurley and Nudds 2006).

One key area of investigation has to do with episodic memory (EM), which is a personal and explicitly conscious kind of remembering involving "mental time travel" such as thinking about myself having experiences at a party last week (Tulving 1983, 1993, 2005). It is often contrasted with *semantic* memory, which need only involve knowing that a given fact is true or what a particular object is, and *procedural* memory, whereby memory of various learned skills is retained. Some notion of self or "I" seems necessary to have a genuine EM. I recognize an EM as *mine* and representing an event in *my* past. We might recall the food caching behavior of scrub jays from Chapter 3 as one example. I have also argued that consciousness entails self-consciousness partly on the basis of EM which involves a temporal and self-referential aspect (Gennaro 1996, chapter nine). The basic idea is that having concepts of outer objects involves understanding those objects as enduring through time (since we do not take them to be mere fleeting subjective states of mind), which, in turn, requires us to think of ourselves as temporally enduring subjects with a past (mainly because we recognize that those objects are the same objects at different times). That is, if a conscious organism can re-identify the same object at different times, then it implicitly understands itself as something that endures through time.

In addition, there is the much-discussed work on uncertainty monitoring with animals such as monkeys and dolphins (Smith, Shields, and Washburn 2003; Smith 2005). For example, a dolphin is trained in a perceptual discrimination task, first learning to identify a particular sound at a fixed frequency (the "sample" sound). Later he learns to match other sounds to the sample sound. When presented with a sound that is either the same or different in pitch as the sample sound, he has to respond in one way if it is the same pitch (such as by pressing one paddle) and another way if it is a different pitch (pressing another paddle). Eventually the dolphin is introduced into a test environment by being forced to make extremely difficult discriminations. To test for the capacity to take advantage of his own uncertainty, the dolphin is presented with a third "uncertain" response that is rewarded if he is uncertain. He is presented with a third paddle, the Escape paddle, which is virtually equivalent to declining the trial. The dolphin chooses the Escape paddle with expected frequency and a similar response pattern to humans and rhesus monkeys, which many researchers take to suggest that the dolphin is aware of his state of uncertainty; that is, he has some knowledge of his own mental state. This is a metacognitive state: the dolphin is aware that he doesn't know something – in this case, whether a sound matches (or is very close to) the sample sound.

Some have also looked to the well-known "mirror recognition test" for evidence of self-awareness (Gallup 1970; Keenan, Gallup, and Falk 2003; DeGrazia 2009). For example, dogs and cats cannot recognize themselves in a mirror (and the same with human children until about eighteen months). Chimps are able to learn that the mirror is reflecting themselves after initially thinking they are seeing other chimps. Much the same is true for orangutans and apes but not for gorillas. Many animals also fail the so-called "spot test" where two red marks are put on the face of animals while anesthetized. When awake, it becomes clear over time whether they recognize the reflection in the mirror as that of their own body; for example, by how often they touch the marks compared with the same spot on the other side of the face. Once again, chimps do well on the spot test but most other animals do not.

My own view on the mirror test is that while these results are interesting, it is not the best test for determining a clear type of self-awareness. It is doubtful that very much should be read into the failure of animals in such experiments. For one thing, these are obviously not the natural conditions or environments of the animals in question. Perhaps failure can be explained in such situations because they don't typically arise in their native environment. In short, many animals may not have ever seen a mirror before. At best, the mirror test might be sufficient for self-awareness even if it is not necessary for self-awareness. Nonetheless, it still seems clear that even those who fail the test seem to be able to distinguish their bodies from the mirror itself, which seems to require a very primitive self-concept.

5.3 Animals and mindreading

Some authors (e.g. Carruthers 2000, 2005) cite experimental work suggesting that even chimps lack the ability to attribute mental states *to others* (Povinelli 2000) which is then treated as necessary for having HOTs about *one's own* experiences. These experiments are sometimes designed to determine if chimps take notice of whether the experimenter is looking at something (say, food) or is unable to see something (for example, due to blindfolding). Chimps were just as likely to ask for food from an experimenter with a bucket over her head as from one who could see. Carruthers argues that animals with HOTs should also be able to have thoughts about the mental states of *other creatures*. However, the evidence seems to be growing that many animals can indeed have I-thoughts and mind-read, and it is not at all clear that having I-thoughts requires being able to read *other* minds.[1]

There also seems to be evidence that at least some animals can mind-read under more familiar conditions. For example, recent work by Laurie Santos and colleagues shows that rhesus monkeys attribute visual and auditory perceptions to others in more competitive paradigms (Flombaum and Santos 2005; Santos, Nissen, and Ferrugia 2006). Rhesus monkeys preferentially attempted to obtain food silently only in conditions in which silence was relevant to obtaining food undetected. While a human competitor was looking away, monkeys would take grapes from a silent container, thus apparently understanding that hearing leads to knowing on the part of human competitors (Santos, Nissen, and Ferrugia 2006). Subjects reliably picked the container that did not alert the experimenter that a grape was being removed. This suggests that monkeys take into account how auditory information can change the knowledge state of the experimenter. In addition, rhesus monkeys also chose to take food from human competitors who could not see them, either because the humans' eyes were facing away or because their faces were blocked by an opaque barrier (Flombaum and Santos 2005). In a similar vein, it has also been argued that many animals' ability to live complex social lives and to take into account another's spatial perspective provides further evidence for mindreading (DeGrazia 2009).

There is also evidence that at least some animals can *deceive* other animals. If this is the case, then we would have some evidence for animal consciousness since deception at least sometimes involves intentionally causing another to believe something false. This is indeed a rather sophisticated psychological capacity. For example, monkeys and baboons sometimes distract the attention of other animals to get food (Byrne and Whiten 1988).

5.4 Lloyd Morgan's canon

Much has been made recently about how considerations of "parsimony" or "simplicity" impact mental state and concept attributions to animals. We should of course be careful not to anthropomorphize, on the one hand, but also not to underestimate animal minds, on the other. The oft-quoted Morgan's canon says that "in no case may we interpret an action as the outcome of the exercise of a higher psychical faculty, if it can be interpreted as the outcome of the exercise of one which stands lower in the psychological scale" (Morgan 1894, 53). On the surface, the canon seems often to favor a less-sophisticated "behavior-reading" hypothesis rather than a mindreading interpretation of the evidence. A behavior-reading interpretation includes references only to the body and behavior of animals under various conditions.

However, many authors have noted serious problems with this conclusion, as well as significant ambiguity in the canon itself (Allen-Hermanson 2005; Montminy 2005; Fitzpatrick 2008). It remains unclear how to interpret Morgan's canon, how it should be used to settle the debate surrounding animal mindreading and metacognition, and how it relates to the associated notions of "parsimony" or "simplicity." For example, Browne (2004) explains that Morgan's canon is thus not quite the same as following a law of parsimony. He rightly recognizes that "it is parsimonious to explain similar, complex, stimulus-response patterns by similar psychological mechanisms" (Browne 2004, 648). So when various animals perform in ways similar to humans on, say, metacognitive tasks, "it is unparsimonious to adopt one kind of lower-level explanation for the animal's response on one task and a different kind of lower-level explanation for the animal's response on [another] task" (Browne 2004, 643–644). Browne thus seems to have in mind what I would consider to be a reasonable *analogical* or *explanatory* notion of simplicity; that is, we ought to attribute mental states to animals (and thus explain their behavior) when they behave similarly to humans under similar conditions. Tomasello and Call (2006, 380–383) also argue that their opponents often propose numerous extremely complex alternative explanations to account for the same data. Thus, considerations of parsimony can actually point *toward* the mindreading hypothesis in many cases and behavior-reading accounts often become quite ad hoc.

Aside from the obvious academic interest, there is also a very practical matter, especially with regard to the morality of animal experimentation and eating animals (Rollin 1989; Singer 1990). At the very least, whether or not an animal can suffer and feel pain should be taken into account with regard to how it ought to be treated. Notice too that pain is a fairly basic and primitive conscious state by comparison to most other kinds of mental states (Allen 2004; Shriver 2006). Billions of animals are killed every year for food and used in research. Many of them are obviously subject to rather cruel conditions. Of course, many argue that even if animals are conscious in some basic sense, they still do not deserve moral consideration, especially compared with humans.

In any case, it is time to turn our attention to the possibility of machine and robot consciousness. One obvious difference is that animals share with us a common biology that machines obviously do not.

5.5 Machine consciousness: an introduction

Machines and robots present some very interesting problems in terms of consciousness. Questions abound: Could a machine think or be conscious? Could a robot really subjectively experience the smelling of a rose or the feeling of pain? Does consciousness have anything to do with what something is made out of? Could a computer be conscious? Can information processors be conscious? Is being alive, or a biological system, necessary for consciousness? Could we upload our consciousness to a machine? If we built conscious robots, how should we treat them? Could robots have free will? These questions have fascinated popular culture and science fiction writers for well over a century, such as in Isaac Asimov's *I Robot* (with the movie in 2004), HAL 9000 in *2001: A Space Odyssey* (1968), and various robots or hybrid humans in the *Terminator* movie series. *The Matrix* of course has also given us a science fiction example of computer-generated simulated experience which raises a host of philosophical questions about the nature of reality. Among television shows, perhaps Commander Data from *Star Trek: The Next Generation* is most familiar to readers.

Hilary Putnam (1967) importantly introduced into philosophy what has come to be known as "machine functionalism" which seemed superior to, say, behaviorism and type-identity theory at the time by allowing for multiple realizability; that is, the idea that the same mental states can be realized in different physical structures or events. Part of the attraction was the notion that, by analogy, the mind is to the brain as a program is to the hardware. But, as we saw in Chapter 1, functionalism also suffers from significant problems if taken as an account of conscious states. It is worth noting again that if the function of a mental state, such as pain, is all that matters, then the physical substrate is entirely irrelevant. This would then certainly allow for robot consciousness given sophisticated enough behavior. As we'll see below, however, some think that consciousness is necessarily biological. A proponent of Tononi's information integration theory might be far more willing to suppose that a robot or machine is capable of having conscious states given enough information integration, as was discussed in Chapter 2.

In the background of philosophical discussion on this topic is what has been called the "computational theory of mind," which says that the mind is basically a computational system and an information processor. The brain is thus thought of as a kind of digital computer. The main characteristic of computational theory is the manipulation of symbols. Of course, the main tool in computer programming is formal logic with its system of well-understood valid and invalid argument patterns. The central mental tasks for which many programs are built involve reasoning and problem solving, such as in chess-playing machines. This approach to cognitive science and artificial intelligence has been called "Good Old-Fashioned AI" or GOFAI (Haugeland 1985). Information and knowledge are entered into a program and then the machine is able to perform various operations in response to questions or commands. Much of this fits well with the notion of explicit representations which, as we saw in Chapter 3, are central to some theories of consciousness as well. Computer programs are basically sets of rules that operate over symbols. If we understand symbols as representations, then we have a clear link between representationalism and the computational theory of mind.

This approach is put to use at the "CYC project" (short for "encyclopedia") in Austin, Texas where a team of researchers have long been engaged in an attempt to assemble a comprehensive ontology and knowledge base with the goal of enabling AI applications to perform human-like reasoning. The project was started in 1984 by Douglas Lenat and is developed by the Cycorp company. But this GOFAI method also has its drawbacks, such as how to program in advance for numerous difficult definitional and philosophical questions, including: What is an object? What is an event? Do fictional objects exist in some sense? What does it mean to say that x causes y? Perhaps most difficult is programming a system to focus only on *relevant* information when attempting to solve a problem, which is a version of the so-called "frame problem." Otherwise, too much time is spent solving the problem and the system is not practically intelligent. Humans are surprisingly good at being able to zero in quickly on what is relevant to a given task or problem. Further, we are also very good at recognizing what common sense and background knowledge are assumed in various contexts.

5.6 Machines: the Turing test

One important early paper was written by the mathematician Alan Turing (1950) who proposed what has come to be known as the "Turing test" for machine intelligence and thought (and perhaps for consciousness as well). The basic idea is that if a machine could fool an interrogator (who could not see the machine) into thinking that it was human, then we should say it thinks or, at least, has intelligence. Turing called it the "imitation game": Suppose that we have a person, a machine, and an interrogator. The interrogator is in a room separated from the other person and the machine. The object of the game is for the interrogator to determine which of the others is the person and which is the machine. The interrogator is allowed to put questions to the person and the machine. The purpose of the machine is to try to cause the interrogator to mistakenly conclude that the machine is the other person. The purpose of the other person is to try to help the interrogator correctly identify the machine.

Part of the problem of course depends on whether one believes that thinking entails consciousness in some way and how one defines "thinking." As we saw in Chapter 3, Descartes held the very strong view that all thought was conscious and Searle argued that all unconscious states are potentially conscious. Still, perhaps a robot could even have all unconscious thoughts. Turing is not very helpful on this point, saying that the question "can machines think?" is perhaps even "too meaningless to deserve discussion." Yet Turing (1950) still conjectured that by the end of the century (that is, 2000), general educated opinion would have altered so much that one would speak of machines thinking without expecting to be contradicted.

Turing was most certainly overly optimistic about whether any machine even today can pass the Turing test. Until fairly recently, most programs were specialized and had very narrow uses. There were "expert systems" such as Weizenbaum's ELIZA (1965), the psychotherapist which can engage with a person in a kind of therapeutic conversational manner via a series of questions and answers (there are of course similar virtual online conversations that one can have today). Most are of course familiar with chess-playing machines, including IBM's impressive Deep Blue which defeated chess champion Gary Kasparov in 1997. There are also very useful programs to aid in medical diagnosis which work by narrowing down causes via an input of symptoms. But obviously one cannot ask these machines about virtually anything, as Turing had envisioned. Perhaps most impressive in recent years has been Watson, which beat top champions on the game show Jeopardy. This is a major programming achievement both for breadth of knowledge and, perhaps even more importantly, the speed of access to information. After all, if a machine cannot act in a timely way, then it is rather useless in many contexts. The same goes for robots: if they cannot respond to stimuli in a fairly timely manner, then what good are they? If we want robots to help the elderly with chores around the house, but it takes hours to bring medicine or water to them, this won't do. Timely intelligent behavior is what we really want. Even Watson was built specifically with the game show in mind and is thus unable to engage in a typical wide-ranging conversation of the sort Turing had in mind.

Moreover, even if a machine or robot could pass the Turing test, many would remain very skeptical as to whether this demonstrates genuine machine thinking, let alone consciousness. For one thing, many philosophers would not take such purely behavioral (i.e. linguistic) evidence to support the conclusion that machines are capable of thought, let alone phenomenal first-person experiences. For example, merely using a word like "red" does not ensure that there is a real grasp of the meaning of "red." If thinking involves the exercise of concepts, then the issue turns on what concepts a robot could possess. One might argue, for example, that having the very concept "red" requires conscious experiences of red. However, it is no easy task to provide criteria of concept possession. If possessing the concept "red" simply involves discriminating red from non-red things and being able to say which things are red, then it seems that a robot could possess such a concept given enough perceptual sophistication. But if we demand some sort of conscious state via sensory organs, then the robot would fall short. The same might apply for concepts like "anger," "love," and the "sound of middle C."

Interestingly, Turing himself considered numerous objections and offered his own interesting replies, some of which are still debated today. For example, he cites a "Theological Objection" based on substance dualists who believe that thinking is a function of a non-physical distinct substance that somehow "combines" with the body to make a person. So creating a physical thing, whether it's a machine or an animal, can never be sufficient to guarantee the presence of thought. Further, this "mind" or "soul" is always the work of the divine creator of the universe, namely God.

But of course there are numerous serious objections to both substance dualism and theism. In addition, even if we assume theism and substance dualism to be true, Turing emphasizes that it is still unclear why thinking machines should be ruled out. Why can't God unite a soul with a machine? Isn't God omnipotent? Why restrict God's power in such an arbitrary way?

Turing also considers what he calls "arguments from various disabilities." He considers a list of capacities that some claim machines will never be able to do, such as have initiative, have a sense of humor, fall in love, enjoy strawberries and cream, learn from experience, use words properly, and do something really new (or be truly "creative"). Most of these abilities seem to require consciousness. Indeed, Turing considers the very similar "argument from consciousness" immediately prior to the arguments from various disabilities. An interesting question to ask first is whether all intelligent or thinking beings must be able to do all of these things. After all, we must be careful not to hold machines to higher standards than is necessary. Why, for example, should we suppose that there must be something deficient about a biological organism or artificial robot who cannot create something new? Is this a necessary condition for being able to think, let alone be conscious?

We then need to ask whether a robot or machine *could* do the other things on the list. Of course, this is just to restate the problem: Could a robot have genuine conscious states such as taste and auditory sensations? In some cases, current machines can arguably do some of the items on the list. For example, there are computers that seem capable of some form of creativity, such as writing poems and composing music. It is also difficult to argue that computers cannot be creative when we are often puzzled as to how exactly humans are creative (think of great artists and composers). Indeed, even defining "creativity" is not as easy as it might seem. Further, as we will see below with connectionist networks, there is already a sense in which current-day robots can "learn" in various ways. Is it learning from "experience" in the sense of *conscious* experience? Again, probably not right now, but how can we rule that out?

In addition to the above, one might question the idea that the Turing test is necessary or sufficient for thinking, intelligence, or consciousness. For example, it is clear that most animals cannot pass the Turing test but at least some seem capable of thought and consciousness. Thus, passing the Turing test wouldn't be *necessary* for thinking or being conscious. In this sense, we might say that the Turing test is too difficult for some genuine thinkers. On the other hand, passing the test also doesn't seem *sufficient* for having genuine thought, according to many. A machine is merely programmed to follow rules and mimic our behavior but it doesn't really have intelligence or genuinely understand the rules or instructions (more on this below with respect to Searle's Chinese room argument). In this case, passing the Turing test seems too easy.

5.7 The Chinese room argument

Another much-discussed argument is John Searle's (1980) famous Chinese room argument, which has spawned an enormous literature since its original publication (see also Searle 1984; Boden 1988; Preston and Bishop 2002). Searle is concerned to reject what he calls "strong AI" which is the view that suitably programmed computers literally have minds; that is, they really understand language and actually have other mental capacities similar to humans. This is contrasted with "weak AI" which is the view that computers are merely useful tools for studying the mind. The gist of Searle's argument is that he imagines himself running a program for using Chinese and then shows that he does not understand Chinese. Therefore, strong AI is false: running the program does not result in any real under-standing (or thought or consciousness, by implication). Searle supports his argument against strong AI by using a thought experiment where he is in a room and follows English instructions for manipulating Chinese symbols to produce appropriate answers to questions in Chinese. Searle argues that, despite the appearance of understanding Chinese (say, from outside the room), he does not understand Chinese at all. He does not thereby know Chinese, but is merely manipulating symbols on the basis of syntax alone. But this is precisely what computers do and so no computer, merely by following a program, genuinely understands anything.

In a little more depth, Searle asks you to imagine that you are a mono-lingual English speaker locked in a room with a large batch of Chinese writing plus a second batch of Chinese script and a set of rules in English for correlating the second batch with the first batch. The rules correlate one set of formal symbols with another set of formal symbols. Formal (or "syntactic") meaning can be identified entirely by their shapes. A third batch of Chinese symbols and more instructions in English enable you to correlate elements of this third batch with elements of the first two batches and instruct you to give back Chinese symbols with certain sorts of shapes in response. You get so good at following the instructions that from the point of view of someone outside the room, your responses are indistin-guishable from those of Chinese speakers. Just by looking at your answers, nobody can tell that you don't speak a word of Chinese. But of course you are providing answers by manipulating uninterpreted formal symbols; that is, you are simply behaving like a computer.

In imagining himself to be the person in the room, Searle thinks it's "quite obvious that . . . I do not understand a word of the Chinese stories. I have inputs and outputs that are indistinguishable from those of the native Chinese speaker, and I can have any formal program you like, but I still understand nothing. . . . For the same reasons . . . [a] computer understands nothing of any stories" since "the computer has nothing more than I have in the case where I understand nothing" (1980, 418). Furthermore, the same "would apply to any [computer] simulation" of any "human mental phenomenon" (1980, 417). Contrary to strong AI, no matter how intelligent a computer behaves, since the symbols it processes are meaningless to it, it is not really intelligent. It's not actually thinking. Its internal states and processes, being purely *syntactic*, lack semantics (or meaning) and so it doesn't really have *intentional* (that is, meaningful) *mental states*. Although Searle acknowledges that there are degrees of "understanding," he argues that there are clear cases in which "understanding" does not apply, including himself in the Chinese room.

Thus, Searle believes the Chinese room argument supports a larger point, which explains the failure of the Chinese room to produce genuine *understanding*. He argues that programs implemented by computers are just syntactical. Computer operations are "formal" in that they respond only to the physical form of the strings of symbols, not to the meaning of the symbols. Minds, on the other hand, have states with meaning: mental contents. We associate meanings with the words or signs in language and we respond to signs because of their meaning, not just their physical appearance. In short, we understand the symbols but computers don't. The key point is that syntax is not by itself sufficient for, or constitutive of, semantics. So although computers may be able to manipulate syntax to produce appropriate responses to natural language, they do not understand the sentences they receive since they cannot associate meanings with the words.

Following up on the above, Searle (1984) presents a summary three-premise argument as follows:

(1) Programs are purely formal (syntactic).
(2) Human minds have mental contents (semantics).
(3) Syntax by itself is neither constitutive of, nor sufficient for, semantic content.
(4) *Therefore*, programs by themselves are not constitutive of or sufficient for minds.

The Chinese room thought experiment is mainly aimed at supporting the third premise.

Searle replies to numerous possible criticisms in his original 1980 paper (which itself comes with extensive peer commentary), but suffice it to say that many are not satisfied with his responses. For example, it might be argued that the entire room or "system" understands Chinese if we are forced to use Searle's analogy and thought experiment. Each part of the room doesn't understand Chinese (including Searle himself) but the entire system does, which includes the instructions and so on. So the *systems reply* says that the real possessor of mental states is the entire Chinese room, not the individual in the room. This may sound strange at first but it's Searle's thought experiment and we have to work with what he gives us.

Searle's response is to "let the individual internalize all . . . of the system" by memorizing the rules and script and doing the lookups and other operations in their head. "All the same," Searle maintains, "he understands nothing of the Chinese, and . . . neither does the system, because there isn't anything in the system that isn't in him. If he doesn't understand then there is no way the system could understand because the system is just part of him" (1980, 420). Searle also insists the systems reply would have the absurd consequence that "mind is everywhere." For instance, "there is a level of description at which my stomach does information processing," there being "nothing to prevent [describers] from treating the input and output of my digestive organs as information if they so desire." Besides, Searle contends, it's just ridiculous to say "that while [the] person doesn't understand Chinese, somehow the conjunction of that person and bits of paper might" (1980, 420).

There is a danger, however, that Searle is committing what is called the "fallacy of composition"; namely, if something is true of the parts, then it must also be true of the whole. So since the parts lack understanding, then the whole lacks understanding. But the conclusion need not follow; for example, oxygen doesn't extinguish a fire but water (H_2O) does. Even better: no materialist would say that any single one of the neurons in my head understands English. But then by Searle's logic, we should conclude that I (or my entire brain) also cannot understand English. But this doesn't seem right. It is certainly not silly or ridiculous to suppose otherwise.

Searle also considers *the robot reply* which says that what prevents the person in the Chinese room from attaching meanings to the Chinese symbols is the disconnection of the symbols to the outside world via the agent's causal relations to outer things. If we "put a computer inside a robot" so as to "operate the robot in such a way that the robot does something very much like perceiving, walking, moving about," however, then the "robot would . . . have genuine understanding and other mental states" (1980, 420).

Searle's counter here is to maintain the same thought experiment applies with only a slight modification. Put it all (including Searle) inside a robot and imagine that some of the Chinese symbols come from a television camera attached to the robot. The Chinese symbols that Searle gives out serve to make the motors move the robot's legs or arms. Searle still insists that he doesn't understand anything except the rules for symbol manipulation. He explains, "by instantiating the program I have no [mental] states of the relevant [meaningful, or intentional] type. All I do is follow formal instructions about manipulating formal symbols." Searle also charges that the robot reply "tacitly concedes that cognition is not solely a matter of formal symbol manipulation" after all, as "strong AI" supposes, since it "adds a set of causal relation[s] to the outside world" (1980, 420).

But at some point it seems reasonable to ask why Searle in the room wouldn't understand Chinese once he becomes so skilled at responding to questions. He can say that he is merely manipulating symbols but he is still meaningfully comparing Chinese symbols to his native language, skillfully answering questions, and so on. How is this so different from what a college student does to genuinely learn Chinese? The point can't be that Searle doesn't *speak* Chinese or understand spoken Chinese. Surely that could be added into the thought experiment if necessary. It seems clear that by "understanding" Searle means, or often means, some kind of *conscious* grasping. After all, if we take the Chinese room scenario at face value, it is Searle himself in the room and he is consciously reporting from the first-person point of view that he doesn't understand Chinese but does understand English. Perhaps, as we'll see below, it all comes back to whether we think a robot can be conscious.

Despite heavy criticism of the argument, two further central issues raised by Searle continue to be of deep interest. First, how and when does one distinguish mere "simulation" of some mental activity or understanding from genuine "duplication"? Searle's view is that computers are, at best, merely simulating understanding and thought, not really duplicating it. Much like we might say that a computerized hurricane or fire simulation does not duplicate a real hurricane or fire (you won't get wet or burned!), Searle insists the same goes for any alleged computer "mental" activity. We do, for example, distinguish between real diamonds or leather and mere simulations which are not the real thing. But Copeland (1993) and others have pointed out that sometimes a simulation can be a duplication; for example, some artificially produced coal (in a lab) might be called simulated coal but it is still real coal in the sense that it is physically indistinguishable. What about simulated "voices"? Isn't artificial light still really light? Copeland makes the following useful distinction:

X is a simulation₁ if it lacks essential features of whatever is being simulated (e.g. diamonds or leather).

X is a simulation₂ if it is exactly like whatever is being simulated except that it hasn't been produced in the usual way but by some non-standard means (such as coal made in a lab).

So a simulated X (simulation₂) can still be an X and Searle can't just assume that simulations of thinking will always be *mere* simulations and can *never* be the real thing. That is, we need a reason to think that simulations of thinking must always be simulation₁ and never simulation₂. However, the problem with mental states is that we would seem first to need to know what the essence of "thinking" or "consciousness" is before we can know if we have simulation₁ or sumulation₂. For this reason and because there is so much disagreement about the essential nature of mental states, it is difficult to see how this can be settled anytime soon. After all, we are still trying to understand what exactly makes *our* mental states conscious! How can we be sure whether a robot could be conscious until we have a better understanding of our own conscious states?

Second, and perhaps even more important, when considering just why computers really can't think or be conscious, Searle interestingly reverts back to a biologically based argument. In essence, he says that computers or robots are just not made of the right stuff with the right kind of "causal powers" to produce genuine thought or consciousness. He ultimately calls his view "biological naturalism" (Searle 2007) and claims that the mind–body problem has a simple solution: "Conscious states are caused by lower level neurobiological processes in the brain and are themselves higher level features of the brain" (Searle 2002, 9). But especially in his early discussion of the Chinese room, Searle's notion of "causal powers" is very unclear. His view seems to be that brain states *cause* consciousness and understanding but he also says that consciousness *is* just a feature of or realized in the brain much like the relationship between the digestive system and the process of digestion.

Searle is sometimes unclear as to the metaphysics involved; for example, how can a brain state cause a mental state and yet still be "realized in" the brain state? On the surface at least, the former claim would seem to imply that brain states and mental states are distinct, which sounds like some form of dualism. However, he insists that he is not even a property dualist (Searle 2002) and does sound more like a materialist when he says that mental states are realized in brain states. We have already seen that most materialists wish to allow for multiple realizability. However, surely there are limits here. After all, a materialist does not have to allow that any kind of physical stuff, even properly interconnected, can produce consciousness any more than any type of physical substance can, say, conduct electricity. Some kinds of things just cannot do the job. Could consciousness be duplicated by a clever arrangement of paper clips and beer cans? Probably not. So Searle might just say that paper clips and beer cans don't have the right "causal powers" to do so. Indeed, Searle sometimes accuses his opponents of holding a latent form of dualism or functionalism since they are the ones who are claiming that biology is irrelevant to mentality.

In any case, it is also important to recognize what Searle is not claiming (1980, 82–84). He is not saying that machines cannot think since we are such machines. Searle is also not saying that a human-made machine cannot think – a machine could think provided it has the same causal powers as our brains. A human clone, for example, would obviously do the trick. However, Searle is saying that something cannot think, understand, and so on solely in virtue of being a computer with the right sort of program. Computation, understood as formal symbol manipulation, is itself not constitutive of thinking.

Of course, this raises a whole host of other questions which go to the heart of the metaphysics of consciousness. To what extent must an organism or system be physiologically like us to be conscious? Why is having a certain biological or chemical make-up necessary for consciousness? Why exactly couldn't an appropriately built robot be capable of having conscious mental states? How could we even know either way? However one answers these questions, it seems that building a truly conscious Commander Data (from Star Trek: The Next Generation) with a "positronic brain" is still just science fiction. Interestingly, even Data does not feel emotions and is fascinated by expressions of human emotion (though an "emotion chip" is sometimes implanted). He also has trouble understanding jokes, sarcasm, and ambiguous statements since Data tends to take everything too literally (how else can you program a robot?).

Perhaps most interesting is the episode "The Measure of a Man" (1989) where the android officer must fight for his right of self-determination in order not to be declared the property of Starfleet and disassembled to create more Datas. Commander Bruce Maddox comes aboard the Enterprise to visit Data, hoping to gain a better understanding of how Data's creator, Dr. Noonien Soong, was able to overcome certain problems in designing and constructing Data's positronic brain. A mini-trial follows because Data, claiming that he has rights, threatens to resign from Starfleet especially since he is skeptical of Maddox's ability. Lieutenant Riker, despite his protests, is forced to act as prosecutor due to Starfleet rules but Captain Picard, acting in Data's defense, turns the discussion to metaphysical matters of Data's "sentience" which typically just means basic consciousness or an ability to feel. Picard points out that Data clearly meets two of the three criteria that Maddox himself used to define "sentient life," namely intelligence and self-awareness. Picard then asks anyone in the court to show a means of measuring consciousness, the third criterion, but no one is able to answer. So the point is to err on the side of caution. As such, Data, by law, must be treated as a sentient being and therefore Data has the right to choose not to undergo dismantling, though he tells Maddox that he might be open to the idea sometime in the future.

A number of articles on this theme in the *International Journal of Machine Consciousness* and *Minds and Machines* will also be of interest to readers. There is little by way of consensus, however. Many authors, in the end, actually agree with Searle in ruling out robot (phenomenal) consciousness while others seem more open to the idea. For example, Chella and Manzotti (2009) explain that to design and build a conscious robot, such features as embodiment, situatedness, emotions and motivations, unity, time, free will, representation, and qualitative experience must be present. Ultimately, however, they are pessimistic about robot consciousness precisely because qualitative experience must be present. Haikonen (2013) argues that consciousness is nothing more than a special way of representing the subjective internal appearance of information. To explain consciousness is to explain how this subjective internal appearance of information can arise in the brain, and so to create a conscious robot would be to create subjective internal appearances of information inside the robot. A useful conscious robot must have a variety of cognitive abilities, but these abilities alone, no matter how advanced, will likely not make the robot conscious since the phenomenal internal appearances must be present as well.

5.8 Connectionism, embodied cognition, and robotics

The growing areas of cognitive science and artificial intelligence can importantly bear on philosophical questions of consciousness. Much current research focuses on how to program a computer to model more closely the workings of the human brain, such as with so-called "neural (or connectionist) networks." This frequently goes hand in hand with the development in labs of so-called "social robots" developed by Honda (such as ASIMO). Sometimes sympathetic to the enactive approach discussed in Chapter 2 and what is often called "embodied (or 'situated') cognition," the basic idea is that a real mind can only be created by interacting with the environment in real time (often called "dynamical systems"). Unlike GOFAI, there are no explicit inner representations or symbols of the outside world. Instead, there are patterns of activity in neural networks. Embodied cognitive science appeals to the idea that cognition deeply depends on aspects of the agent's body other than the brain. By the early 1990s, work in computational intelligence had started to explore ways of generating intelligent action in robots, which became known as the embodied approach to robotics. Rodney Brooks (1991) had presented an overview of a kind of intelligent computational architecture that he characterized as providing "intelligence without representation." Those working in "biorobotics" will, for example, build machines which model biological organisms, such as insects, that reflect basic design principles such as foraging and locomotion.

Much of the work in robotics by Brooks and others tends to favor a connectionist approach to AI where the emphasis is on patterns of neural activity augmented by backpropagation and resulting in concept learning and application (Rumelhart and McClelland 1986; Waskan 2010). Connectionism is an AI approach to the study of human cognition that hopes to explain human abilities using artificial neural networks (or "neural nets"). This approach is also sometimes called parallel distributed processing (PDP). Neural networks are simplified models of the brain composed of large numbers of neuron-like units, together with weights that measure the strength of connections between the units. These weights are meant to model the effects of the synapses that link one neuron to another. Although there are many different ways of building networks, units in a net are normally grouped into three classes: input units, which receive information to be processed, output units, where the results of the processing are found, and units in between called hidden units. Experiments with these models have, for example, demonstrated an ability to learn skills such as face recognition, reading, and simple grammatical structure. One influential early connectionist model was a neural net trained by Rumelhart and McClelland (1986) to predict the past tense of English verbs. The pattern of activation set up by a net is determined by the weights.

Now, when activation flows directly from inputs to hidden units and then on to the output units, this is called a "feedforward net." It is well understood that a truly realistic model of the brain would have to include many more layers of hidden units, as well as recurrent connections that send signals back from higher to lower levels. However, one of the most widely used training methods in PDP is called "backpropagation." To use this method, one needs a training set consisting of many examples of inputs and their desired outputs for a given task. This allows for backpropagation learning, where an error signal propagates backward through multiple layers to guide weight modifications. Finding the right set of weights to accomplish a given task is the main goal in connectionist research. Networks can be trained to discriminate new instances of a given input, such as a new face or perceptual object. Further, there is an emphasis on the way that human infants learn both in terms of cognition and bodily behavior. Like human infants and children, robots learn how to do certain things over time, often by a kind of trial and error. For example, infants learn how to walk and children learn how to catch a ball without all the relevant information first programmed into the system. Instead, adjustments are made to the system when errors occur so as to avoid falling over when learning how to walk or overreaching for a thrown ball.

On the positive side, connectionist networks promise some interesting similarities with the way our brains actually work. Perhaps most obvious is the notion of backpropagation, which at least seems to have the analog of feedback loops in the brain. There is also the central notion that through increasingly strengthened connections and patterns of activity, a system can ideally learn new concepts and behaviors. The "parallel" aspect of PDP seems similar to many of the independently operating brain sub-systems. However, there are also significant differences between connectionist networks and the way our brains work. For example, the "nodes" in connectionist networks are very simple and homogenous compared with real neurons, for example, in terms of the number of connections to other "neurons" and in the complete lack of any analog to brain neurochemistry and neurotransmitters. Further, some human learning doesn't really require very much repetition or "training" and is not in need of an outside "supervisor" to keep checking on the accuracy of the backpropagation.

One well-known dispute over the years is about whether connectionist networks can still be viewed as genuinely "representational," at least with regard to compositionality (productivity) and systematicity (Fodor and Pylyshyn 1988). In short, the problem is that connectionist architecture cannot account for essential aspects of thought, such as the ability to think many thoughts by simply recombining or reordering their concepts, which, in turn, requires the systematicity of syntax and semantics. Like language, the productivity and systematicity of thought, as well as reasoning and inference, are explained by its combinatorial and recursive syntax and semantics. If one can think "John loves Mary," then one can think "Mary loves John." There is at least no guarantee of systematicity for a given network. Moreover, if concepts and thus thoughts are distributed states of networks, it begins to look as if they are not explicitly represented at all in the connectionist units. Nonetheless, some have forcefully argued that connectionist networks are compatible with classical models of mental representation and can make sense of the requisite compositionality (Hawthorne 1989; Chalmers 1993). It is not clear to me that connectionist models must be inconsistent with classical models, but I will not enter into this debate here as it will take me too far afield from the topic of consciousness. Obviously, however, if any theory of human cognition does not allow for genuine mental representation, then it cannot realize a representational theory, and I would be inclined to reject it given my preference for HOR theory.

Interestingly, connectionism has been used to offer yet another reply to Searle's Chinese room argument. Paul and Patricia Churchland (1990) criticize the lack of neurophysiological analogy in the thought experiment. Instead of imagining Searle working alone with paper in the room, they invite us to imagine a more brain-like connectionist architecture. Imagine Searle-in-the-room as just one among many agents, all working in parallel, and each doing their own small bit of processing (like the many neurons of the brain). Since Searle-in-the-room does only a very small portion of the total computational job of generating appropriate Chinese replies in response to Chinese input, he of course would not comprehend the whole process. So we shouldn't expect him to grasp or to be conscious of the meanings of the communications he is involved in processing. But the entire room could still rightly be said to understand Chinese.

Searle (1990) counters that we could then imagine a "Chinese gym" with many English speakers working in parallel, producing output indistinguishable from that of native Chinese speakers. Each English speaker follows their own limited set of instructions in English. Still, Searle insists that since none of the individuals understands, neither does the whole group collectively. It's utterly obvious, Searle maintains, that no one and nothing in the revised Chinese gym experiment understands a word of Chinese either individually or collectively. Nothing is being done in the Chinese gym except meaningless syntactic manipulations from which intentionality and consequently meaningful thought could not conceivably arise. Once again, however, we might then object that the same is true for both our individual neurons and our entire brains.

5.9 Ethical issues

Could a futuristic robot exercise free will and thus start to behave in ways that might be wrong or very damaging to humans and other robots (as in I Robot)? We might suppose that robots could never have libertarian free will partly because they are determinist machines with pre-determined programming and perhaps because they are not conscious. Of course, as we saw in Chapter 1, many do not think that humans have libertarian free will either even though we are conscious and capable of deliberation and making choices. Perhaps we too are deterministic machines despite the fact that we feel like we have libertarian free will. In that case, however, perhaps it wouldn't be so far-fetched to suppose that robots have compatibilist free will. If a robot is doing what it wants without external coercion, for example, perhaps that is all we need for free will. But the real question then becomes whether robots having free will of either kind requires consciousness. After all, much of the discussion about what is involved in exercising free will presupposes at least some level of consciousness, for example a conscious deliberative process or conscious choice among options. Also, as we saw in the previous chapter, some believe that moral responsibility requires consciousness of some kind. Should robots then be held morally responsible for their decisions and actions? Should they be prosecuted and put in jail?

Recognizing the worry here, Asimov set forth his three laws of robotics:

(1)   A robot may not injure a human being or, through inaction, allow a human being to come to harm.
(2)   A robot must obey the orders given it by human beings except where such orders would conflict with the First Law.
(3)   A robot must protect its own existence as long as such protection does not conflict with the First or Second Laws.

Actually, Asimov himself found it necessary to add a fourth, or "zeroth" law, to precede the others:

(0) A robot may not harm humanity, or, by inaction, allow humanity to come to harm.

Wallach and Allen (2009) explore a very wide range of potential dangers of "autonomous moral agents" (AMAs) against the background of standard ethical theories (see also Muller 2015). For example, they warn against the potential for robots to shut down an electrical power grid, cause an economic crisis, or even to commit terrorist acts and war crimes when used in place of humans in a decision-making role. Yet Wallach and Allen are surprisingly uninterested in the role of phenomenal consciousness which they say "is irrelevant to the development of AMAs. Functional equivalence of behavior is all that can possibly matter for the practical issues of designing AMAs" (Wallach and Allen 2009, 68). But, again, if consciousness is necessary for moral consideration as well as for being held morally responsible, then we must be careful not to put the cart before the horse. A related worry would be the formation of a kind of slave class of conscious robots who themselves don't have any rights against our potential abuse. Much like animals, if we really come to believe that robots are conscious (even just with basic sentience), then this should have at least some bearing on how we should treat them. Shouldn't we care if robots really can suffer and feel pain?

One prominent contemporary figure who has thought and written extensively about the future of technology and robots is Ray Kurzweil. For example, in The Singularity is Near (2005), Kurzweil describes his "law of accelerating returns" which predicts an exponential increase in technologies like computers, genetics, nanotechnology, robotics, and artificial intelligence.

He says this will lead to a technological "singularity" in the year 2045, a point where progress is so rapid it goes beyond humans' ability to comprehend it. Kurzweil predicts the technological advances will transform people as we alter our brains and bodies genetically, with nanotechnology, and with artificial intelligence. Although Kurzweil recognizes the potential for abuse and various other ethical worries, he is mostly optimistic in offering bold predictions such as the possibility of reversing the aging process as well as curing cancer, heart disease, and other illnesses. Perhaps our minds can even eventually be downloaded into a machine for permanent safe-keeping such that a kind of digital immortality can be achieved. It is also possible that we will even morph into machines ourselves via the regular replacement of our body parts over time (such as cochlear implants now). But being able to replace neurons and their activity is of course the real difficulty. It is difficult to know now just how likely these futuristic scenarios are.

Chapter summary

This chapter addressed the extent to which animals are conscious and whether machines could be conscious. Regarding animals, we examined various criteria that can be used when inferring that an animal is conscious, such as similarities in brain structure and behavior. There also seems to be increasing evidence that most animals have episodic memory, are capable of metacognitive states, and perhaps more controversially also have "mindreading" ability. The possibility of machine (or robot) consciousness has intrigued philosophers and non-philosophers for decades. We first examined what has come to be known as the "Turing test" for machine intelligence and thought (and seemingly consciousness also to some extent). We then critically discussed John Searle's Chinese room argument, which was designed to show that "strong AI," the view that suitably programmed computers literally have a mind or "understanding," is false. The similarities and differences between human brains and computer programs (and robots) were also assessed partly via a discussion of connectionist networks. Finally, some ethical worries about the future of robotics and AI research were raised.

Further reading

For more on the "brain structure" line of argument with animals, see Baars 2005, Edelman, Baars, and Seth 2005, and Beshkar 2008. Beshkar 2008 also brings together a plethora of supporting evidence regarding animal tool use, communication, problem solving, and deceptive behavior, especially for various mammals, birds, spiders, and bees. See also Beckoff, Allen, and Burghardt 2002, Keenan, Gallup, and Falk 2003, Lurz 2009, and Andrews 2015.

For more on episodic memory, see the 2014 special issue of *Review of Philosophy and Psychology* (vol. 5). See also Zentall 2005 and DeGrazia 2009 for further evidence of both episodic memory and anticipation of future events in various animals. See Raby and Clayton 2009 for an interesting related discussion and Shea and Heyes 2010 for an argument that meta-memory is evidence of animal consciousness.

For more on the Turing test and the history between 1950 and 2000, see Saygin, Cicekli, and Akman 2000. See also Aleksander 2013 and the special 2012 issue (no. 4) on "Mind Uploading" in the *International Journal of Machine Consciousness*. For much more on the singularity, see Chalmers' 2010 target article in the *Journal of Consciousness Studies* as well as two subsequent issues devoted to this topic with a reply from Chalmers 2012, vol. 19 (1–2) and vol. 19 (7–8).

Note

1 For much more on the overall issue of mindreading and metacognition in animals and infants, see Carruthers 2009 (and the peer commentary that follows), as well as Nichols and Stich 2003, Goldman 2006, and Gennaro 2012 (chapters seven and eight). For further defense of the view that self-attribution of mental states (metacognition) is prior to our capacity to attribute mental states to others (mindreading), see Goldman 2006. A more modest view, offered by Nichols and Stich 2003, is that the two capacities are independent and dissociable. Carruthers 2009, however, argues at length that mindreading is actually prior to metacognition. I am not convinced that the evidence supports his view better than, say, Nichols and Stich's position. Two related opposing views are simulation theory (ST) and theory-theory (TT). ST holds that mindreading involves the ability to imaginatively take the perspective of another. TT holds that metacognition results from one's "theory of mind" being directed at oneself. So which of the three views is closest to the truth? I am not sure that we have enough evidence to decide, but I think it is premature to suppose that mindreading is *prior to* metacognition, as Carruthers thinks.

CONCLUDING
THOUGHTS AND
FUTURE DIRECTIONS

So where are we now? As was mentioned in the Introduction, it is always important to be careful with respect to the confusing terminology in this field, such as the difference between creature and state consciousness. Recall that I also made a plea for more uniform usage, whenever possible, for terms like "experience" and "phenomenal." There is enough real disagreement in philosophy and psychology – we needn't create artificial ones by using terms so differently without good reason. In Chapters 1 and 2, we examined the relative pros and cons of numerous versions of materialism and dualism as well as critically discussing a number of specific theories of consciousness.

As I mentioned in Chapter 3 and have argued elsewhere (Gennaro 2012), I personally favor a version of the higher-order thought (HOT) theory of consciousness. HOT theory says that what makes a mental state conscious is that a higher-order thought is directed at that state. I think HOT theory is plausibly motivated by the transitivity principle and it offers a nice way to differentiate conscious and unconscious mental states.

I do not think that directly reducing consciousness to neurophysiology is, at least currently, the best strategy to take, but this is not because of the standard objections to materialism discussed in Chapter 1 (section 1.7). I agree with Carruthers that those who currently attempt to reduce consciousness more directly in neural or physical terms "leap over too many explanatory levels at once" (2005, 6). This is a point missed by Hardcastle (2004), for example, who mistakenly supposes that HOT theorists are chiefly motivated by the alleged nonreductionist divide between mind and brain or by a mysterious permanent explanatory gap. Hardcastle seems not to appreciate that HOT theorists are very much open to a later second-step reduction to the neurophysiological, a point made by Rosenthal on several occasions and echoed in Chapter 3.

The hard problem might be hard but there is little reason to suppose that it is impossible to solve. How long has it really been so far? Shouldn't we at least give it another fifty years or so? Humans believed that the Earth was the center of the solar system, not to mention the entire universe, for centuries. I am very glad that biologists didn't give up so quickly in solving the mystery of "life." I am also happy that we now recognize the natural causes of seizures and auditory hallucinations in schizophrenia, no longer attributing them to demon possession or insanity. Perhaps there is at most a moderately interesting *epistemic* gap between the physical and mental but there isn't a *metaphysical* gap. As we saw in Chapter 1, with the exception of David Chalmers, many authors who put forth such arguments are not really challenging the metaphysics of materialism. Further, whether or not a theory is false depends upon how it is defined. The stronger one defines terms like "physicalism" and "materialism," the easier they would be to falsify.

Although there certainly are some serious objections to HOT theory, such as the misrepresentation problem and the issue of animal consciousness, I think that it has the resources to handle them. Recall also that HOT theory is immune to Chalmers' version of the hard problem anyway. So I think that some form of HOT theory will remain a viable option for many years to come. I expect significant work on the neural correlates of consciousness (NCCs) to be continued with fervor for the foreseeable future. This work should also bear on the neural realization of HOT theory. In particular, it will not only be interesting to learn how and where various conscious states are realized, but also to what extent (if any) the prefrontal cortex (PFC) is *required* for first-order conscious states. As we saw in Chapter 3, this is also relevant to the problem of animals and infants. For my own part, I have previously made the following concession:

> *If* all HOTs occur in the PFC, *and if* PFC activity is necessary for all conscious experience, *and if* there is little or no PFC activity in infants and most animals, then either (a) infants and most animals do not have conscious experience or (b) HOT theory is false. Unlike Carruthers, and perhaps Rosenthal, I would opt for (b). I think I am more sure of animal and infant consciousness than I am of any philosophical theory of consciousness.
>
> (Gennaro 2012, 281–282)

However, I think that a good case can be made for the falsity of one or more of the conjuncts in the antecedent of the foregoing conditional.

It is also worth mentioning that there is no reason in principle to rule out the possibility of experimental data supporting HOT theory. Despite her scathing but somewhat misdirected criticism of HOT theory, Hardcastle (2004, 290–294) suggests that the ubiquitous presence of unconscious HOTs could find empirical support via a modified priming task. There is no reason why some of the methods used to indicate the presence of unconscious first-*order* mental states could not, if suitably modified, also be used to indicate the presence of unconscious HOTs. For example, one well-known method is *subliminal priming*, which refers to the effects on subsequent behavior of stimuli that are not consciously detected (Marcel 1983). Unconscious mental processes can influence our conscious mental states in very specific ways. For example, Jacoby, Lindsay, and Toth (1992) briefly presented completed words before presenting a target word stem, such as presenting RESPOND followed by ___OND. But then subjects were told *not* to use the completed word in suggesting that it would complete the stem. Subjects would also be primed unconsciously to give the flashed word although they were instructed to disregard it. In such an opposition condition, subjects would take longer to answer questions for which they had just been primed with an answer that they could not use. But when they were told to use the completed word, priming would work to their advantage and their reaction times were shorter. By comparing response times between the two conditions, as well as their respective error rates, we get some idea of the influence that unconscious states can have on their conscious answers.

Hardcastle suggests that we

> can and should use a similar methodology to determine whether we have unconscious HOTs . . . co-active with any conscious states. . . . We need a priming task that would test whether we can recognize that we were aware of a series of target conscious events faster or with fewer errors than other aspects of the same events. If we can, then that would be some evidence that we are unconsciously aware that we are aware.
>
> (2004, 292)

She gives an example of one possible experiment. We flash a series of simple scenes (such as a cat on a mat or a dog with a bone) for a half second or so, long enough to reach consciousness. Each scene is then replaced by the same masking stimulus, which prevents subjects from studying the stimulus. We can then ask about their conscious experience (did you see a bone?) or about the scene (was the dog next to the bone?). With appropriate controls in place, if we have unconscious HOTs "accompanying all conscious experiences, then HOTs should prime our behavior with regard to reacting to the fact that we are conscious" (Hardcastle 2004, 292), and we should answer the former questions (about conscious experience) with fewer errors than the latter (about the scene). To my knowledge, however, these kinds of experiments have not been done to date. Aside from this specific suggestion, there should be some way to design experiments that could serve as experimental evidence for or against HOT theory.

Overall, though, I still do find myself much more in sympathy with some form of materialism, at least in opposition to dualism (especially substance dualism). While we may argue about the validity of the usual arguments against materialism, it is rather puzzling to me how few openly wonder: "How does dualism help to explain why we experience certain smells and colors instead of other smells and colors at a given time?" "How can a conscious state have a structure of any kind (such as a 'unity') if it is realized in a non-physical substance without parts?" "Why should neural activity in my visual cortex, as opposed to my hippocampus, cause (non-physical) visual experiences?" We might also ask: What would even count as an "explanation" or "reduction" of consciousness? In some cases, it seems that the bar is set much higher for materialism than for other views. I have been personally somewhat surprised by the recent increased interest in, for example, panpsychism and emergence. On the one hand,

I think it is very healthy that philosophers (and non-philosophers) entertain and critically examine virtually all possible positions, even re-examining some historically minority and unpopular views in light of new data or arguments. On the other hand, my sense is that the initial motivation for many of these views is primarily negative; that is, materialism can't be true ("you know, there's a hard problem and zombies are possible") so let's theorize about the alternatives. Still, there is of course nothing wrong with the usual philosophical "argument by elimination" and each of us probably dismisses other views too quickly at times.

In some circles, idealism is also perhaps a surprising contender. As a philosopher, I very much enjoy reading and thinking about Berkeley, Leibniz, and Indian philosophy. I often tell my non-philosopher friends that we teach and discuss philosophical views that we disagree with all the time. Kant is perhaps my favorite historical figure but I am not a transcendental idealist (though I am tempted at times). I love Leibniz but don't believe in monads. However, it is very important for all sides to understand the landscape of historical and current positions on mind and metaphysics (the "logical space," as philosophers sometimes put it). As we saw in Chapter 1, there are numerous versions of both materialism and dualism (how many "isms" can we come up with?), not to mention idealism and panpsychism. Further, it is not even always clear what the difference is between, say, property dualism and non-reductive materialism.

It is crucial to keep in mind the big picture in terms of direct realism, representatational realism, transcendental idealism, and idealism. If one is not aware of all these alternatives and the standard objections to each, one might mistakenly set up a false dilemma. For example, one might argue that if direct realism is false, then we should embrace idealism. The difference between "material" and "physical" is also important. For example, one might argue that materialism is false because of what we now know from quantum physics or because there really is only energy which appears like matter. But we need to be careful not to conflate levels of reality or erroneously rule out some *other* kind of "physicalism" by opting too quickly for idealism. As we saw in Chapter 1, there are also serious objections to idealism. There is, recall, a kind of "reverse hard problem"; namely, how can our conscious experiences explain the *appearance* of a material world? As interesting as other alternative theories are (such as the integrated information and sensorimotor theories), I am not convinced that they have enough *advantages* over HOT theory or even identity theory. Nonetheless, I do find attempts to tie consciousness to information, quantum results, and attention to be very interesting and worth exploring.

I cannot help but wonder at times about the background psychology involved when we argue for our preferred positions. We are all familiar with confirmation bias and other common habits of the mind, which are surely not ideally rational. A theist believes in God and so (probably) immortality. Won't the theist be predisposed to opt for some form of dualism and accept near-death experience (NDE) reports at face value? Recall, however, that contemporary property dualists are not normally motivated by considerations about an afterlife. On the other hand, an atheist will probably be more likely to take a more skeptical look at reports of NDEs. In one sense, there is nothing wrong with this. Some views more naturally go together, for example atheism, materialism, and determinism. Although this is not without exception, perhaps it is no surprise that those who hold one of these views tend to embrace them all. It is even sometimes difficult to know which, if any, belief is the most central to us. The same might be said for theism, dualism, and libertarian free will. Ideally, we should be totally objective in evaluating arguments on both sides, but this is indeed an ideal. Nonetheless, people do change their minds throughout their lives, and entire cultures can change beliefs over long periods of time as well. We also see this with respect to our views on various ethical issues.

Having said all that, perhaps future experiments using superior technology could help to settle the debate between (interactionist) substance dualists and materialists. For example, if it turns out that neurons frequently fire in the absence of *any* physical cause, such as any pre-synaptic neural firing, then we would seem to have some evidence for substance dualism (if we agree that neural firings always have causes). After all, if neurons fire without any physical cause, then one might reasonably infer that there is a non-physical cause, such as that which is posited by a substance dualist. From the third-person point of view, there would appear to be spontaneous, even random, neural firings. Similar experiments could cast doubt not only on materialism but also on other versions of substance dualism such as epiphenomenalism and parallelism. I am not aware of any such evidence at the present time and it may even be incredibly difficult to gather such data at the neuronal level.

The search for NCCs and attempts to solve the binding problem are also still works in progress. It may turn out that some combination of extant theories is narrowing in on answers and solutions. Indeed, I suspect that the hard problem, the binding problem, and the search for NCCs are really three aspects of the very same problem. I think that work in philosophical psychopathology and philosophy of psychiatry is an extremely exciting area of current research. I would expect these sub-areas to continue to yield important results over the next few decades. Each of the pathologies we discussed in Chapter 4 is not only interesting in its own right, but also bears on important philosophical and psychological problems pertaining to consciousness. For example, dissociative identity disorder (DID) and conscious unity, synesthesia and multimodal conscious perception, and schizophrenia and self-consciousness. I am also very concerned with what should even count as a "mental illness" and how to differentiate these from what are more typically called "physical diseases." After all, if all mental activity is really neural activity, then mental illnesses just are brain illnesses in some sense. Just as brain damage results seem to be best (or at least "more simply") explained by a materialist position, so too should be the case for mental illnesses.

Like most philosophers, I have a deep metaphysical interest in the traditional and contemporary free will–determinism debate (though I admit that my patience is sometimes tested as I read through the abundance of thought experiments!). Perhaps most intriguing to me is the current work on moral and legal responsibility in light of the free will–determinism debate and especially any connection to consciousness. The cutting-edge areas of neuroethics and neurolaw are also crucially important: Under what circumstances (if any) should neuroimaging data be used in a court of law, for example, to show a lack of moral responsibility, a mental illness, or some kind of diminished capacity? Should we rethink the way the legal system assumes libertarian free will and seems largely based on retributive justice? What, if any, legal or prison reforms could be put in place? Perhaps most important: What can be done to prevent mass casualty crimes committed by the truly mentally ill?

It is fairly obvious that the quest to build better machines and human-like robots will be at the forefront of AI and consciousness research for many decades to come. Turing was clearly overly optimistic in his 1950 prediction about machine "thinking" but still raised many of the central issues. There are also certainly numerous ethical issues raised by this research, some of which were described in Chapter 5. Much like in genetic engineering, researchers in robotics must try not to let the technology get too far ahead of careful ethical considerations. It is difficult to know when, or if, we might succeed in building genuinely conscious robots. Perhaps it will be even difficult to know one way or another. Alternatively, we may reach a point where human body parts (including the brain) are systematically replaced by artificial parts. I am not convinced that Searle's Chinese room argument is successful; however, I find myself often in agreement with Searle that consciousness is tied to biology or neurobiology in some important way. I confess that I am not entirely clear why and so I remain hesitant to rule out robot consciousness forever.

In any case, the twenty-first century promises to be an incredibly exciting time for all those interested and working in consciousness research. I am very glad to be just a small part of it.

GLOSSARY

Achromatopsia – The loss of color vision.

Agnosia – A loss of ability to recognize objects, persons, sounds, shapes, or smells while the specific sense itself is not defective, nor is there any significant memory loss.

Akinetopsia – The loss of motion perception.

Alexithymia – A deficiency in understanding, processing, or describing emotions. It is common to around 85 percent of people on the autism spectrum and can be difficult to distinguish from or co-occur with social-emotional agnosia.

Amnesia – A condition in which one's memory is lost. *Anterograde* amnesia is the loss of short-term memory, the loss or impairment of the ability to form new memories through memorization. *Retrograde* amnesia is the loss of pre-existing memories to conscious recollection, beyond an ordinary degree of forgetfulness. The person may be able to memorize new things that occur after the onset of amnesia (unlike in anterograde amnesia), but be unable to recall some or all of their life or identity prior to the onset.

Anarchic hand syndrome – A neurological disorder caused by brain lesion in which individuals frequently perform seemingly voluntary movements that they do not consciously intend and cannot directly inhibit.

Anosognosia – A condition in which a person who suffers from a disability seems unaware of the existence of the disability.

Anton's syndrome – A form of anosognosia in which a person with partial or total blindness denies being visually impaired, despite medical evidence to the contrary. The patient typically confabulates; that is, contrives excuses for the inability to see.

Apraxia – A form of motor (body) agnosia involving the neurological loss of ability to map out physical actions to repeat them in functional activities. It is a form of body-disconnectedness and takes several different forms.

Asomatognosia – A lack of awareness of the condition of all or part of one's body. A lack of awareness of paralysis because the brain is damaged.

Attended intermediate-level representation (AIR) theory – Jesse Prinz's theory that a conscious perception must represent basic "intermediate" features of external objects such as colors, shapes, tones, and feels. This is the "IR" aspect of AIR. To be conscious, however, the represented content must also be attended (the "A").

Autism – A disorder characterized by impaired social interaction and communication, and by restricted and repetitive behavior.

Behaviorism – The view that mental states are nothing more than behavioral dispositional states.

Binding problem – The problem of how the brain integrates information processed by different regions of the brain.

Blindsight – Occurs when partially cortically blind patients can successfully guess at some characteristics of a stimulus that is not consciously seen.

Body swap illusion – People can be tricked into the false perception of owning another body. An illusion that can make people feel that another body, be it a mannequin or an actual person, is really theirs.

Capgras syndrome – A disorder in which a person holds a delusion that a friend, spouse, parent, or other close family member has been replaced by an identical-looking impostor.

Change blindness – Occurs when normal subjects fail to notice what would seem to be an obvious change in some object or scene.

Charles Bonnet syndrome – A condition that causes patients with visual loss to have complex and vivid visual hallucinations in which the characters or objects are smaller than normal (such as faces or cartoons).

Chinese room argument – Searle's argument based on imagining himself running a program for using Chinese and then showing that he does not understand Chinese. Strong AI is false because merely running the program does not result in any real understanding (or thought or consciousness, by implication). Searle uses a thought experiment whereby he is in a room and follows English instructions for manipulating Chinese symbols to produce appropriate answers to questions in Chinese.

Compatibilism (sometimes also called "soft determinism") – The view that the very *same* action can be *both* free and determined. Freedom is best understood as something more like "the absence of external constraint" or "acting in accordance with one's desires and beliefs."

Conceptualism – The view that the representational content of a perceptual experience is fully conceptual in the sense that what the experience represents (and how it represents it) is entirely determined by the conceptual capacities the perceiver brings to bear in her experience.

Confabulation – The unconscious filling of gaps in one's memory by fabrications that one accepts as facts. Rationalizing what would seem to be delusional behavior.

Connectionism – The approach to AI where the emphasis is on patterns of neural activity augmented by backpropagation and resulting in concept learning and application. This approach is also sometimes called parallel distributed processing (PDP) and attempts to explain human abilities by using artificial neural networks (or "neural nets"). Neural networks are simplified models of the brain composed of large numbers of neuron-like units, together with weights that measure the strength of connections between the units.

Connection principle – John Searle's view that every unconscious intentional state is at least potentially conscious.

Conscious ("what it is like" sense) – Thomas Nagel's famous characterization of when I am in a conscious mental state, namely that there is "something it is like" for me to be in that state from the subjective or first-person point of view.

Consciousness, access – Ned Block's term for a mental state's relationship with other mental states; for example, a mental state's availability for use in reasoning and rationality guiding speech and action. Contrasted with phenomenal consciousness (or "phenomenality") which is similar to Nagel's "what it is like" sense of consciousness.

Consciousness, creature – Refers to the fact that an organism is awake, as opposed to sleeping or in a coma.

Consciousness, hard problem of – Coined by David Chalmers, this refers to the difficulty of explaining just how physical processes in the brain give rise to subjective conscious experiences.

Consciousness, Intransitive – Based on the expression "x is conscious," in contrast to transitive consciousness, where the locution "x is conscious of y" is used.

Consciousness, state – Refers to when an individual mental state, such as a pain or perception, is conscious.

Consciousness, unity of – There are many different senses of "unity" of consciousness but perhaps most common is the notion that, from the first-person point of view, we experience the world in an integrated way and as a single phenomenal field of experience.

Cotard syndrome – A rare neuropsychiatric disorder in which people hold a delusional belief that they are dead (either figuratively or literally), do not exist, are putrefying, or have lost their blood or internal organs.

Determinism (general) – The more general view about cause and effect in nature such that given the state of the universe (or any causally closed part of it) at any given time and the laws of nature, the next state of the universe (or part of it) is uniquely fixed. That is, there is only one physically possible future.

Determinism, psychological – The idea that given the entire conscious and unconscious psychological make-up of a person P at a particular time (which results jointly from P's heredity *and* past experiences), P is compelled to do what P actually does *at that time.*

Dissociative identity disorder (DID) – A psychiatric diagnosis that describes a condition in which a person displays multiple distinct identities (known as "alters" or "parts"), each with its own pattern of perceiving and interacting with the environment. DID was previously called "multiple personality disorder."

Dualism (general) – The view that the conscious mind or a conscious mental state is non-physical in some sense.

Dualism, interactionist (or simply "interactionism") – The most common form of "substance dualism"; its name derives from the widely accepted fact that mental states and bodily states causally interact with each other. It is sometimes referred to as "Cartesian dualism" due to the influence of Descartes.

Dualism, property – The view that there are mental *properties* (i.e. characteristics or aspects of things), as opposed to substances, that are neither identical nor reducible to physical properties.

Dualism, substance – The view that the mind is a non-physical substance distinct from the body.

Dysexecutive syndrome – Consists of a group of symptoms that fall into cognitive, behavioral, and emotional categories that tend to occur together. A dysfunction in executive functions, such as planning, abstract thinking, flexibility, and behavioral control.

Emergentism – The view that consciousness is an emergent property of physical systems. A property is emergent if it is a novel property of a system or an entity that arises when that system or entity has reached a certain level of complexity. An emergent property is itself distinct from and not reducible to the properties of the parts of the system from which it emerges. We might say that the emergent "whole" is greater than the sum of the "parts." In this case, the claim is that consciousness is an emergent property of the brain.

Enactive (or "sensorimotor") theory – The view that conscious experiences are inseparable from bodily activities and sensorimotor expectations. On this view, what we feel is determined by what we do and what we know how to do. It explicitly rejects the notion that consciousness can be explained by brain activity and even that conscious states arise from brain states alone.

Epiphenomenalism – The view that mental events are caused by, but not reducible to, brain events such that mental events are mere "epiphenomena." Mental states or events are caused by physical states or events in the brain but do not themselves cause anything.

Explanatory gap – Joseph Levine's way of expressing the difficulty for any materialistic attempt to explain consciousness due to the gap in our ability to explain the connection between phenomenal properties and brain properties.

Feedback loops – Also referred to as recurrent processing or reentrant feedback. Many neurons not only connect and transmit from early processing areas to higher areas but also *feed back* from the higher areas to the early areas.

First-order representationalism (FOR) – Theories that attempt to explain conscious experience primarily in terms of world-directed (or first-order) intentional states.

Free will, libertarian – The view that a person P does act A freely when, and only when, P could have done some other action B at that same time *and* P had some control over doing A.

Fregoli delusion – The belief that various people who the believer meets are actually the same person in disguise.

Functionalism – The view that conscious mental states should only be identified with the functional role they play within an organism rather than what physically makes them up.

Global workspace theory (GWT) of consciousness – Bernie Baars' view that we should think of the entire cognitive system as built on a "blackboard architecture" which is a kind of global workspace. Unconscious processes and mental states compete for the spotlight of attention, from which information is "broadcast globally" throughout the system. We experience a conscious state precisely when such information is globally available.

Hemispatial neglect – Also called hemiagnosia, hemineglect, unilateral neglect, spatial neglect, unilateral visual inattention, hemi-inattention, or neglect syndrome. A neuropsychological condition in which there is a deficit in attention to and awareness of one side of space. It is defined by the inability for a person to process and perceive stimuli on one side of the body or environment that is not due to a lack of sensation.

Higher-order global states (HOGS) – Robert Van Gulick's view that an unconscious state becomes conscious when the unconscious state is "recruited" into a larger state such that there is implicit self-awareness that one is in the lower-order state.

Higher-order perception (HOP) theory – A theory that says that what makes a mental state M conscious is that it is the object of a higher-order perceptual or experiential state of some kind, which does not require the kind of conceptual content invoked by HOT theorists.

Higher-order representationalism (HOR) – Any theory that holds that what makes a mental state M conscious is that it is the object of some kind of HOR directed at M. A HOR is a "meta-psychological" or "metacognitive" state; that is, a mental state directed at another mental state.

Higher-order thought (HOT) theory – A theory that says that what makes a mental state M conscious is that it is the object of a higher-order thought (with conceptual components) directed at M.

Higher-order thought theory, Dispositional – Peter Carruthers' theory that the conscious status of an experience is due to its availability to higher-order thought.

Idealism – The view that there are *only* non-physical mental substances and states. It denies the existence of mind-independent physical substances altogether.

Idealism, transcendental – The Kantian view that there are mind-independent objects or things but we cannot know what they are like "in themselves."

Identity theory, Token-token – The view that each particular conscious mental *event* in some organism is identical to some particular brain process or event in that organism.

Identity theory, Type-type – The view that mental *properties*, such as "having a desire to drink some water" or "being in pain," are literally identical to a brain property of some kind.

Inattentional blindness – Occurs when a subject is not conscious of objects within their visual fields because they are paying close attention to something.

Integrated information theory (IIT) – Giulio Tononi's theory that consciousness is a purely information-theoretic property of systems. He uses a mathematical measure, "ϕ" (*phi*, pronounced "fi"), that measures not only the information in the parts of a given system but also the information in the organization of the entire system.

Intensional contexts – Instances where replacing one co-referring term with another can change a statement's truth-value.

Inverted spectrum – An objection to functionalism which maintains that there could be an individual who, for example, satisfies the functional definition of our experience of red but is experiencing yellow, and yet is behaviorally indistinguishable from someone with normal color vision.

Leibniz's Law – If x and y have any different properties, then x cannot be identical to y.

Mania – A state of abnormally elevated or irritable mood, arousal, and/or energy levels. In a sense, it is the opposite of depression.

Materialism (general) – The view that the mind is the brain or, more specifically, that conscious mental activity is identical with neural activity (identity theory).

Materialism, eliminative – The view that there really are no mental states, at least in the sense that the very concept of consciousness is muddled or that the mentalistic notions found in "folk psychology," such as desires and beliefs, will eventually be eliminated and replaced by physicalistic terms as neurophysiology matures into the future.

Metaphysics – The branch of philosophy concerned with the ultimate nature of reality.

Mindreading – The ability to attribute mental states to others or have a thought about another's mental state.

Mirror self-misidentification – The belief that one's reflection in a mirror is some other person.

Monism – The view that there is only one type of thing in the universe.

Monism, neutral – The view that most fundamental entities in the world are neither mental nor physical.

Multiple drafts model (MDM) of consciousness – Dennett's view that all kinds of cognitive activities occur in the brain via parallel processes of *interpretation* which are under frequent revision. The MDM rejects the idea of a "self" as an inner observer; rather, the self is the product or construction of a narrative which emerges over time, which Dennett calls the "center of narrative gravity." Various streams of information compete for "fame in the brain" and the winner simply gets expressed via behavioral outputs and verbal reports.

Mysterianism – The view that we are simply not capable of solving the problem of consciousness (McGinn). Mysterians believe that the hard problem can *never* be solved because of human cognitive limitations.

Narcissistic personality disorder – A pervasive pattern of grandiosity, need for admiration, and a lack of empathy.

Near-death experience (NDE) – This occurs when some patients, often in cardiac arrest at a hospital, experience a peaceful moving through a tunnel-like structure to a light, among other things.

Obsessive compulsive disorder (OCD) – An anxiety disorder in which people have unwanted and repeated thoughts, feelings, ideas, sensations (obsessions), or behaviors that make them feel driven to do something (compulsions).

Orchestrated objective reduction ("Orch OR") – Penrose and Hammeroff's view that consciousness arises through quantum effects occurring in subcellular neural structures known as "microtubules" which are structural proteins in cell walls.

Out of body experience (OBE) – Instances where one seems to perceive the world (and often one's own body) from above or outside one's body.

Panpsychism – The view that all things in physical reality, even down to microparticles, have some degree of mentality or consciousness.

Parallelism – A version of substance dualism which denies the causal interaction between the non-physical mental and physical bodily realms (often attributed to Leibniz). The idea is our minds and bodies run along parallel tracks, so to speak, with each unfolding according to its own laws.

Leibniz used the analogy of two watches which are perfectly synchronized so that mental states and bodily states are timed perfectly.

Paranoia – A psychotic disorder characterized by delusions of persecution with or without grandeur, often strenuously defended with apparent logic and reason.

Phantom limb pain/sensation – Sensations (such as cramping pain) described as perceptions that an individual experiences relating to a limb or an organ that is no longer physically part of the body. These sensations are recorded most frequently following the amputation of an arm or a leg, but may also occur following the removal of a breast or an internal organ. Phantom limb pain is the feeling of pain in an absent limb or a portion of a limb.

Phenomenal concepts – Concepts that use a phenomenal or "first-person" property to refer to some conscious mental state.

Principle of alternative possibilities (PAP) – A person is morally responsible for what she does do only if she can do otherwise.

Prosopagnosia – Also known as "faceblindness" and "facial agnosia." Patients cannot consciously recognize very familiar faces, sometimes even including their own.

Psychopathy – A mental disorder characterized primarily by a lack of empathy and remorse, shallow emotions, egocentricity, and deceptiveness.

Qualia (singular, quale) – Qualitative or phenomenal properties of mental states. Most often understood as the felt properties or qualities of conscious states.

Qualia, absent – An objection mainly to functionalism that it seems possible to have two functionally equivalent creatures, one of whom lacks qualia entirely. There could be creatures functionally equivalent to normal humans whose mental states have no qualitative character at all.

Realism, representational (or indirect) – The view, associated with Locke for example, that there are mind-independent objects or things and that we can know something about what they are really like.

Realism, transcendental – Kant's view that there are mind-independent objects or things but we cannot know what they are like "in themselves."

Reductionism – A relation between theories such that one theory (the reduced theory) is derivable from another theory (the reducing theory) usually with the help of "bridging principles."

Representational theories of consciousness – Theories that attempt to reduce consciousness to "mental representations" rather than directly to neural or other physical states.

Rubber hand illusion – People can be convinced that a rubber hand is their own by putting it on a table in front of them while stroking it in the same way as their real hand.

Schizophrenia – A mental disorder characterized by disintegration of thought processes and of emotional responsiveness. It most commonly manifests itself as auditory hallucinations, paranoid or bizarre delusions, or disorganized speech and thinking, and it is accompanied by significant social or occupational dysfunction. *Thought insertion* is the delusion that some thoughts are not one's own and are somehow being inserted into one's mind.

Self-deception – A process of denying or rationalizing away the relevance, significance, or importance of opposing evidence and logical argument. Self-deception involves convincing oneself of a truth (or lack of truth) so that one does not reveal any self-knowledge of the deception. A *delusion* is a false belief held with absolute conviction despite superior evidence. Unlike hallucinations, delusions are always pathological (the result of an illness or illness process). A delusion is distinct from a belief based on false or incomplete information, dogma, poor memory, illusion, or other effects of perception.

Self-representational theory of consciousness – The view that a conscious mental state represents both an outer object but also is directed back at itself.

Simplicity, principle of (or "Occam's razor") – If two theories can equally explain a given phenomenon, then we should accept the one which posits fewer objects or forces.

Simultanagnosia – Patients can recognize objects or details in their visual field, but only one at a time. They cannot make out the scene they belong to or a whole image out of the details. They literally "cannot see the forest for the trees." Simultanagnosia is a common symptom of *Balint's syndrome*.

Somatoparaphrenia – A type of delusion where one denies ownership of a limb or an entire side of one's body. A body delusion.

Split-brain cases – Those patients where severing the corpus callosum blocks the inter-hemispheric transfer of perceptual, sensory, motor, and other forms of information in a dramatic way.

Strong AI – The view that suitably programmed computers literally have a mind; that is, they really understand language and actually have other mental capacities similar to humans. This is contrasted with "weak AI" which is the view that computers are merely useful tools for studying the mind.

Supervenience – A highly technical notion with many variations, but the basic idea is one of *dependence* (instead of identity), for example that the mental depends on the physical in the sense that any mental change must be accompanied by some physical change.

Synesthesia – The "union of the senses" whereby two or more of the five senses that are normally experienced separately are involuntarily and automatically joined together in experience. For example, some synesthetes experience a color when they hear a sound or see a letter.

Transitivity principle (TP) – A conscious state is a state whose subject is, in some way, aware of being in it.

Turing test – The basic idea is that if a machine could fool an interrogator (who could not see the machine) into thinking that it was human, then we should say it thinks or, at least, has intelligence.

Wide intrinsicality view (WIV) – Rocco Gennaro's version of HOT theory which says that first-order conscious states are complex states with a world-directed part and a meta-psychological component.

Zombie – The philosophical notion of a "zombie" refers to conceivable creatures which are physically and behaviorally indistinguishable from us but lack consciousness entirely.

BIBLIOGRAPHY

Aleksander, I. 2013. Phenomenal Consciousness and Biologically Inspired Systems. *International Journal of Machine Consciousness* 5: 3–9.

Alexander, E. 2012. *Proof of Heaven*. New York: Simon and Schuster.

Alkire, M., Hudetz, A., and Tononi, G. 2008. Consciousness and Anesthesia. *Science* 322: 876–880.

Allen, C. 2004. Animal Pain. *Nous* 38: 617–643.

Allen, C. 2013. Fish Cognition and Consciousness. *Journal of Agricultural and Environmental Ethics* 26: 25–39.

Allen-Hermanson, S. 2005. Morgan's Canon Revisited. *Philosophy of Science* 72: 608–631.

Alter, T. 2005. The Knowledge Argument against Physicalism. *Internet Encyclopedia of Philosophy*. Available at http://www.iep.utm.edu/know-arg/

Alter, T. and Howell, R. 2009. *A Dialogue on Consciousness*. New York: Oxford University Press.

Alter, T. and Howell, R. eds. 2012. *Consciousness and the Mind-Body Problem*. New York: Oxford University Press.

Alter, T. and Nagasawa, Y. 2012. What is Russellian Monism? *Journal of Consciousness Studies* 19 (9–10): 67–95.

Alter, T. and Walter, S. eds. 2007. *Phenomenal Concepts and Phenomenal Knowledge: New Essays on Consciousness and Physicalism*. New York: Oxford University Press.

American Psychiatric Association. 2013. *Diagnostic and Statistical Manual of Mental Disorders*, 5th edition. Washington, D.C.: American Psychiatric Association.

Andersen, H. and Grush, R. 2009. A Brief History of Time-Consciousness: Historical Precursors to James and Husserl. *Journal of the History of Philosophy* 47: 277–307.

Andrews, K. 2015. *The Animal Mind: An Introduction to the Philosophy of Animal Cognition*. New York: Routledge.

Anton, A. 2013. The Virtue of Psychopathy: How to Appreciate the Neurodiversity of Psychopaths and Sociopaths Without Becoming A Victim. In *Ethics and Neurodiversity*. Newcastle: Cambridge Scholars Publishing.

Armstrong, D. 1968. *A Materialist Theory of Mind*. London: Routledge and Kegan Paul.

Armstrong, D. 1981. What is Consciousness? In *The Nature of Mind*. Ithaca, NY: Cornell University Press.

Arpaly, N. 2002. Moral Worth. *Journal of Philosophy* 99: 223–245.

Augustine, K. 2015. Near-Death Experiences are Hallucinations. In Martin and Augustine 2015.

Baars, B. 1988. *A Cognitive Theory of Consciousness*. Cambridge, MA: Cambridge University Press.

Baars, B. 1997. *In The Theater of Consciousness*. New York: Oxford University Press.

Baars, B. 2005. Subjective Experience is Probably not Limited to Humans: The Evidence from Neurobiology and Behavior. *Consciousness and Cognition* 14: 7–21.

Baars, B. and Gage, N. 2010. *Cognition, Brain, and Consciousness: Introduction to Cognitive Neuroscience*, 2nd edition. Oxford: Elsevier.

Baars, B., Banks, W., and Newman, J. eds. 2003. *Essential Sources in the Scientific Study of Consciousness*. Cambridge, MA: MIT Press.

Babiak, P., Neumann, C., and Hare, R. 2010. Corporate Psychopathy: Talking the Walk. *Behavioral Sciences and the Law* 28: 174–193.

Baker, L. 1987. *Saving Belief*. Princeton, NJ: Princeton University Press.

Balog, K. 1999. Conceivability, Possibility, and the Mind-Body Problem. *Philosophical Review* 108: 497–528.

Baron-Cohen, S. 1995. *Mindblindness*. Cambridge, MA: MIT Press.

Barrett, D. 2014. Consciousness, Attention, and Working Memory: An Empirical Evaluation of Prinz's Theory of Consciousness. *Journal of Consciousness Studies* 21 (9–10): 7–29.

Baumeister, R., Mele, A., and Vohs, K. 2010. *Free Will and Consciousness: How Might they Work?* New York: Oxford University Press.

Bayne, T. 2004. Self-Consciousness and the Unity of Consciousness. *The Monist* 87: 219–236.

Bayne, T. 2008. The Unity of Consciousness and the Split-Brain Syndrome. *The Journal of Philosophy* 105: 277–300.

Bayne, T. 2010. *The Unity of Consciousness.* New York: Oxford University Press.

Bayne, T. and Chalmers, D. 2003. What is the Unity of Consciousness? In Cleeremans 2003.

Bayne, T. and Fernandez, J. eds. 2009. *Delusion and Self-Deception.* Abingdon: Psychology Press.

Bayne, T. and Pacherie, E. 2005. In Defence of the Doxastic Conception of Delusion. *Mind and Language* 20: 163–188.

Bayne, T., Cleeremans, A., and Wilken, P. eds. 2009. *Oxford Companion to Consciousness.* New York: Oxford University Press.

Beck, F. and Eccles, J. 1992. Quantum Aspects of Brain Activity and the Role of Consciousness. *Proceedings of the National Academy of Sciences of the USA* 89: 11357–11361.

Bekoff, M., Allen, C., and Burghardt, G. eds. 2002. *The Cognitive Animal: Empirical and Theoretical Perspectives on Animal Cognition.* Cambridge, MA: MIT Press.

Bennett, D. and Hill, C. eds. 2014. *Sensory Integration and the Unity of Consciousness.* Cambridge, MA: MIT Press.

Bentall, R. 2004. Sideshow? Schizophrenia Construed by Szasz and the neoKrapelinians. In J. A. Schaler ed. *Szasz under Fire: The Psychiatric Abolitionist Faces His Critics.* Peru, IL: Open Court.

Beran, M., Brandl, J., Perner, J., and Proust, J. eds. 2012. *Foundations of Metacognition.* New York: Oxford University Press.

Beshkar, M. 2008. Animal Consciousness. *Journal of Consciousness Studies* 15 (3): 5–33.

Bickle, J. 2003. *Philosophy and Neuroscience: A Ruthlessly Reductive Account.* Berlin: Kluwer.

Billon, A. and Kriegel, U. 2015. Jaspers' Dilemma: The Psychopathological Challenge to Subjectivity Theories of Consciousness. In Gennaro 2015b.

Blackmore, S. 2012. *Consciousness: An Introduction, 2nd edition.* Oxford: Oxford University Press.

Blaney, P., Krueger, R., and Millon, T. eds. 2014. *Oxford Textbook of Psychopathology*, 3rd edition. Oxford: Oxford University Press.

Blanke, O. and Arzy, S. 2005. The Out-of-Body Experience: Disturbed Self-Processing at the Temporo-Parietal Junction. *Neuroscientist* 11: 16–24.

Blanke, O., Ortigue, S., Spinelli, L., and Seeck, M. 2004. Out-of-Body Experience and Autoscopy of Neurological Origin. *Brain* 127: 243–258.

Block, N. 1980. Are Absent Qualia Impossible? *Philosophical Review* 89: 257–274.

Block, N. 1990. Inverted Earth. In J. Tomberlin ed. *Philosophical Perspectives*, 4 Atascadero, CA: Ridgeview Publishing Company.

Block, N. 1995. On a Confusion about the Function of Consciousness. *Behavioral and Brain Sciences* 18: 227–247.

Block, N. 1996. Mental Paint and Mental Latex. *Philosophical Issues* 7: 19–49.

Block, N. 2005. Review of Alva Noe's *Action in Perception. Journal of Philosophy* 102: 259–272.

Block, N. 2007. Consciousness, Accessibility, and the Mesh between Psychology and Neuroscience. *Behavioral and Brain Sciences* 30: 481–499.

Block, N. 2011. The Higher Order Approach to Consciousness is Defunct. *Analysis* 71: 419–431.

Block, N. and Stalnaker, R. 1999. Conceptual Analysis, Dualism, and the Explanatory Gap. *Philosophical Review* 108: 1–46.

Block, N., Flanagan, O., and Güzeldere, G. eds. 1997. *The Nature of Consciousness*. Cambridge, MA: MIT Press.

Boden, M. 1988. Escaping From the Chinese Room. In J. Heil ed. *Computer Models of Mind*. Cambridge: Cambridge University Press.

Bolton, D. 2008. *What is Mental Disorder?* Oxford: Oxford University Press.

Bortolotti, L. 2009. *Delusions and Other Irrational Beliefs*. New York: Oxford University Press.

Bortolotti, L. 2013. Delusion. *The Stanford Encyclopedia of Philosophy (Winter 2013 Edition)*. Edward N. Zalta ed. Available at http://plato.stanford.edu/archives/win2013/entries/delusion/

Bortolotti, L. and Broome, M. 2009. A Role for Ownership and Authorship in the Analysis of Thought Insertion. *Phenomenology and the Cognitive Sciences* 8: 205–224.

Botterell, A. 2001. Conceiving What is Not There. *Journal of Consciousness Studies* 8 (8): 21–42.

Bottini, G., Bisiach, E., Sterzi, R., and Vallar, G. 2002. Feeling Touches in Someone Else's Hand. *NeuroReport* 13: 249–252.

Boucher, J. 2001. "Lost in a Sea of Time": Time-Parsing and Autism. In C. Hoerl and T. McCormack eds. *Time and Memory*. New York: Oxford University Press.

Boyd, R. 1980. Materialism Without Reductionism: What Physicalism Does Not Entail. In N. Block ed. *Readings in the Philosophy of Psychology, Volume 1*. Cambridge, MA: Harvard University Press.

Breen, N., Caine, D., Coltheart, M., Hendy, J., and Roberts, C. 2000. Towards an Understanding of Delusions of Misidentification: Four Case Studies. *Mind and Language* 15: 74–110.

Brentano, F. 1874/1973. *Psychology From an Empirical Standpoint*. New York: Humanities.

Brewer, B. 1999. *Perception and Reason*. Oxford: Oxford University Press.

Brewer, B. 2005. Do Sense Experiential States have Conceptual Content? In E. Sosa and M. Steup eds. *Contemporary Debates in Epistemology*. Oxford: Blackwell.

Broadbent, D. 1958. *Perception and Communication*. London: Pergamon Press.

Brink, D. and Nelkin, D. 2013. Fairness and the Architecture of Responsibility. In D. Shoemaker ed. *Oxford Studies in Agency and Responsibility*, volume 1. New York: Oxford University Press.

Brook, A. 1994. *Kant and the Mind*. New York: Cambridge University Press.

Brook, A. 2005. Kant, Cognitive Science, and Contemporary neo-Kantianism. *Journal of Consciousness Studies* 11 (10–11): 1–25.

Brook, A. 2015. Disorders of Unified Consciousness: Brain Bisection and Dissociative Identity Disorder. In Gennaro 2015b.

Brooks, R. 1991. Intelligence Without Representation. *Artificial Intelligence* 47: 139–159.

Broome, M. and Bortolotti, L. eds. 2009. *Psychiatry as Cognitive Neuroscience: Philosophical Perspectives*. New York: Oxford University Press.

Browne, D. 2004. Do Dolphins Know Their Own Minds? *Biology and Philosophy* 19: 633–653.

Brugger, E. 2012. The Problem of Fetal Pain and Abortion: Toward an Ethical Consensus for Appropriate Behavior. *Kennedy Institute of Ethics Journal* 22: 263–287.

Bullier, J. 2001. Feedback Connections and Conscious Vision. *Trends in Cognitive Sciences* 9: 369–370.

Byrne, A. 1997. Some like it HOT: Consciousness and Higher-Order Thoughts. *Philosophical Studies* 86: 103–129.

Byrne, A. 2001. Intentionalism Defended. *Philosophical Review* 110: 199–240.

Byrne, A. 2004. What Phenomenal Consciousness is Like. In Gennaro 2004a.

Byrne, A. 2005. Perception and Conceptual Content. In E. Sosa and M. Steup eds. *Contemporary Debates in Epistemology*. Oxford: Blackwell.

Byrne, R. and Whiten, A. 1988. *Machiavellian Intelligence: Social Expertise and the Evolution of Intellect in Monkeys, Apes, and Humans*. New York: Oxford University Press.

Carruthers, P. 1989. Brute Experience. *Journal of Philosophy* 86: 258–269.

Carruthers, P. 1996. Autism as Mindblindness: An Elaboration and Partial Defence. In P. Carruthers, and P. Smith eds. 1996. *Theories of Theories of Mind*. New York: Cambridge University Press.

Carruthers, P. 1999. Sympathy and Subjectivity. *Australasian Journal of Philosophy* 77: 465–482.

Carruthers, P. 2000. *Phenomenal Consciousness*. Cambridge: Cambridge University Press.

Carruthers, P. 2004. HOP over FOR, HOT Theory. In Gennaro 2004a.

Carruthers, P. 2005. *Consciousness: Essays from a Higher-Order Perspective*. New York: Oxford University Press.

Carruthers, P. 2008. Meta-Cognition in Animals: A Skeptical Look. *Mind and Language* 23: 58–89.

Carruthers, P. 2009. How We Know Our Own Minds: The Relationship Between Mindreading and Metacognition. *Behavioral and Brain Sciences* 32: 121–138.

Carruthers, P. and Veillet, B. 2007. The Phenomenal Concept Strategy. In Gennaro 2007.

Caruso, G. 2012. *Free Will and Consciousness: A Determinist Account of the Illusion of Free Will*. Lanham, MD: Lexington Books.

Caston, V. 2002. Aristotle on Consciousness. *Mind* 111: 751–815.

Chalmers, D. 1993. Connectionism and Compositionality: Why Fodor and Pylyshyn Were Wrong. *Philosophical Psychology* 6: 305–319.

Chalmers, D. 1995. Facing Up to the Problem of Consciousness. *Journal of Consciousness Studies* 2: 200–219.

Chalmers, D. 1996. *The Conscious Mind*. Oxford: Oxford University Press.

Chalmers, D. 1999. Materialism and the Metaphysics of Modality. *Philosophy and Phenomenological Research* 59: 473–497.

Chalmers, D. 2000. What is a Neural Correlate of Consciousness? In Metzinger 2000.

Chalmers, D. ed. 2002. *Philosophy of Mind: Classical and Contemporary Readings*. New York: Oxford University Press.

Chalmers, D. 2004. The Representational Character of Experience. In B. Leiter ed. *The Future for Philosophy*. Oxford: Oxford University Press.

Chalmers, D. 2007. Phenomenal Concepts and the Explanatory Gap. In Alter and Walter 2007.

Chalmers, D. 2010a. *The Character of Consciousness*. New York: Oxford University Press.

Chalmers, D. 2010b. The Singularity: A Philosophical Analysis. *Journal of Consciousness Studies* 14 (9–10): 7–65.

Chalmers, D. 2012. The Singularity: A Reply to Commentators. *Journal of Consciousness Studies* 16 (7–8): 141–167.

Chalmers, D. 2016. The Combination Problem for Panpsychism. In G. Bruntrup and L. Jaskolla eds. *Panpsychism*. New York: Oxford University Press.

Chalmers, D. and Jackson, F. 2001. Conceptual Analysis and Reductive Explanation. *Philosophical Review* 110: 315–361.

Chella, A. and Manzotti, R. 2009. Machine Consciousness: A Manifesto for Robotics. *International Journal of Machine Consciousness* 1: 33–51.

Chuard, P. 2006. Demonstrative Concepts without Re-Identification. *Philosophical Studies* 130: 153–201.

Chuard, P. 2007. The Riches of Experience. In Gennaro 2007.

Chudnoff, E. 2015. *Cognitive Phenomenology*. New York: Routledge.

Churchland, P. M. 1981. Eliminative Materialism and the Propositional Attitudes. *Journal of Philosophy* 78: 67–90.

Churchland, P. M. 1985. Reduction, Qualia, and the Direct Introspection of Brain States. *Journal of Philosophy* 82: 8–28.

Churchland, P. M. 2013. *Matter and Consciousness*, 3rd edition. Cambridge, MA: MIT Press.

Churchland, P. M. and Churchland, P. S. 1990. Could a Machine Think? *Scientific American* 262: 32–37.

Churchland, P. S. 1986. *Neurophilosophy*. Cambridge, MA: MIT Press.

Churchland, P. S. 1996. The Hornswoggle Problem. *Journal of Consciousness Studies* 3 (5–6): 402–408.

Churchland, P. S. 2002. *Brain-Wise*. Cambridge, MA: MIT Press.

Churchland, P. S. 2011. *Braintrust: What Neuroscience Tells Us about Morality*. Princeton, NJ: Princeton University Press.

Churchland, P. S. 2013. *Touching a Nerve*. New York: W.W. Norton.

Clark, A. 2001. Visual Experience and Motor Action: Are the Bonds Too Tight? *The Philosophical Review* 110: 495–519.

Clark, A. 2008. *Supersizing the Mind*. New York: Oxford University Press.

Clark, A. and Chalmers, D. 1998. The Extended Mind. *Analysis* 58: 7–19.

Clark, A., Kiverstein, J., and Vierkant, T. eds. 2013. *Decomposing the Will*. New York: Oxford University Press.

Clayton, N., Bussey, T., and Dickinson, A. 2003. Can Animals Recall the Past and Plan for the Future? *Nature Reviews Neuroscience* 4: 685–691.

Clayton, N., Emery, N., and Dickinson, A. 2006. The Rationality of Animal Memory: Complex Caching Strategies of Western Scrub Jays. In Hurley and Nudds 2006.

Cleeremans, A. ed. 2003. *The Unity of Consciousness: Binding, Integration and Dissociation*. Oxford: Oxford University Press.

Coleman, S. 2015. Quotational Higher-Order Thought Theory. *Philosophical Studies* 172: 2705–2733.

Cooper, R. 2007. *Psychiatry and Philosophy of Science*. London: Acumen.

Copeland, J. 1993. *Artificial Intelligence: A Philosophical Introduction*. Cambridge, MA: Blackwell.

Coseru, C. 2012. *Perceiving Reality: Consciousness, Intentionality, and Cognition in Buddhist Philosophy*. New York: Oxford University Press.

Crick, F. 1994. *The Astonishing Hypothesis: The Scientific Search for the Soul*. New York: Scribners.

Crick, F. and Koch, C. 1990. Toward a Neurobiological Theory of Consciousness. *Seminars in Neuroscience* 2: 263–275.

Crick, F. and Koch, C. 2003. A Framework for Consciousness. *Nature Neuroscience* 6: 119–126.

Cullen, F. and Agnew, R. eds. 2011. *Criminology Theory: Past to Present, 4th edition*. New York: Oxford University Press.

Cytowic, R. 2003. *The Man Who Tasted Shapes*. Cambridge, MA: MIT Press.

Dainton, B. 2000. *Stream of Consciousness*. New York and London: Routledge.

Dainton, B. 2007. Coming Together: The Unity of Conscious Experience. In Velmans and Schneider 2007.

Dainton, B. 2008. *The Phenomenal Self*. New York: Oxford University Press.

Dainton, B. 2010. "Temporal Consciousness". *The Stanford Encyclopedia of Philosophy (Spring 2014 edition)*. Edward N. Zalta ed. Available at http://plato.stanford.edu/archives/spr2014/entries/consciousness-temporal/

Damasio, A. 1994. *Descartes' Error: Emotion, Reason, and the Human Brain*. Mahopac, NY: Putnam.

Damasio, A. 1999. *The Feeling of What Happens*. New York: Harcourt.

Davies, M. and Coltheart, M. 2000. Introduction: Pathologies of Belief. *Mind and Language* 15: 1–46.

de Gardelle, V., Sackur, J., and Kouider, S. 2009. Perceptual Illusions in Brief Visual Presentations. *Consciousness and Cognition* 18: 569–577.

DeGrazia, D. 2009. Self-Awareness in Animals. In Lurz 2009.

Dehaene, S. 2014. *Consciousness and the Brain*. New York: Viking.

Dehaene, S. and Changeux, J. 2011. Experimental and Theoretical Approaches to Conscious Processing. *Neuron* 70: 200–227.

Dehaene, S. and Naccache, L. 2001. Towards a Cognitive Neuroscience of Consciousness: Basic Evidence and a Workspace Framework. *Cognition* 79: 1–37.

Dehaene, S., Changeux, J., Nacchache, L., Sackut, J., and Sergent, C. 2006. Conscious, Preconscious, and Subliminal Processing: A Testable Taxonomy. *Trends in Cognitive Science* 10: 204–211.

Del Cul, A., Baillet, S., and Dehaene, S. 2007. Brain Dynamics Underlying the Nonlinear Threshold for Access to Consciousness. *PLOS Biology* 5: 2408–2423.

Dennett, D. 1978. *Brainstorms*. Cambridge, MA: MIT Press.

Dennett, D. 1987. *The Intentional Stance*. Cambridge, MA: MIT Press.

Dennett, D. 1988. Quining Qualia. In A. Marcel and E. Bisiach eds. *Consciousness and Contemporary Science*. New York: Oxford University Press.

Dennett, D. 1991. *Consciousness Explained*. Boston: Little, Brown, and Co.

Dennett, D. 2003. *Freedom Evolves*. New York: Penguin.

Dennett, D. 2005. *Sweet Dreams*. Cambridge, MA: MIT Press.

Dennett, D. and Kinsbourne, M. 1992. Time and the Observer: The Where and When of Consciousness in the Brain. *Behavioral and Brain Sciences* 15: 183–201.

DeQuincey, C. 2006. Switched-On Consciousness. *Journal of Consciousness Studies* 13 (4): 7–12.

Dere, E., Kart-Teke, E., Huston, J., and Silva, D. 2006. The Case for Episodic Memory in Animals. *Neuroscience and Biobehavioral Reviews* 30: 1206–1224.

Descartes, R. 1641/1993. *Meditations on First Philosophy*. Indianapolis: Hackett.

de Vignemont, F. 2010. Body Schema and Body Image – Pros and Cons. *Neuropsychologia* 48: 669–680.

Dolan, M. and Fullam, R. 2010. Moral/Conventional Transgression Distinction and Psychopathy in Conduct Disordered Adolescent Offenders. *Personality and Individual Differences* 49: 995–1000.

Dretske, F. 1993. Conscious Experience. *Mind* 102: 263–283.

Dretske, F. 1995. *Naturalizing the Mind*. Cambridge, MA: MIT Press.

Dretske, F. 2004. Change Blindness. *Philosophical Studies* 120: 1–18.

Dretske, F. 2007. What Change Blindness Teaches About Consciousness. In J. Hawthorne ed. *Philosophical Perspectives: Philosophy of Mind (Vol. 21)*. Malden, MA: Blackwell.

Droege, P. 2003. *Caging the Beast*. Philadelphia and Amsterdam: John Benjamins Publishers.

Droege, P. 2015. From Darwin to Freud: Confabulation as an Adaptive Response to Dysfunctions of Consciousness. In Gennaro 2015b.

Edelman, G. 1989. *The Remembered Present: A Biological Theory of Consciousness*. New York: Basic Books.

Edelman, G. and Seth, A. 2009. Animal Consciousness: A Synthetic Approach. *Trends in Neurosciences* 32: 476–484.

Edelman, G. and Tononi, G. 2000a. Reentry and the Dynamic Core: Neural Correlates of Conscious Experience. In Metzinger 2000.

Edelman, G. and Tononi, G. 2000b. *A Universe of Consciousness*. New York: Basic Books.

Edelman, G., Baars, B., and Seth, A. 2005. Identifying Hallmarks of Consciousness in Non-Mammalian Species. *Consciousness and Cognition* 14: 169–187.

Edwards, C. 2009. Ethical Decisions in the Classification of Mental Conditions as Mental Illness. *Philosophy, Psychiatry, and Psychology* 16: 73–90.

Eichenbaum, H., Fortin, N., Ergorul, C., Wright, S., and Agster, K. 2005. Episodic Recollection in Animals: "If it walks like a duck and quacks like a duck . . . " *Learning and Motivation* 36: 190–207.

Eilan, N., Hoerl, C., McCormack, T., and Roessler, J. eds. *Joint Attention: Communication and Other Minds*. New York: Oxford University Press.

Emery, N. and Clayton, N. 2001. Effects of Experience and Social Context on Prospective Caching Strategies in Scrub Jays. *Nature* 414: 443–446.

Emery, N. and Clayton, N. 2009. Comparative Social Cognition. *Annual Review of Psychology* 60: 87–113.

Evans, G. 1982. *Varieties of Reference*. New York: Oxford University Press.

Fahrenfort, J., Scholte, H., and Lamme, V. 2007. Masking Disrupts Reentrant Processing in Human Visual Cortex. *Journal of Cognitive Neuroscience* 19: 1488–1497.

Farah, M. 2004. *Visual Agnosia*, 2nd edition. Cambridge, MA: The MIT Press.

Farah, M. ed. 2010. *Neuroethics: An Introduction with Readings*. Cambridge, MA: The MIT Press.

Feinberg, T. 2000. The Nested Hierarchy of Consciousness: A Neurobiological Solution to the Problem of Mental Unity. *Neurocase* 6: 75–81.

Feinberg, T. 2001. *Altered Egos: How the Brain Creates the Self.* New York: Oxford University Press.

Feinberg, T. 2009. *From Axons to Identity: Neurological Explorations of the Nature of the Self.* New York: W.W. Norton and Company.

Feinberg, T. 2011. Neuropathologies of the Self: Clinical and Anatomical Features. *Consciousness and Cognition* 20: 75–81.

Feinberg, T. and Keenan, J. eds. 2005. *The Lost Self: Pathologies of the Brain and Identity.* New York: Oxford University Press.

Fischer, J. and Ravizza, M. 1998. *Responsibility and Control: A Theory of Moral Responsibility.* New York: Cambridge University Press.

Fitzpatrick, S. 2008. Doing Away with Morgan's Canon. *Mind and Language* 23: 224–246.

Fitzpatrick, S. 2009. The Primate Mindreading Controversy: A Case Study in Simplicity and Methodology in Animal Psychology. In Lurz 2009.

Flanagan, O. 1992. *Consciousness Reconsidered.* Cambridge, MA: MIT Press.

Flohr, H. 1995. An Information Processing Theory of Anaesthesia. *Neuropsychologia* 33: 1169–1180.

Flohr, H. 2000. NMDA Receptor-Mediated Computational Processes and Phenomenal Consciousness. In Metzinger 2000.

Flombaum, J. and Santos, L. 2005. Rhesus Monkeys Attribute Perceptions to Others. *Current Biology* 15: 447–452.

Fodor, J. 1974. Special Sciences. *Synthese* 28: 77–115.

Fodor, J. 1983. *Modularity of Mind.* Cambridge, MA: MIT Press.

Fodor, J. and Pylyshyn, Z. 1988. Connectionism and Cognitive Architecture: A Critical Analysis. *Cognition* 28: 3–71.

Ford, J. and Smith, D. W. 2006. Consciousness, Self, and Attention. In Kriegel and Williford 2006.

Foster J. 1996. *The Immaterial Self: A Defence of the Cartesian Dualist Conception of Mind.* London: Routledge.

Frankfurt, H. 1969. Alternate Possibilities and Moral Responsibility. *Journal of Philosophy* 66: 829–839.

Frankfurt, H. 1971. Freedom of the Will and the Concept of a Person. *Journal of Philosophy* 68: 5–20.

Frith, C. 1992. *The Cognitive Neuropsychology of Schizophrenia.* Abingdon: Psychology Press.

Frith, C. and Happé, F. 1999. Theory of Mind and Self-Consciousness: What is it Like to be Autistic? *Mind and Language* 14: 1–22.

Frith, C. and Hill, E. eds. 2003. *Autism: Mind and Brain*. New York: Oxford University Press.

Fuchs, T. 2013. Temporality and Psychopathology. *Phenomenology and the Cognitive Sciences* 12: 75–104.

Fulford, K., Thornton, T., and Graham, G. eds. 2006. *Oxford Textbook of Philosophy and Psychiatry*. Oxford: Oxford University Press.

Fulford, K., Davies, M., Gipps, R., Graham, G., Sadler, J., Stanghellini, G., and Thornton, T. 2013. *The Oxford Handbook of Philosophy and Psychiatry*. New York: Oxford University Press.

Gallagher, S. 2000. Philosophical Conceptions of the Self. *Trends in Cognitive Sciences* 4: 14–21.

Gallagher, S. 2004. Agency, Ownership, and Alien Control in Schizophrenia. In D. Zahavi, T. Grunbaum, and J. Parnas eds. *The Structure and Development of Self-Consciousness: Interdisciplinary Perspectives*. Amsterdam: John Benjamins.

Gallup, G. 1970. Chimpanzees: Self-Recognition. *Science* 167: 86–87.

Gazzaniga, M. 1992. Brain Modules and Belief Formation. In F. Kessel, P. M. Cole, and D. L. Johnson eds. *Self and Consciousness: Multiple Perspectives*. Mahwah, NJ: Lawrence Erlbaum.

Gazzaniga, M. ed. 2000. *The New Cognitive Neurosciences*. Cambridge, MA: The MIT Press.

Gendler, T. and Hawthorne, J. eds. 2002. *Conceivability and Possibility*. New York: Oxford University Press.

Gendler, T. and Hawthorne, J. eds. 2006. *Perceptual Experience*. New York: Oxford University Press.

Gennaro, R. 1992. Consciousness, Self-Consciousness, and Episodic Memory. *Philosophical Psychology* 5: 333–347.

Gennaro, R. 1993. Brute Experience and the Higher-Order Thought Theory of Consciousness. *Philosophical Papers* 22: 51–69.

Gennaro, R. 1995. Does Mentality Entail Consciousness? *Philosophia* 24: 331–358.

Gennaro, R. 1996. *Consciousness and Self-Consciousness: A Defense of the Higher-Order Thought Theory of Consciousness*. Amsterdam and Philadelphia: John Benjamins.

Gennaro, R. 1999. Leibniz on Consciousness and Self-Consciousness. In R. Gennaro and C. Huenemann eds. *New Essays on the Rationalists*. New York: Oxford University Press.

Gennaro, R. 2002. Jean-Paul Sartre and the HOT Theory of Consciousness. *Canadian Journal of Philosophy* 32: 293–330.

Gennaro, R. ed. 2004a. *Higher-Order Theories of Consciousness: An Anthology.* Amsterdam and Philadelphia: John Benjamins.

Gennaro, R. 2004b. Higher-Order Thoughts, Animal Consciousness, and Misrepresentation: A Reply to Carruthers and Levine. In Gennaro 2004a.

Gennaro, R. 2005. The HOT Theory of Consciousness: Between a Rock and a Hard Place? *Journal of Consciousness Studies* 12 (2): 3–21.

Gennaro, R. 2006. Between Pure Self-Referentialism and the (Extrinsic) HOT Theory of Consciousness. In U. Kriegel and K. Williford eds. *Self-Representational Approaches to Consciousness.* Cambridge, MA: MIT Press.

Gennaro, R. ed. 2007. *The Interplay Between Consciousness and Concepts.* Exeter: Imprint Academic. [This is also a special double issue of the *Journal of Consciousness Studies* 14 (9–10).]

Gennaro, R. 2008a. Representationalism, Peripheral Awareness, and the Transparency of Experience. *Philosophical Studies* 139: 39–56.

Gennaro, R. 2008b. Are There Pure Conscious Events? In C. Chakrabarti and G. Haist eds. *Revisiting Mysticism.* Newcastle: Cambridge Scholars Press.

Gennaro, R. 2009. Animals, Consciousness, and I-Thoughts. In R. Lurz ed. *Philosophy of Animal Minds.* New York: Cambridge University Press.

Gennaro, R. 2012. *The Consciousness Paradox: Consciousness, Concepts, and Higher-Order Thoughts.* Cambridge, MA: The MIT Press.

Gennaro, R. 2013. Defending HOT Theory and the Wide Intrinsicality View: A Reply to Weisberg, Van Gulick, and Seager. *Journal of Consciousness Studies* 20 (11-12): 82–100.

Gennaro, R. 2014, revised. Consciousness. *Internet Encyclopedia of Philosophy.* Available at http://www.iep.utm.edu/consciou/

Gennaro, R. 2015a. The 'of' of Intentionality and the 'of' of Acquaintance. In S. Miguens, G. Preyer, and C. Morando eds. *Pre-Reflective Consciousness: Sartre and Contemporary Philosophy of Mind.* New York: Routledge Publishers.

Gennaro, R. ed. 2015b. *Disturbed Consciousness: New Essays on Psychopathology and Theories of Consciousness.* Cambridge, MA: The MIT Press.

Gennaro, R. 2015c. Somatoparaphrenia, Anosognosia, and Higher-Order Thoughts. In Gennaro 2015b.

Gennaro, R. and Fishman, Y. 2015. The Argument from Brain Damage Vindicated. In Martin and Augustine 2015.

Gennaro, R., Herrmann, D., and Sarapata, M. 2006. Aspects of the Unity of Consciousness and Everyday Memory Failures. *Consciousness and Cognition* 15: 372–385.

Georgalis, N. 2006. *The Primacy of the Subjective*. Cambridge, MA: MIT Press.

Gerken, M. 2008. Is There a Simple Argument for Higher-Order Representation Theories of Awareness Consciousness? *Erkenntnis* 69: 243–259.

Gertler, B. 2002. Explanatory Reduction, Conceptual Analysis, and Conceivability Arguments about the Mind. *Nous* 36: 22–49.

Gertler, B. 2012. In Defense of Mind-Body Dualism. In Alter and Howell 2012.

Gibson, J. J. 1979. *The Ecological Approach to Visual Perception*. Boston: Houghton Mifflin.

Glannon, W. 2008. Moral Responsibility and the Psychopath. *Neuroethics* 1: 158–166.

Goff, P. 2006. Experiences Don't Sum. *Journal of Consciousness Studies* 13 (10–11): 53–61.

Goff, P. 2009. Why Panpsychism Doesn't Help Us Explain Consciousness. *Dialectica* 63: 289–311.

Goldberg, I., Harel, M., and Malach, R. 2006. When the Brain Loses Its Self: Prefrontal Inactivation during Sensorimotor Processing. *Neuron* 50: 329–339.

Goldman, A. 1993. Consciousness, Folk Psychology and Cognitive Science. *Consciousness and Cognition* 2: 264–282.

Goldman, A. 2006. *Simulating Minds*. New York: Oxford University Press.

Goodale, M. 2007. Duplex Vision: Separate Cortical Pathways for Conscious Perception and the Control of Action. In Velmans and Schneider 2007.

Graham, G. 2013. *The Disordered Mind: An Introduction into Philosophy of Mind and Mental Illness*, 2nd edition. London: Routledge.

Graham, G. and Stephens, G. L. eds. 1994. *Philosophical Psychopathology*. Cambridge, MA: MIT Press.

Graham, G. and Stephens, G. L. 2000. *When Self-Consciousness Breaks*. Cambridge, MA: MIT Press.

Graham, G., Horgan, T., and Tienson, J. 2007. Consciousness and Intentionality. In Velmans and Schneider 2007.

Graziano, M. 2013. *Consciousness and the Social Brain*. New York: Oxford University Press.

Greenspan, P. 2003. Responsible Psychopaths. *Philosophical Psychology* 16: 417–429.

Griffin, D. and Speck, G. 2004. New Evidence of Animal Consciousness. *Animal Cognition* 7: 5–18.

Grill-Spector, K. and Malach, R. 2004. The Human Visual Cortex. *Annual Review of Neuroscience* 7: 649–677.

Grossenbacher, P. ed. 2001. *Finding Consciousness in the Brain*. Amsterdam and Philadelphia: John Benjamins.

Grossenbacher, P. and Lovelace, C. 2001. Mechanisms of Synesthesia: Cognitive and Physiological Constraints. *Trends in Cognitive Science* 5: 36–41.

Gunther, Y. ed. 2003. *Essays on Nonconceptual Content*. Cambridge, MA: MIT Press.

Haikonen, P. 2013. Consciousness and Sentient Robots. *International Journal of Machine Consciousness* 5: 11–26.

Hameroff, S. and Penrose, R. 1996. Conscious Events as Orchestrated Spacetime Selections. *Journal of Consciousness Studies* 3 (1): 36–53.

Hameroff, S. and Penrose, R. 2014. Consciousness in the Universe: A Review of the Orch OR Theory (with commentaries and replies). *Physics of Life Reviews* 11: 39–112.

Hameroff, S., Pylkkanen, P., and Gennaro, R. 2014. From HOT to DOT: A "Deeper-Order Thought" Theory of Consciousness. In D. Chopra ed. *Brain, Mind, Cosmos: The Nature of our Existence and the Universe*. Trident Media Group, Ebook, August 2014.

Hampton, R. 2005. Can Rhesus Monkeys Discriminate Between Remembering and Forgetting? In Terrace and Metcalfe 2005.

Hardcastle, V. 2000. *The Myth of Pain*. Cambridge, MA: MIT Press.

Hardcastle, V. 2004. HOT Theories of Consciousness: More Sad Tales of Philosophical Intuitions Gone Astray. In Gennaro 2004a.

Hare, B. and Tomasello, M. 2004. Chimpanzees are More Skilled in Competitive Than in Cooperative Cognitive Tasks. *Animal Behavior* 68: 571–581.

Hare, B., Call, J., Agnetta, B., and Tomasello, M. 2000. Chimpanzees Know What Conspecifics Do and Do Not See. *Animal Behavior* 59: 771–785.

Hare, B., Call, J., and Tomasello, M. 2001. Do Chimpanzees Know What Conspecifics Know? *Animal Behavior* 61: 139–151.

Hare, R. D. 2003. *The Hare Psychopathy Checklist-Revised*, 2nd edition. Toronto: Multi-Health Systems.

Harman, G. 1990. The Intrinsic Quality of Experience. In J. Tomberlin ed. *Philosophical Perspectives* 4. Atascadero, CA: Ridgeview Publishing.

Haugeland, J. 1985. *Artificial Intelligence: The Very Idea*. Cambridge, MA: MIT Press.

Hawthorne, J. 1989. On the Compatibility of Connectionist and Classical Models. *Philosophical Psychology* 2: 5–15.

Heck, R. 2000. Non-Conceptual Content and the "Space of Reasons." *The Philosophical Review* 109: 483–523.

Heck, R. 2007. Are There Different Kinds of Content? In McLaughlin and
    Cohen 2007.
Heidegger, M. 1927/1962. *Being and Time (Sein und Zeit)*. Translated by
    J. Macquarrie and E. Robinson. New York: Harper and Row.
Hill, C. 1991. *Sensations*. Cambridge, MA: Cambridge University Press.
Hill, C. 1997. Imaginability, Conceivability, Possibility, and the Mind-Body
    Problem. *Philosophical Studies* 87: 61–85.
Hill, C. and McLaughlin, B. 1998. There are Fewer Things in Reality than are
    Dreamt of in Chalmers' Philosophy. *Philosophy and Phenomenological
    Research* 59: 445–454.
Hillier, A. and Allinson, L. 2002. Understanding Embarrassment Among Those with
    Autism: Breaking Down the Complex Emotion of Embarrassment Among
    Those with Autism. *Journal of Autism and Developmental Disorders* 32: 583–592.
Hirstein, W. 2005. *Brain Fiction: Self-Deception and the Riddle of Confabulation*.
    Cambridge, MA: MIT Press.
Hirstein, W. ed. 2009. *Confabulation: Views from Neuroscience, Psychiatry,
    Psychology, and Philosophy*. Oxford: Oxford University Press.
Hirstein, W. 2015. Consciousness Despite Network Underconnectivity in
    Autism: Another Case of Consciousness Without Prefrontal Activity? In
    Gennaro 2015b.
Hochstein, S. and Ahissar, M. 2002. View from the Top: Hierarchies and
    Reverse Hierarchies in the Visual System. *Neuron* 36: 791–804.
Hodgson, D. 2012. *Rationality + Consciousness = Free Will*. New York: Oxford
    University Press.
Hoerl, C. 2009. Time and Tense in Perceptual Experience. *Philosopher's Imprint*
    9: 1–18.
Hohwy, J. 2007. The Search for Neural Correlates of Consciousness. *Philosophy
    Compass* 2/3: 461–474.
Hohwy, J. 2009. The Neural Correlates of Consciousness: New Experimental
    Approaches Needed? *Consciousness and Cognition* 18: 428–438.
Horgan, T. 1984. Jackson on Physical Information and Qualia. *Philosophical
    Quarterly* 34: 147–152.
Horgan, T. and Tienson, J. 2002. The Intentionality of Phenomenology and the
    Phenomenology of Intentionality. In Chalmers 2002.
Humphreys, G. 2003. Conscious Visual Representations Built from Multiple
    Binding Processes: Evidence from Neuropsychology. In Cleeremans 2003.
Hurley, S. 2003. Action, the Unity of Consciousness, and Vehicle Externalism.
    In Cleeremans 2003.

Hurley, S. and Nudds, M. eds. 2006. *Rational Animals?* New York: Oxford University Press.

Husserl, E. 1913/1931. *Ideas: General Introduction to Pure Phenomenology (Ideen au einer reinen Phänomenologie und phänomenologischen Philosophie).* Translated by W. Boyce Gibson. New York: MacMillan.

Hutto, D. and Myin, E. 2012. *Radicalizing Enactivism.* Cambridge, MA: MIT Press.

Huxley, T. 1874. On the Hypothesis That Animals Are Automata, and its History. *Fortnightly Review* 95: 555–580.

Illes, J. and Sahakian, B. eds. 2011. *Oxford Handbook of Neuroethics.* Oxford: Oxford University Press.

Jackendoff, R. 1987. *Consciousness and the Computational Mind.* Cambridge, MA: MIT Press.

Jackson, F. 1982. Epiphenomenal Qualia. *Philosophical Quarterly* 32: 127–136.

Jackson, F. 1986. What Mary Didn't Know. *Journal of Philosophy* 83: 291–295.

Jackson, F. 1998. Postscript on Qualia. In F. Jackson, *Mind, Method, and Conditionals.* London: Routledge.

Jackson, F. 2004. Postscripts. In Ludlow, Nagasawa, and Stoljar 2004.

Jacoby, L., Lindsay, D., and Toth, J. 1992. Unconscious Influences Revealed: Attention, Awareness, and Control. *American Psychologist* 47: 802–809.

James, W. 1890. *The Principles of Psychology.* New York: Henry Holt & Company.

Janzen, G. 2008. *The Reflexive Nature of Consciousness.* Amsterdam and Philadelphia: John Benjamins.

Jeannerod, M. 2004. From Self-Recognition to Self-Consciousness. In Zahavi, Grünbaum, and Parnas 2004.

Jehle, D. and Kriegel, U. 2006. An Argument Against Dispositional HOT Theory. *Philosophical Psychology* 19: 462–476.

Jennings, C. 2015. Consciousness without Attention. *Journal of the American Philosophical Association* 1: 276–295.

Jiang, Y., Costello, P., Fang, F., Huang, M., He, S., and Purves, D. 2006. A Gender- and Sexual Orientation-Dependent Spatial Attentional Effect of Invisible Images. *Proceedings of the National Academy of Sciences* 1003: 17048–17052.

Jorgensen, L. 2010. "Seventeenth-Century Theories of Consciousness," *The Stanford Encyclopedia of Philosophy (Fall 2010 Edition)*, Edward N. Zalta ed. Available at http://plato.stanford.edu/archives/fall2010/entries/consciousness-17th/

Kane, R. ed. 2011. *Oxford Handbook on Free Will*, 2nd edition. New York: Oxford University Press.

Kant, I. 1781/1965. *Critique of Pure Reason.* Translated by N. Kemp Smith. New York: MacMillan.

Keenan, J., Gallup, G., and Falk, D. 2003. *The Face in the Mirror*. New York: HarperCollins.

Kelly, S. 2001a. Demonstrative Concepts and Experience. *The Philosophical Review* 110: 397–420.

Kelly, S. 2001b. The Non-Conceptual Content of Perceptual Experience: Situation Dependence and Fineness of Grain. *Philosophy and Phenomenological Research* 62: 601–608.

Kemeny, J. and Oppenheim, P. 1956. On Reduction. *Philosophical Studies* 7: 6–19.

Kennett, J. and Matthews, J. 2002. Identity, Control and Responsibility: The Case of Dissociative Identity Disorder. *Philosophical Psychology* 15: 509–526.

Kentridge, R. 2011. Attention without Awareness: A Brief Review. In Mole et al. 2011.

Kiehl, K. and Sinnott-Armstrong, W. eds. 2013. *Handbook on Psychopathy and the Law*. New York: Oxford University Press.

Kim, J. 1989. The Myth of Nonreductive Materialism. *Proceedings of the Addresses of the American Philosophical Association* 63: 31–47.

Kim, J. 1993. *Supervenience and Mind*. Cambridge, MA: Cambridge University Press.

Kim, J. 1999. *Mind in a Physical World*. Cambridge, MA: MIT Press.

Kincaid, H. and Sullivan, J. 2014. *Classifying Psychopathology: Mental Kinds and Natural Kinds*. Cambridge, MA: MIT Press.

Kind, A. 2003. What's so Transparent about Transparency? *Philosophical Studies* 115: 225–244.

Kind, A. 2008. Qualia. *Internet Encyclopedia of Philosophy*. Available at http://www.iep.utm.edu/qualia/

Kind, A. 2014. The Case Against Representationalism About Moods. In U. Kriegel ed. *Current Controversies in Philosophy of Mind*. New York: Routledge Press.

Kinsbourne, M. 2005. A Continuum of Self-Consciousness that Emerges in Phylogeny and Ontogeny. In Terrace and Metcalfe 2005.

Kircher, T. and Leube, D. 2003. Self-Consciousness, Self-Agency, and Schizophrenia. *Consciousness and Cognition* 12: 656–669.

Kirk, R. 1994. *Raw Feeling*. New York: Oxford University Press.

Kirk, R. 2005. *Zombies and Consciousness*. New York: Oxford University Press.

Kitcher, P. 1990. *Kant's Transcendental Psychology*. New York: Oxford University Press.

Kitcher, P. 2010. *Kant's Thinker*. New York: Oxford University Press.

Koch, C. 2004. *The Quest for Consciousness: A Neurobiological Approach*. Englewood, CO: Roberts and Company.

Koch, C. 2012. *Consciousness*. Cambridge, MA: MIT Press.

Koch, C. and Tsuchiya, N. 2007. Attention and Consciousness: Two Distinct Brain Processes. *Trends in Cognitive Sciences* 11: 16–22.

Koriat, A. 2007. Metacognition and Consciousness. In Zelazo, Moscovitch, and Thompson 2007.

Kouider, S. 2009. Neurobiological Theories of Consciousness. In W. Banks ed. *Encyclopedia of Consciousness*. Oxford: Elsevier.

Kouider, S. and Dehaene, S. 2007. Levels of Processing During Non-Conscious Perception: A Critical Review of Visual Masking. *Philosophical Transactions of the Royal Society* 362: 857–875.

Kozuch, B. 2014. Prefrontal Lesion Evidence Against Higher-Order Theories of Consciousness. *Philosophical Studies* 167: 721–746.

Kriegel, U. 2002. PANIC Theory and the Prospects for a Representational Theory of Phenomenal Consciousness. *Philosophical Psychology* 15: 55–64.

Kriegel, U. 2003a. Consciousness, Higher-Order Content, and the Individuation of Vehicles. *Synthese* 134: 477–504.

Kriegel, U. 2003b. Consciousness as Intransitive Self-Consciousness: Two Views and an Argument. *Canadian Journal of Philosophy* 33: 103–132.

Kriegel, U. 2004. Consciousness and Self-Consciousness. *Monist* 87: 182–205.

Kriegel, U. 2005. Naturalizing Subjective Character. *Philosophy and Phenomenological Research* 71: 23–56.

Kriegel, U. 2006. The Same Order Monitoring Theory of Consciousness. In U. Kriegel and K. Williford eds. *Self-Representational Approaches to Consciousness*. Cambridge, MA: MIT Press.

Kriegel, U. 2007. A Cross-Order Integration Hypothesis for the Neural Correlate of Consciousness. *Consciousness and Cognition* 16: 897–912.

Kriegel, U. 2009. *Subjective Consciousness*. New York: Oxford University Press.

Kriegel, U. 2013. *Phenomenal Intentionality*. New York: Oxford University Press.

Kriegel, U. and Williford, K. eds. 2006. *Self-Representational Approaches to Consciousness*. Cambridge, MA: MIT Press.

Kripke, S. 1972. *Naming and Necessity*. Cambridge, MA: Harvard University Press.

Kurzweil, R. 2005. *The Singularity is Near*. New York: Viking.

Lamme, V. 2003. Why Visual Attention and Awareness are Different. *Trends in Cognitive Science* 7: 12–18.

Lamme, V. 2004. Separate Neural Definitions of Visual Consciousness and Visual Attention: A Case for Phenomenal Awareness. *Neural Networks* 17: 861–872.

Lamme, V. and Roelfsema, P. 2000. The Distinct Modes of Vision Offered by Feedforward and Recurrent Processing. *Trends in Neuroscience* 23: 571–579.

Lane, T. 2015. Self, Belonging, and Conscious Experience: A Critique of Subjectivity Theories of Consciousness. In Gennaro 2015b.

Lane, T. and Liang, C. 2010. Mental Ownership and Higher-Order Thought. *Analysis* 70: 496–501.

Lau, H. and Passingham, R. 2006. Relative Blindsight in Normal Observers and the Neural Correlate of Visual Consciousness. *Proceedings of the National Academy of Sciences* 103: 18763–18768.

Leekam, S. 2005. Why Do Children with Autism have a Joint Attention Impairment? In Eilan, Hoerl, McCormack, and Roessler 2005.

Leibniz, G. W. 1686/1991. *Discourse on Metaphysics.* Translated by D. Garber and R. Ariew. Indianapolis: Hackett.

Leibniz, G. W. 1720/1925. *The Monadology.* Translated by R. Lotte. London: Oxford University Press.

Le Poidevin, R. 2000. "The Experience and Perception of Time". *The Stanford Encyclopedia of Philosophy (Winter 2009 Edition).* Edward N. Zalta ed. Available at http://plato.stanford.edu/archives/win2009/entries/time-experience/

Levin, D. 2002. Change Blindness as Visual Metacognition. *Journal of Consciousness Studies* 9 (5–6): 111–130.

Levin, J. 1985. Functionalism and the Argument from Conceivability. *Canadian Journal of Philosophy* 11: 85–104.

Levine, J. 1983. Materialism and Qualia: The Explanatory Gap. *Pacific Philosophical Quarterly* 64: 354–361.

Levine, J. 2001. *Purple Haze: The Puzzle of Conscious Experience.* Cambridge, MA: MIT Press.

Levy, N. 2011. *Hard Luck: How Luck Undermines Free Will and Moral Responsibility.* New York: Oxford University Press.

Levy, N. 2014. *Consciousness and Moral Responsibility.* New York: Oxford University Press.

Levy, N. and Savulescu, J. 2009. Moral Significance of Phenomenal Consciousness. *Progress in Brain Research* 177: 361–370.

Lewis, D. 1983. Postscript to Mad Pain and Martian Pain. In D. Lewis ed. *Philosophical Papers,* volume 1. New York: Oxford University Press.

Lewis, D. 1988. What Experience Teaches. In the *Proceedings of Russellian Society, University of Sydney.* Reprinted in Block, Flanagan, and Güzeldere 1997.

Liang, L. and Lane, T. 2009. Higher-Order Thought and Pathological Self: The Case of Somatoparaphrenia. *Analysis* 69: 661–668.

Libet, B. 1985. Unconscious Cerebral Initiative and the Role of Conscious Will in Voluntary Action. *Behavioral and Brain Sciences* 8: 529–566.

Libet, B. 1999. Do We Have Free Will? *Journal of Consciousness Studies* 6 (8–9): 47–57.

Llinas, R. 2001. Consciousness and the Brain: The Thalamocortical Dialogue in Health and Disease. *Annals of the New York Academy of Sciences* 929: 166–175.

Loar, B. 1997. Phenomenal States. In Block, Flanagan, and Güzeldere 1997.

Loar, B. 1999. David Chalmers's *The Conscious Mind*. *Philosophy and Phenomenological Research* 59: 465–472.

Locke, J. 1689/1975. *An Essay Concerning Human Understanding*. P. Nidditch ed. Oxford: Clarendon.

Ludlow, P., Nagasawa, Y., and Stoljar, D. eds. 2004. *There's Something about Mary*. Cambridge, MA: MIT Press.

Lurz, R. ed. 2009. *The Philosophy of Animal Minds*. Cambridge, MA: Cambridge University Press.

Lurz, R. 2011. *Mindreading Animals*. Cambridge, MA: MIT Press.

Lycan, W. 1996. *Consciousness and Experience*. Cambridge, MA: MIT Press.

Lycan, W. 2001. A Simple Argument for a Higher-Order Representation Theory of Consciousness. *Analysis* 61: 3–4.

Lycan, W. 2004. The Superiority of HOP to HOT. In R. Gennaro ed. *Higher-Order Theories of Consciousness: An Anthology*. Amsterdam: John Benjamins.

Lycan, W. and Ryder, Z. 2003. The Loneliness of the Long-Distance Truck Driver. *Analysis* 63: 132–136.

Mack, A. and Rock, I. 1998. *Inattentional Blindness*. Cambridge, MA: MIT Press.

MacPherson, F. 2005. Colour Inversion Problems for Representationalism. *Philosophy and Phenomenological Research* 70: 127–152.

Maibom, H. 2005. Moral Unreason: The Case of Psychopathy. *Mind and Language* 20: 237–257.

Malatesti, L. and McMillan, J. eds. 2010. *Responsibility and Psychopathy: Interfacing Law, Psychiatry, and Philosophy*. Oxford: Oxford University Press.

Mandelovici, A. 2014. Pure Intentionalism about Moods and Emotions. In U. Kriegel ed. *Current Controversies in Philosophy of Mind*. New York: Routledge Press.

Marcel, A. 1983. Conscious and Unconscious Perception: Experiments on Visual Masking and World Recognition. *Cognitive Psychology* 15: 197–237.

Margolis, E. and Laurence, S. eds. 1999. *Concepts: Core Readings*. Cambridge, MA: MIT Press.

Marks, C. 1981. *Commissurotomy, Consciousness and Unity of Mind*. Cambridge, MA: MIT Press.

Marshall, I. and Zohar, D. 1990. *The Quantum Self: Human Nature and Consciousness Defined by the New Physics*. New York: Morrow.

Martin, M. and Augustine, K. eds. 2015. *The Myth of an Afterlife*. New York: Rowman and Littlefield.

Martinez-Conde, S. and Macknik, S. 2008. Magic and the Brain. *Scientific American*. December Issue: 72–79.

Mashour, G. ed. 2010. *Consciousness, Awareness, and Anesthesia*. Cambridge: Cambridge University Press.

Mashour, G. and LaRock, E. 2008. Inverse Zombies, Anesthesia Awareness, and the Hard Problem of Unconsciousness. *Consciousness and Cognition* 17: 1163–1168.

McDowell, J. 1994. *Mind and World*. Cambridge, MA: Harvard University Press.

McDowell, J. 1998. Having the World in View: Sellars, Kant, and Intentionality. *Journal of Philosophy* 95: 431–491.

McDowell, J. 2002. Responses. In N. Smith ed. *Reading McDowell on Mind and World*. New York: Routledge.

McGinn, C. 1989. Can We Solve the Mind-Body Problem? *Mind* 98: 349–366.

McGinn, C. 1991. *The Problem of Consciousness*. Oxford: Blackwell.

McKenna, M. and Coates, D. J. 2004. "Compatibilism". *The Stanford Encyclopedia of Philosophy (Summer 2015 Edition)*. Edward N. Zalta ed. Available at http://plato.stanford.edu/archives/sum2015/entries/compatibilism/

McLaughlin, B. and Cohen, J. eds. 2007. *Contemporary Debates in the Philosophy of Mind*. Oxford: Blackwell.

Mele, A. 2014. *A Dialogue on Free Will and Science*. New York: Oxford University Press.

Menzel, C. 2005. Progress in the Study of Chimpanzee Recall and Episodic Memory. In Terrace and Metcalfe 2005.

Merleau-Ponty, M. 1945. *Phenomenology of Perception*. Paris: Gallimard.

Metcalfe, J. and Shimamura, A. P. eds. 1994. *Metacognition: Knowing about Knowing*. Cambridge, MA: MIT Press.

Metzinger, T. ed. 1995. *Conscious Experience*. Paderborn: Ferdinand Schöningh.

Metzinger, T. ed. 2000. *Neural Correlates of Consciousness: Empirical and Conceptual Questions*. Cambridge, MA: MIT Press.

Metzinger, T. 2003. *Being No One: The Self-Model Theory of Subjectivity*. Cambridge, MA: MIT Press.

Metzinger, T. 2011. The No-Self Alternative. In S. Gallagher ed. *The Oxford Handbook of the Self*. Oxford: Oxford University Press.

Milner, A. and Goodale, M. 1995. *The Visual Brain in Action*. Oxford: Oxford University Press.

Mitchell-Yellin, B. and Fischer, J. 2014. The Near-Death Experience Argument Against Physicalism. *Journal of Consciousness Studies* 21 (7–8): 158–183.

Mole, C. 2008. Attention and Consciousness. *Journal of Consciousness Studies* 15 (4): 86–104.

Mole, C. 2011. *Attention is Cognitive Unison*. New York: Oxford University Press.

Mole, C., Smithies, D., and Wu, W. eds. 2011. *Attention: Philosophical and Psychological Essays*. New York: Oxford University Press.

Montemayor, C. and Haladjian, H. 2015. *Consciousness, Attention, and Conscious Attention*. Cambridge, MA: MIT Press.

Montminy, M. 2005. What Use is Morgan's Canon? *Philosophical Psychology* 18: 339–414.

Moody, R. 1975. *Life After Life*. Atlanta, GA: Mockingbird.

Moore, G. E. 1903. The Refutation of Idealism. In G. E. Moore, *Philosophical Studies*. Totowa, NJ: Littlefield, Adams, and Company.

Morgan, C. L. 1894. *An Introduction to Comparative Psychology*. London: Walter Scott.

Morin, A. 2006. Levels of Consciousness and Self-Awareness: A Comparison and Integration of Various Neurocognitive Views. *Consciousness and Cognition* 15: 358–371.

Morse, S. 2010. Psychopathy and the Law: The United States Experience. In Malatesti and McMillan 2010.

Muller, V. 2015. *Risks of Artificial Intelligence*. Boca Raton, FL: Taylor and Francis, CRC Press.

Munkata, Y. and McClelland, J. 2003. Connectionist Models of Development. *Development Science* 6: 413–429.

Murphy, D. 2006. *Psychiatry in the Scientific Image*. Cambridge, MA: MIT Press.

Murphy, D. 2009. Psychiatry and the Concept of Disease as Pathology. In M. Broome and L. Bortolotti eds. *Psychiatry as Cognitive Neuroscience: Philosophical Perspectives*. New York: Oxford University Press.

Murphy, D. 2013. Delusions, Modernist Epistemology and Irrational Belief. *Mind and Language* 28: 113–124.

Murphy, G. 2002. *The Big Book of Concepts*. Cambridge, MA: MIT Press.

Murphy, J. 1972. Moral Death: A Kantian Essay on Psychopathy. *Ethics* 82: 284–298.

Mylopoulos, M. 2015. Consciousness, Action, and Pathologies of Agency. In Gennaro 2015b.

Nadelhoffer, T. ed. 2013. *The Future of Punishment*. New York: Oxford University Press.

Nagel, T. 1971. Brain Bisection and the Unity of Consciousness. *Synthese* 22: 396–413.

Nagel, T. 1974. What is it Like to be a Bat? *Philosophical Review* 83: 435–456.

Neander, K. 1998. The Division of Phenomenal Labor: A Problem for Representational Theories of Consciousness. *Philosophical Perspectives* 12: 411–434.

Nemirow, L. 1990. Physicalism and the Cognitive Role of Acquaintance. In W. Lycan ed. *Mind and Cognition: A Reader*. Oxford: Blackwell.

Newen, A. and Bartels, A. 2007. Animal Minds and the Possession of Concepts. *Philosophical Psychology* 20: 283–308.

Newen, A. and Vogeley, K. 2003. Self-representation: Searching for a Neural Signature of Self-Consciousness. *Consciousness and Cognition* 12: 529–543.

Nichols, S. 2004. *Sentimental Rules: On the Natural Foundations of Moral Judgment*. New York: Oxford University Press.

Nichols, S. and Stich, S. 2003. *Mindreading*. New York: Oxford University Press.

Nisbett, R. and Wilson, T. 1977. Telling More Than We Can Know. *Psychological Review* 84: 231–295.

Noë, A. ed. 2002. *Is the Visual World a Grand Illusion? Special Issue: Journal of Consciousness Studies* 9 (5/6): 1–12.

Noë, A. 2004. *Action in Perception*. Cambridge, MA: MIT Press.

Noë, A. 2009. *Out of Our Heads: Why You Are Not Your Brain, and Other Lessons From the Biology of Consciousness*. New York: Hill and Wang.

Noë, A. and Thompson, E. 2004. Are There Neural Correlates of Consciousness? *Journal of Consciousness Studies* 11 (1): 3–28.

O'Regan, K. 2011. *Why Red Doesn't Sound Like a Bell*. New York: Oxford University Press.

O'Regan, K. and Noë, A. 2001. A Sensorimotor Account of Vision and Visual Consciousness. *Behavioral and Brain Sciences* 24: 883–917.

O'Reilly, R., Busby R., and Soto, R. 2003. Three Forms of Binding and Their Neural Substrates: Alternatives to Temporal Synchrony. In Cleeremans 2003.

Papineau, D. 1998. Mind the Gap. In J. Tomberlin ed. *Philosophical Perspectives* 12. Atascadero, CA: Ridgeview Publishing Company.

Papineau, D. 2002. *Thinking about Consciousness*. Oxford: Oxford University Press.

Parnas, J. and Sass, L. 2011. Bodily Awareness and Self-Consciousness. In S. Gallagher ed. *The Oxford Handbook of the Self*. New York: Oxford University Press.

Pascual-Leone, A. and Walsh, V. 2001. Fast Backprojections from the Motion to the Primary Visual Area Necessary for Visual Awareness. *Science* 292: 510–513.

Peacocke, C. 2001. Does Perception Have a Nonconceptual Content? *Journal of Philosophy* 98: 239–264.

Penn, D. and Povinelli, D. 2007. On the Lack of Evidence that Non-Human Animals Possess Anything Remotely Resembling a "Theory of Mind." *Philosophical Transactions of the Royal Society B* 362: 731–744.

Penrose, R. 1989. *The Emperor's New Mind*. Oxford: Oxford University Press.

Penrose, R. 1994. *Shadows of the Mind*. Oxford: Oxford University Press.

Pereboom, D. ed. 2009. *Free Will*, 2nd edition. Indianapolis: Hackett.

Pereboom, D. 2011. *Consciousness and the Prospects for Physicalism*. New York: Oxford University Press.

Pereboom, D. 2014. *Free Will, Agency, and Meaning in Life*. New York: Oxford University Press.

Perry, E., Ashton, H., and Young, A. eds. 2002. *Neurochemistry of Consciousness*. Amsterdam and Philadelphia: John Benjamins.

Perry, J. 2001. *Knowledge, Possibility, and Consciousness*. Cambridge, MA: MIT Press.

Phillips, I. 2011. Attention and Iconic Memory. In Mole et al. 2011.

Piccinini, G. and Bahar, S. 2015. No Mental Life after Brain Death: The Argument from the Neural Localization of Mental Functions. In Martin and Augustine 2015.

Picciuto, V. 2011. Addressing Higher-Order Misrepresentation with Quotational Thought. *Journal of Consciousness Studies* 18 (3–4): 109–136.

Pink, T. 2004. *Free Will: A Very Short Introduction*. New York: Oxford University Press.

Place, U. T. 1956. Is Consciousness a Brain Process? *British Journal of Psychology* 47: 44–50.

Pliushch, I. and Metzinger, T. 2015. Self-Deception and the Dolphin Model of Cognition. In Gennaro 2015b.

Pockett, S., Banks, W., and Gallagher, S. eds. 2009. *Does Consciousness Cause Behavior?* Cambridge, MA: MIT Press.

Poland, J. 2014. Deeply Rooted Sources of Error and Bias in Psychiatric Classification. In H. Kincaid and J. Sullivan eds. *Classifying Psychopathology: Mental Kinds and Natural Kinds*. Cambridge, MA: MIT Press.

Polger, T. 2004. *Natural Minds*. Cambridge, MA: MIT Press.

Pollen, D. 1999. On the Neural Correlates of Visual Perception. *Cerebral Cortex* 9: 4–19.

Pollen, D. 2003. Explicit Neural Representations, Recursive Neural Networks and Conscious Visual Perception. *Cerebral Cortex* 13: 807–814.

Povinelli, D. 2000. *Folk Physics for Apes.* New York: Oxford University Press.

Povinelli, D. and Vonk, J. 2006. We Don't Need a Microscope to Explore the Chimpanzee's Mind. In Hurley and Nudds 2006.

Premack, D. and Woodruff, G. 1978. Does the Chimpanzee Have a Theory of Mind? *Behavioral and Brain Sciences* 1: 515–526.

Preston, J. and Bishop, J. eds. 2002. *Views Into the Chinese Room: New Essays on Searle and Artificial Intelligence.* New York: Oxford University Press.

Prinz, J. 2007. The Intermediate Level Theory of Consciousness. In Velmans and Schneider 2007.

Prinz, J. 2011. Is Attention Necessary and Sufficient for Consciousness? In Mole et al. 2011.

Prinz, J. 2012. *The Conscious Brain.* New York: Oxford University Press.

Proust, J. 2006. Rationality and Metacognition in Non-Human Animals. In Hurley and Nudds 2006.

Proust, J. 2009. The Representational Basis of Brute Metacognition: A Proposal. In Lurz 2009.

Proust, J. 2013. *The Philosophy of Metacognition: Mental Agency and Self-Awareness.* New York: Oxford University Press.

Puccetti, R. 1973. Brain Bisection and Personal Identity. *British Journal for the Philosophy of Science* 24: 339–355.

Puccetti, R. 1981. The Case for Mental Duality: Evidence From Split-Brain Data and Other Considerations. *Behavioral and Brain Sciences* 4: 93–123.

Putnam, H. 1967. The Mental Life of Some Machines. In Hector-Neri Castaneda ed. *Intentionality, Minds and Perception.* Detroit: Wayne State University Press.

Putnam, H. 1975. The Meaning of "Meaning." In *Mind, Language, and Reality: Philosophical Papers Vol. 2.* Cambridge, MA: Cambridge University Press.

Raby, C. and Clayton, N. 2009. Prospective Cognition in Animals. *Behavioural Processes* 80: 314–324.

Raby, C., Alexis, D., Dickinson, A., and Clayton, N. 2007. Planning for the Future by Western Scrub-Jays. *Nature* 445: 919–921.

Radden, J. 1996. *Divided Minds and Successive Selves.* Cambridge, MA: MIT Press.

Radden, J. ed. 2004. *The Philosophy of Psychiatry: A Companion.* New York: Oxford University Press.

Radden, J. 2010. *On Delusion.* Abingdon and New York: Routledge.

Ramachandran, V. 2004. *A Brief Tour of Human Consciousness.* London: Pearson Education.

Ramachandran, V. and Blakeslee, S. 1998. *Phantoms in the Brain.* New York: Quill.

Ramachandran, V. and Hubbard, E. 2001. Synaesthesia: A Window into Perception, Thought and Language. *Journal of Consciousness Studies* 8 (12): 3–34.

Revonsuo, A. 2006. *Inner Presence: Consciousness as a Biological Phenomenon.* Cambridge, MA: MIT Press.

Revonsuo, A. 2010. *Consciousness: The Science of Subjectivity.* New York: Psychology Press.

Riddoch, M. and Humphreys, G. 1987. A Case of Integrative Visual Agnosia. *Brain* 110: 1431–1462.

Ridge, M. 2001. Taking Solipsism Seriously: Nonhuman Animals and Meta-Cognitive Theories of Consciousness. *Philosophical Studies* 103: 315–340.

Roberts, W. 2002. Are Animals Stuck in Time? *Psychological Bulletin* 128: 473–489.

Robertson, C. and Sagiv, N. eds. 2005. *Synesthesia: Perspectives from Cognitive Neuroscience.* New York: Oxford University Press.

Robinson, W. 2004. *Understanding Phenomenal Consciousness.* New York: Cambridge University Press.

Rochat, P. 2001. *The Infant's World.* Cambridge, MA: Harvard University Press.

Rochat, P. 2003. Five Levels of Self-Awareness as they Unfold Early in Life. *Consciousness and Cognition* 12: 717–731.

Rollin, B. 1989. *The Unheeded Cry: Animal Consciousness, Animal Pain, and Science.* New York: Oxford University Press.

Rolls, E. 2004. A Higher Order Syntactic Thought (HOST) Theory of Consciousness. In Gennaro 2004a.

Rosenthal, D. M. 1986. Two Concepts of Consciousness. *Philosophical Studies* 49: 329–359.

Rosenthal, D. M. 1990. On Being Accessible to Consciousness. *The Behavioral and Brain Sciences* 13: 621–622.

Rosenthal, D. M. 1991. The Independence of Consciousness and Sensory Quality. *Philosophical Issues* 1: 15–36.

Rosenthal, D. M. 1993. State Consciousness and Transitive Consciousness. *Consciousness and Cognition* 2: 355–363.

Rosenthal, D. M. 1997. A Theory of Consciousness. In N. Block, O. Flanagan, and G. Güzeldere eds. *The Nature of Consciousness.* Cambridge, MA: MIT Press.

Rosenthal, D. M. 2002. Explaining consciousness. In D. Chalmers ed. *Philosophy of Mind: Classical and Contemporary Readings.* New York: Oxford University Press.

Rosenthal, D. M. 2003. Unity of Consciousness and the Self. *Proceedings of the Aristotelian Society* 103: 325–352.

Rosenthal, D. M. 2004. Varieties of Higher-Order Theory. In R. Gennaro ed. *Higher-Order Theories of Consciousness: An Anthology*. Amsterdam: John Benjamins.

Rosenthal, D. M. 2005. *Consciousness and Mind*. New York: Oxford University Press.

Rosenthal, D. M. 2010. Consciousness, the Self and Bodily Location. *Analysis* 70: 270–276.

Rosenthal, D. M. 2011. Exaggerated Reports: Reply to Block. *Analysis* 71: 431–437.

Rosenthal, D. M. 2012. Awareness and Identification of Self. In J. Liu and J. Perry eds. *Consciousness and the Self: New Essays*. Cambridge, MA: Cambridge University Press.

Rumelhart, D. and McClelland, J. 1986. *Parallel Distributed Processing* Vols. I and II. Cambridge, MA: MIT Press.

Russell, B. 1927. *The Analysis of Matter*. London: Kegan Paul.

Russell, P. 2004. Responsibility and the Condition of Moral Sense. *Philosophical Topics* 32: 287–305.

Ryle, G. 1949. *The Concept of Mind*. London: Hutchinson.

Sabanz, N. and Prinz, W. eds. 2006. *Disorders of Volition*. Cambridge, MA: The MIT Press.

Sacks, O. 1987. *The Man Who Mistook His Wife for a Hat and Other Clinical Tales*. New York: Harper and Row.

Saenz, M. and Koch, C. 2008. The Sound of Change: Visually-Induced Auditory Synesthesia. *Current Biology* 18: R650–51.

Santos, L., Nissen, A., and Ferrugia, J. 2006. Rhesus Monkeys, *Macaca Mulatta*, Know What Others Can and Cannot Hear. *Animal Behavior* 71: 1175–1181.

Sartre, J. 1956. *Being and Nothingness*. New York: Philosophical Library.

Sauret, W. and Lycan, W. 2014. Attention and Internal Monitoring: A Farewell to HOP. *Analysis* 74: 363–370.

Saygin, A., Cicekli, I., and Akman, V. 2000. Turing Test: 50 Years Later. *Minds and Machines* 10: 463–518.

Schechter, E. 2010. Individuating Mental Tokens: The Split-Brain Case. *Philosophia* 38: 195–216.

Schechter, E. 2012. The Switch Model of Split-Brain Consciousness. *Philosophical Psychology* 25: 203–226.

Schmidt, E. 2015. *Modest Nonconceptualism*. Cham: Springer International Publishing.

Schramme, T. 2014. *Being Amoral: Psychopathology and Moral Incapacity*. Cambridge, MA: The MIT Press.

Schwartz, B. 2005. Do Nonhuman Primates Have Episodic Memory? In Terrace and Metcalfe 2005.

Seager, W. 2004. A Cold Look at HOT Theory. In R. Gennaro ed. *Higher-Order Theories of Consciousness: An Anthology*. Amsterdam: John Benjamins.

Seager, W. 2016. *Theories of Consciousness*, 2nd edition. New York and London: Routledge.

Searle, J. 1980. Minds, Brains and Programs. *Behavioral and Brain Sciences* 3: 417–457.

Searle, J. 1984. *Minds, Brains, and Science*. Cambridge, MA: Harvard University Press.

Searle, J. 1990. Is the Brain's Mind a Computer Program? *Scientific American* 262: 26–31.

Searle, J. 1992. *The Rediscovery of the Mind*. Cambridge, MA: MIT Press.

Searle, J. 2002. Why I Am Not a Property Dualist. *Journal of Consciousness Studies* 9 (12): 57–64.

Searle, J. 2004. *Mind: A Brief Introduction*. New York: Oxford University Press.

Searle, J. 2007. Biological Naturalism. In M. Velmans and S. Schneider eds. *The Blackwell Companion to Consciousness*. New York: Blackwell.

Sellars, W. 1956. Empiricism and the Philosophy of Mind. *Minnesota Studies in the Philosophy of Science* 1: 253–329.

Seth, A. and Baars, B. 2005. Neural Darwinism and Consciousness. *Consciousness and Cognition* 14: 140–168.

Seth, A., Baars, B., and Edelman, D. 2005. Criteria for Consciousness in Humans and Other Mammals. *Consciousness and Cognition* 14: 119–139.

Shani, I. 2007. Consciousness and the First Person. *Journal of Consciousness Studies* 14 (12): 57–91.

Shani, I. 2008. Against Consciousness Chauvinism. *The Monist* 91: 294–323.

Shea, N. and Bayne, T. 2010. The Vegetative State and the Science of Consciousness. *British Journal for the Philosophy of Science* 61: 459–484.

Shea, N. and Heyes, C. 2010. Metamemory as Evidence of Animal Consciousness: The Type That Does the Trick. *Biology and Philosophy* 25: 95–110.

Shear, J. ed. 1997. *Explaining Consciousness: The Hard Problem*. Cambridge, MA: MIT Press.

Sher, G. 2009. *Who Knew? Responsibility without Awareness.* New York: Oxford University Press.

Shoemaker, D. 2011. Psychopathy, Responsibility, and the Moral/Conventional Distinction. *Southern Journal of Philosophy* 49: 99–124.

Shoemaker, S. 1981. Absent Qualia Are Impossible – A Reply to Block. *Philosophical Review* 90: 581–599.

Shoemaker, S. 1982. The Inverted Spectrum. *Journal of Philosophy* 79: 357–381.

Shoemaker, S. 1994. Self-Knowledge and "Inner Sense." *Philosophy and Phenomenological Research* LIV: 249–314.

Shoemaker, S. 2003. Consciousness and Co-Consciousness. In Cleeremans 2003.

Shriver, A. 2006. Minding Mammals. *Philosophical Psychology* 19: 433–442.

Siderits, M., Thompson, E., and Zahavi, D. eds. 2011. *Self, No Self?: Perspectives from Analytical, Phenomenological, and Indian Traditions.* New York: Oxford University Press.

Siegel, S. 2010. *The Contents of Visual Experience.* New York: Oxford University Press.

Sierra, M. and Berrios, G. 2000. The Cambridge Depersonalisation Scale: A New Instrument for the Measurement of Depersonalisation. *Psychiatry Research* 93: 153–164.

Siewart, C. 1998. *The Significance of Consciousness.* Princeton: Princeton University Press.

Silberstein, M. 1998. Emergence and the Mind-Body Problem. *Journal of Consciousness Studies* 5: 464–482.

Silberstein, M. 2001. Converging on Emergence: Consciousness, Causation and Explanation. *Journal of Consciousness Studies* 8: 61–98.

Simner, J. and Hubbard, E. eds. 2013. *The Oxford Handbook of Synesthesia.* Oxford: Oxford University Press.

Simons, D. 2000. Current Approaches to Change Blindness. *Visual Cognition* 7: 1–15.

Simons, D. and Chabris, C. 1999. Gorillas in our Midst: Sustained Inattentional Blindness for Dynamic Events. *Perception* 28: 1059–1074.

Singer, P. ed. 1990. *Animal Liberation.* New York: Avon Books.

Sinnott-Armstrong, W. ed. 2014. *Moral Psychology: Volume 4.* Cambridge, MA: MIT Press.

Sinnott-Armstrong, W. and Nadel, L. 2011. *Conscious Will and Responsibility.* New York: Oxford University Press.

Skinner, B. F. 1953. *Science and Human Behavior*. New York: MacMillan.

Skrbina, D. 2005. *Panpsychism in the West*. Cambridge, MA: MIT Press.

Skrbina, D. 2014. Panpsychism. *Internet Encyclopedia of Philosophy*. Available at http://www.iep.utm.edu/panpsych/

Smart, J. J. C. 1959. Sensations and Brain Processes. *The Journal of Philosophy* 68: 141–156.

Smith, D. W. 1989. *The Circle of Acquaintance*. Dordrecht: Kluwer.

Smith, D. W. 2004. *Mind World: Essays in Phenomenology and Ontology*. Cambridge, MA: Cambridge University Press.

Smith, J. D. 2005. Studies of Uncertainty Monitoring and Metacognition in Animals. In Terrace and Metcalfe 2005.

Smith, J. D., Shields, W., and Washburn, D. 2003. The Comparative Psychology of Uncertainty Monitoring and Metacognition. *Behavioral and Brain Sciences* 26: 317–373.

Smith, Q. and Jokic, A. eds. 2003. *Consciousness: New Philosophical Perspectives*. New York: Oxford University Press.

Smithies, D. 2011. Attention is Rational-Access Consciousness. In Mole et al. 2011.

Smithies, D. and Stoljar, D. eds. 2012. *Introspection and Consciousness*. New York: Oxford University Press.

Sober, E. 1998. Morgan's Canon. In D. Cummins and C. Allen eds. *The Evolution of Mind*. Oxford: Oxford University Press.

Sosa, E. and Steup, M. eds. 2005. *Contemporary Debates in Epistemology*. Oxford: Blackwell.

Sperling, G. 1960. The Information Available in Brief Visual Presentations. *Psychological Monographs* 74: 1–29.

Sperry, R. 1984. Consciousness, Personal Identity and the Divided Brain. *Neuropsychologia* 22: 611–673.

Stapp, H. 1999. On Quantum Theories of the Mind. *Journal of Consciousness Studies* 6 (1): 61–65.

Stapp, H. 2007. Quantum Approaches to Consciousness. In Zelazo, Moscovitch, and Thompson 2007.

Stephens, G. and Graham, G. 2000. *When Self-Consciousness Breaks: Alien Voices and Inserted Thoughts*. Cambridge, MA: The MIT Press.

Stephens, G. and Graham, G. 2007. Philosophical Psychopathology and Self-Consciousness. In Velmans and Schneider 2007.

Stoljar, D. 2006. *Ignorance and Imagination*. New York: Oxford University Press.

Stoljar, D. 2008. *Physicalism*. London: Routledge.

Strawson, G. 2004. Real Intentionality. *Phenomenology and the Cognitive Sciences* 3: 287–313.

Strawson, G. 2006. Realistic Monism: Why Physicalism Entails Panpsychism. *Journal of Consciousness Studies* 13 (10–11): 3–31.

Strawson, P. 1962. Freedom and Resentment. *Proceedings of the British Academy* 48: 1–25.

Stubenberg, L. 1998. *Consciousness and Qualia*. Philadelphia and Amsterdam: John Benjamins.

Suddendorf, T. and Corballis, M. 2007. The Evolution of Foresight: What is Mental Time Travel, and is it Unique to Humans? *Behavioral and Brain Sciences* 30: 299–313.

Swinburne, R. 1986. *The Evolution of the Soul*. New York: Oxford University Press.

Szasz, T. 1974. *The Myth of Mental Illness*. New York: Harper & Row.

Terrace, H. and Metcalfe, J. eds. 2005. *The Missing Link in Cognition: Origins of Self-Reflective Consciousness*. New York: Oxford University Press.

Teuber, H. 1968. Alteration of Perception and Memory in Man. In L. Weiskrantz ed. *Analysis of Behavioral Change*. New York: Harper & Row.

Textor, M. 2006. Brentano (and Some Neo-Brentanians) on Inner Consciousness. *Dialectica* 60: 411–432.

Titchener, E. 1901. *An Outline of Psychology*. New York: Macmillan.

Tomasello, M. and Call, J. 2006. Do Chimpanzees Know What Others See – Or Only What They Are Looking At? In Hurley and Nudds 2006.

Tomasello, M., Call, J., and Hare, B. 2003. Chimpanzees Understand Psychological States: The Question is Which Ones and To What Extent. *Trends in Cognitive Sciences* 7: 153–156.

Tong, F. 2003. Primary Visual Cortex and Visual Awareness. *Nature Reviews Neuroscience* 4: 219–229.

Tononi, G. 2004. An Information Integration Theory of Consciousness. *BMC Neuroscience* 5: 42.

Tononi, G. 2008. Consciousness as Integrated Information: A Provisional Manifesto. *Biological Bulletin* 215: 216–242.

Tononi, G. and Koch, C. 2015. Consciousness: Here, There and Everywhere? *Philosophical Transactions Royal Society B*: 370.

Treisman, A. 1993. The Perception of Features and Objects. In A. Baddeley and L. Weiskrantz eds. *Attention: Selection, Awareness and Control*. New York: Oxford University Press.

Treisman, A. 2003. Consciousness and Perceptual Binding. In Cleeremans 2003.

Tulving, E. 1983. *Elements of Episodic Memory*. Oxford: Oxford University Press.

Tulving, E. 1993. What is Episodic Memory? *Current Perspectives in Psychological Science* 2: 67–70.

Tulving, E. 2005. Episodic Memory and Autonoesis: Uniquely Human? In Terrace and Metcalfe 2005.

Turing, A. 1950. Computing Machinery and Intelligence. *Mind* 59: 433–460.

Tye, M. 1995. *Ten Problems of Consciousness*. Cambridge, MA: MIT Press.

Tye, M. 2000. *Consciousness, Color, and Content*. Cambridge, MA: MIT Press.

Tye, M. 2002. Representationalism and the Transparency of Experience. *Nous* 36: 137–151.

Tye, M. 2003. *Consciousness and Persons*. Cambridge, MA: MIT Press.

Tye, M. 2006. Nonconceptual Content, Richness, and Fineness of Grain. In Gendler and Hawthorne 2006.

Tye, M. 2009. *Consciousness Revisited: Materialism without Phenomenal Concepts*. Cambridge, MA: MIT Press.

Tye, M. 2015. "Qualia," *The Stanford Encyclopedia of Philosophy (Fall 2015 Edition)*, Edward N. Zalta ed. Available at http://plato.stanford.edu/archives/fall2015/entries/qualia/

Vallar, G. and Ronchi, R. 2009. Somatoparaphrenia: A Body Delusion. A Review of the Neuropsychological Literature. *Experimental Brain Research* 192: 533–551.

Van Gulick, R. 1985. Physicalism and the Subjectivity of the Mental. *Philosophical Topics* 13: 51–70.

Van Gulick, R. 1992. Nonreductive Materialism and the Nature of Inter-theoretical Constraint. In A. Beckermann, H. Flohr, and J. Kim eds. *Emergence or Reduction?: Prospects for Nonreductive Physicalism*. Berlin: De Gruyter.

Van Gulick, R. 1993. Understanding the Phenomenal Mind: Are We All Just Armadillos? In M. Davies and G. Humphreys eds. *Consciousness: Psychological and Philosophical Essays*. Oxford: Blackwell.

Van Gulick, R. 1995a. How Should We Understand the Relation Between Intentionality and Phenomenal Consciousness? *Philosophical Perspectives* 9: 271–289.

Van Gulick, R. 1995b. Why the Connection Argument Doesn't Work. *Philosophy and Phenomenological Research* 55: 201–207.

Van Gulick, R. 1995c. What Would Count as Explaining Consciousness? In Metzinger 1995.

Van Gulick, R. 2000. Inward and Upward: Reflection, Introspection and Self-Awareness. *Philosophical Topics* 28: 275–305.

Van Gulick, R. 2001. Reduction, Emergence and Other Recent Options on the Mind/Body Problem: A Philosophic Overview. *Journal of Consciousness Studies* 8 (9–10): 1–34.

Van Gulick, R. 2004. Higher-Order Global States (HOGS): An Alternative Higher-Order Model of Consciousness. In R. Gennaro ed. *Higher-Order Theories of Consciousness: An Anthology*. Amsterdam: John Benjamins.

Van Gulick, R. 2006. Mirror mirror – is that all? In U. Kriegel and K. Williford eds. *Self- Representational Approaches to Consciousness*. Cambridge, MA: MIT Press.

Van Gulick, R. 2015. Altogether Now – Not! Integration Theories of Consciousness and Pathologies of Disunity. In Gennaro 2015b.

Van Lommel, P. 2010. *Consciousness Beyond Life: The Science of Near-Death Experience*. New York: Harper Collins.

Varela, F. and Thompson, E. 2003. Neural Synchrony and the Unity of Mind: A Neurophenomenological Perspective. In Cleeremans 2003.

Velmans, M. and Schneider, S. eds. 2007. *The Blackwell Companion to Consciousness*. Malden, MA: Blackwell.

Vincent, N. ed. 2013. *Neuroscience and Legal Responsibility*. Oxford: Oxford University Press.

Wallach, W. and Allen, C. 2009. *Moral Machines: Teaching Robots Right From Wrong*. New York: Oxford University Press.

Waller, B. 2015. *The Stubborn System of Moral Responsibility*. Cambridge, MA: MIT Press.

Waskan, J. 2010. Connectionism. *Internet Encyclopedia of Philosophy*. Available at http://www.iep.utm.edu/connect/

Watson, G. 1996. Two Faces of Responsibility. *Philosophical Topics* 24: 227–248.

Watson, G. ed. 2007. *Free Will*, 2nd edition. New York: Oxford University Press.

Watson, J. 1913. Psychology as the Behaviorist Views It. *Psychological Review* 20: 158–177.

Wegner, D. 2002. *The Illusion of Conscious Will*. Cambridge, MA: MIT Press.

Weisberg, J. 2008. Same Old, Same Old: The Same-Order Representation Theory of Consciousness and The Division of Phenomenal Labor. *Synthese* 160: 161–181.

Weisberg, J. 2011. Misrepresenting Consciousness. *Philosophical Studies* 154: 409–433.

Weisberg, J. 2014. *Consciousness*. Malden, MA: Polity Press.

Weiskrantz, L. 1986. *Blindsight*. Oxford: Clarendon.

Wilkes, K. 1988. Yishi, Duh, Um and Consciousness. In A. Marcel and E. Bisiach eds. *Consciousness in Contemporary Science*. New York: Oxford University Press.

Williford, K. 2006. The Self-Representational Structure of Consciousness. In Kriegel and Williford 2006.

Wright, E. ed. 2008. *The Case for Qualia*. Cambridge, MA: MIT Press.

Wu, W. 2014. *Attention*. New York: Oxford University Press.

Wundt, W. 1897. *Outlines of Psychology*. Leipzig: W. Engleman.

Yablo, S. 1999. Concepts and Consciousness. *Philosophy and Phenomenological Research* 59: 455–463.

Young, A. 2003. Face Recognition With and Without Awareness. In Cleeremans 2003.

Zachar, P. 2014. *A Metaphysics of Psychopathology*. Cambridge, MA: MIT Press.

Zahavi, D. 1998. Brentano and Husserl on Self-Awareness. *Etudes Phénoménologiques* 27–28: 127–169.

Zahavi, D. ed. 2000. *Exploring the Self*. Amsterdam and Philadelphia: John Benjamins.

Zahavi, D. 2004. Back to Brentano? *Journal of Consciousness Studies* 11 (10–11): 66–87.

Zahavi, D. 2005. *Subjectivity and Selfhood*. Cambridge, MA: MIT Press.

Zahavi, D. 2007. The Heidelberg School and the Limits of Reflection. In S. Heinämaa, V. Lähteenmäki, and P. Remes eds. *Consciousness: From Perception to Reflection in the History of Philosophy*. Dordrecht: Springer.

Zahavi, D., Grünbaum, T., and Parnas, J. eds. 2004. *The Structure and Development of Self-Consciousness*. Amsterdam and Philadelphia: John Benjamins.

Zeki, S. 2001. Localization and Globalization in Conscious Vision. *Annual Review of Neuroscience* 24: 57–86.

Zeki, S. 2007. A Theory of Micro-Consciousness. In Velmans and Schneider 2007.

Zelazo, P., Gao, H., and Todd, R. 2007. The Development of Consciousness. In Zelazo, Moscovitch, and Thompson 2007.

Zelazo, P., Moscovitch, M., and Thompson, E. eds. 2007. *The Cambridge Handbook of Consciousness*. Cambridge, MA: Cambridge University Press.

Zentall, T. 2005. Animals May Not Be Stuck in Time. *Learning and Motivation* 36: 208–225.

INDEX

Made in the USA
Lexington, KY
30 June 2019